ACTIVATING DEMOCRACY IN BRAZIL

RECENT TITLES FROM THE HELEN KELLOGG INSTITUTE
FOR INTERNATIONAL STUDIES

Scott Mainwaring, *series editor*

The University of Notre Dame Press gratefully thanks the Helen Kellogg Institute for International Studies for its support in the publication of titles in this series.

Carlos Guevara Mann
Political Careers, Corruption, and Impunity: Panama's Assembly, 1984–2009 (2011)

Gabriela Ippolito-O'Donnell
The Right to the City: Popular Contention in Contemporary Buenos Aires (2012)

Susan Fitzpatrick-Behrens
The Maryknoll Catholic Mission in Peru, 1943–1989: Transnational Faith and Transformation (2012)

Barry S. Levitt
Power in the Balance: Presidents, Parties, and Legislatures in Peru and Beyond (2012)

Sérgio Buarque de Holanda
Roots of Brazil (2012)

José Murilo de Carvalho
The Formation of Souls: Imagery of the Republic in Brazil (2012)

Douglas Chalmers and Scott Mainwaring, eds.
Problems Confronting Contemporary Democracies: Essays in Honor of Alfred Stepan (2012)

Peter K. Spink, Peter M. Ward, and Robert H. Wilson, eds.
Metropolitan Governance in the Federalist Americas: Strategies for Equitable and Integrated Development (2012)

Natasha Borges Sugiyama
Diffusion of Good Government: Social Sector Reforms in Brazil (2012)

Ignacio Walker
Democracy in Latin America: Between Hope and Despair (2013)

Laura Gómez-Mera
Power and Regionalism in Latin America: The Politics of MERCOSUR (2013)

Erik Ching
Authoritarian El Salvador: Politics and the Origins of the Military Regimes, 1880–1940 (2013)

For a complete list of titles from the Helen Kellogg Institute for International Studies, see http://www.undpress.nd.edu

ACTIVATING DEMOCRACY IN BRAZIL

Popular Participation, Social Justice,
and Interlocking Institutions

Brian Wampler

University of Notre Dame Press
Notre Dame, Indiana

Published in the United States of America

Library of Congress Cataloging-in-Publication Data

Wampler, Brian.
  Activating democracy in Brazil : popular Participation, Social Justice,
and Interlocking Institutions / Brian Wampler.
      pages   cm. —
  (From the helen kellogg institute for international studies)
  Includes bibliographical references and index.
  ISBN 978-0-268-04430-5 (pbk. : alk. paper) —
  ISBN 0-268-04430-9 (pbk. : alk. paper)
    1. Democracy—Brazil.   2. Political participation—Brazil.
3. Social justice—Brazil.   I. Title.
  JL2481.W36   2015
  320.981—dc23

                                                    2014047955

FOR SEBASTIAN AND GINGER:

for your curiosity in exploring new places, cultures, and ideas

for helping me to see Brazil with fresh eyes

Contents

List of Abbreviations   ix
List of Tables and Figures   xi
Acknowledgments   xiii

ONE   Activating Democracy in Brazil   1

TWO   Establishing the Participatory Citizenship Regime   33

THREE   Rebuilding the Local State   63

FOUR   Innovation and Renewal of Participatory Budgeting   93

FIVE   Councils and Conferences: Health Care, Housing,   131
           and Social Services

SIX   Transforming the Engagement of Civil Society   169
           Organizations: Adopting New Strategies in the
           Participatory Citizenship Regime

SEVEN   Transforming Favelas   209

EIGHT   Activating Democracy: Belo Horizonte and Beyond   245

           Notes   273
           References   277
           Index   293

Abbreviations

BNDES	Brazilian Development Bank (Banco Nacional de Desenvolvimento Econômico e Social)
CEB	ecclesial base community (*comunidade eclesiais de base*)
DEM	Democrats (Democratas)
HDI	Human Development Index
IBGE	Brazilian Institute of Geography and Statistics (Instituto Brasileiro de Geografia e Estatística)
IQVU	Index of the Quality of Urban Life (Índice de Qualidade de Vida Urbana)
MDB	Brazilian Democratic Movement (Movimento Democrático Brasileiro)
MST	Landless Workers' Movement (Movimento dos Trabalhores Sem Terra)
NGO	nongovernmental organization
PB	participatory budgeting (*orçamento participativo*)
PCB	Brazilian Communist Party (Partido Comunista Brasileiro)
PC do B	Communist Party of Brazil (Partido Comunista do Brazil)
PDS	Social Democratic Party (Partido Social Democrata)

PDT   Democratic Workers' Party (Partido Democrático Trabalhista)

PFL   Liberal Front Party (Partido de Frente Liberal)

PMDB   Brazilian Democratic Movement Party (Partido do
        Movimento Democrático Brasileiro)

PSB   Socialist Party of Brazil

PSDB   Brazilian Social Democratic Party (Partido da Social
        Democracia Brasiliera)

PT   Workers' Party (Partido dos Trabalhadores)

PTB   Brazilian Labor Party (Partido Trabalhista Brasileiro)

TSE   Tribunal Superior Eleitoral

Tables and Figures

TABLES

1.1	Participatory Design Principles to Promote Social Justice	25
1.2	Basic Social Indicators in Major Brazilian Cities	26
3.1	Mayoral Vote: First Round, 1992–2008	69
3.2	Mayoral Vote: Second Round, 1992–2008	69
3.3	Party Affiliation of Mayor and Vice Mayor	70
3.4	Budget Amendments Presented by Belo Horizonte City Council Members, 2003–2010	74
3.5	Public Policy Management Councils: Venues and Formal Representation for Citizens, Government Officials, and Unions in 2009–2010	79
3.6	Participatory Budgeting, 2008–2009	80
4.1	Number of Participants in Participatory Budgeting	110
4.2	Demographic Profile of Participatory Budgeting Delegates	111
4.3	Resources Allocated through Participatory Budgeting, 1994–2012	112
4.4	Resource Allocation across Communities, 1994–2008	113
4.5	Distribution of Participatory Budgeting Projects by Policy Sector, 1994–2010	116
4.6	Participatory Budgeting Housing Participants	122
4.7	Participation in Participatory Budgeting Digital	125
4.8	Distribution of Participation in Participatory Budgeting Digital by IQVU, 2006	126

5.1   Public Policy Management Councils and Seats, 2009–2010   142
5.2   Distribution of Seats by Civil Society Sector
        (Municipal Level)   142
5.3   Distribution of Regional-Level Seats   144
5.4   Distribution of Local-Level Seats   144
6.1   Demographic Profile of Survey Respondents   180
6.2   Internal Activities of CSOs   183
6.3   Formal Contracts to Provide Service   184
6.4   CSO Contacts with Other Associations   185
6.5   Engaging in Participatory Democracy Venues   186
6.6   Contact with Municipal Legislature   189
6.7   Contact with Mayoral Administration Officials   191
6.8   Campaign Activities   193
6.9   Demonstrations and Contentious Politics   195
7.1   CSOs in Morro de Papagaio and Alto Vera Cruz   213
7.2   Demographic Profile of Citizens   234
7.3   Activity within Civil Society   237
7.4   Access to Public Institutions   239
7.5   Sharing Information   240
7.6   Campaigns and Elections   241
8.1   Participatory Budgeting, 1989–2012 (Municipalities with
        at Least 50,000 Residents)   262
8.2   Public Policy Management Councils in Brazil   264
8.3   Municipalities Voluntarily Adopting Councils   265
8.4   Voluntarily Adopting Councils (by Municipality Size)   266

FIGURES

1.1   Interlocking Institutions   20
3.1   Distribution of Seats on Belo Horizonte's Municipal Council,
        1997–2012   71
3.2   Belo Horizonte's Municipal Budget, 1999–2008   73
4.1   Participation Flow with Participatory Budgeting   98
4.2   Resource Allocation in Micro-Regions, 2002–2008   118
5.1   Activation of the Participatory Citizenship Regime: Outcomes
        Across Six New Democratic Institutions   168

Acknowledgments

I am grateful to a number of individuals and institutions for their support over the six-year period that involved applying for research support, conducting research, analyzing the results, and drafting the book. I was fortunate to live in Brazil during two key phases of working on this book, conducting research during the 2009–2010 academic year and the final revision stage in 2014.

To support the research, Boise State University provided me with sabbatical leave and research funding to hire research assistants and administer a survey; Dean Melissa Lavitt was particularly supportive. The Fulbright program, supported by the US government and administered in conjunction with the Brazilian government, granted me the opportunity to conduct research and teach a graduate course at the Federal University of Minas Gerais. Professor Leonardo Avritzer, with whom I team-taught the graduate course, was a welcoming host. Avritzer leads the Center for Participatory Democracy, an extremely vibrant place of research and learning. My thanks to Leonardo Avritzer and his excellent team for helping me as I conducted research in the city of Belo Horizonte. Several enthusiastic and smart research assistants contributed significantly to the project. In Brazil, Uriella Coelho Ribeiro carried out innumerable tasks that ensured the project would move forward. William Soares, Daniela Linhares, and Roberto Michael administered a survey in Morro de Papagaio and helped me to navigate its complex politics. At Boise State, Michelle Wilson, Sam Pagano, and Sally Sargeant provided timely and high-quality support to pull different streams of evidence together. John Loveday, the program administrator for the University Studies Abroad Consortium, provided great hospitality as I was finishing the book in Florianopolis.

I presented this book in different venues over four years. Thanks to the institutional support of National University of Brasilia, CEBRAP, Fundação Getúlio Vargas, Instituto de Pesquisa Econômica Aplicada, University of Pittsburgh, Syracuse University, University of Texas, University of Washington, Woodrow E. Wilson International Center for Scholars, and conferences hosted by the American Political Science Association, Latin American Studies Association, and the Brazilian Studies Association. Timely and helpful feedback came from Rebecca Abers, Leonardo Avritzer, Sonia Alvarez, Cathy Boone, Zach Elkins, Frank Fischer, Archon Fung, Chris Gibson, Benjamin Goldfrank, Michael Goodhart, Patrick Heller, Wendy Hunter, Sunila Kale, Margaret Keck, Adrian Lavalle Gurza, Tony Lucero, Stephanie McNulty, Tina Nabatchi, Carole Pateman, Debora Rezende, Blair Ruble, Wager Romão, Peter Spink, Arthur Scaritt, George Stetson, Jose Leon Szwako, Mike Touchton, Marco Antonio Teixeira, Jonathan Warren, Kurt Weyland, and Wendy Wolford. The title went through several iterations, so I am particularly grateful to Wendy Hunter, who suggested it. Finally, several anonymous reviewers provided feedback that significantly improved my analysis. Stephen Little from the University of Notre Dame Press provided excellent guidance and strong support. I appreciate Scott Mainwaring's decision to include this book in the Helen Kellogg Institute for International Studies series.

This book and my life were enriched by having my children, Sebastian and Ginger, spend eighteen months in Brazil. Living abroad with children is an eye-opening, enriching, and challenging experience. I learned different things about Brazil as a result of their presence (patience and flexibility). Of course, my deepest appreciation goes to my wonderful wife and their mother, Paula Perry, who sustained our family through the project. My heartfelt thanks to Paula, Sebastian, and Ginger for their willingness to share these adventures.

CHAPTER ONE

Activating Democracy in Brazil

*Democracy is not a static concept, whose essence could ever be decided
once and for all. Rather, it is a dynamic and open-ended project.* . . . *Those
faithful to the democratic project should look at the range of constraints
and possibilities for furthering that project in particular times and places.*
— John Dryzek, *Deliberative Democracy and Beyond*

*All power emanates from the people, who exercise it by means of elected
representatives or directly, as provided by this Constitution.*
— Article 1, Brazil's 1988 constitution

Brazilian citizens, civil society organizations, and public officials are adopting and adapting new democratic institutions in the hopes of improving
ordinary citizens' quality of life, expanding their voice and vote, changing the distribution of public goods, and deepening the quality of democracy. Civil society activists and ordinary citizens now participate in a multi-
tude of state-sanctioned institutions, including public policy management
councils, public policy conferences, participatory budgeting programs,
and legislative hearings. The proliferation of democratic institutions has
demonopolized how and where citizens gain access to public officials, thus
limiting the power of clientelistic gatekeepers and allowing civil society

1

organizations (CSOs) to diversify the political strategies used to secure public goods. Citizens now attend deliberative hearings, exercise voice and vote over public resources, and monitor government officials' implementation of policies. This book demonstrates how the proliferation of multiple democratic institutions transforms when, where, and who citizens, CSOs, and public officials engage each other.

The book's central argument is that the promulgation of Brazil's 1988 constitution initiated a participatory citizenship regime, thereby altering the political and policy terrain through which citizens express political voice, claim social rights, engage their fellow citizens and public officials, and hold government officials accountable. "Citizenship regimes define *who* has political membership, *which* rights they possess, and *how* interest intermediation with the state is structured" (Yashar 2005, 6; italics in original). Brazil's participatory citizenship regime significantly expands *who* participates in formal policymaking institutions, *which* political rights can be used to secure social rights, and *how* citizens and government officials negotiate over the allocation of public resources and public goods.

I am arguing here that citizens, activists, and public officials must *activate* the participatory citizenship regime to ensure that citizens can access rights formally guaranteed under Brazil's 1988 constitution. Activating such a regime is a contested, highly politicized process through which citizens, CSOs, and political parties seek to adopt new democratic institutions and transform the existing state. Their efforts to activate these rights are resisted by political rivals, unresponsive bureaucracies, short-term political alliances, and the difficulties of sustaining collective action. Because of this resistance, there is broad variation across Brazil with regard to who can access new rights and new democratic new institutions. By focusing on multiple democratic institutions over a twenty-year period, this book illustrates how the participatory citizenship regime generates political and social change.

The participatory citizenship regime draws attention to the central role of the state in convening institutions that mediate disputes among citizens, CSOs, and government officials. Across Brazil, government officials now administer an extensive participatory architecture, which incorporates millions of citizens and CSO activists directly into policymaking venues. At least 300,000 Brazilian citizens are elected to participatory institutions in which citizens have some authority over public funds and policymaking (Baretto 2011). Between 2004 and 2012, some six to eight million Brazilians participated in public policy conferences sponsored by the federal government (Avritzer and Souza 2013). Although participants did not exercise specific decision-making authority, they contributed to agenda setting that affects governments' policy choices (Avritzer 2012; Pogrebinschi and Samuels 2014). In addition, hundreds of thousands of Brazilians participate in municipal-level participatory budgeting programs on a biannual basis (Wampler and Avritzer 2005; Avritzer 2009; Spada, Wampler, and Coelho 2013).

The 1988 constitution marks the formal start of the participatory citizenship regime, but there is tremendous variation in how citizens and public officials have been able to activate it. This book demonstrates that the variation results from the interplay of five factors: state formation, the development of civil society, government support for citizens' use of voice and vote, the degree of public resources available for spending on services and public goods, and finally, the rules that regulate forms of participation, representation, and deliberation within participatory venues. The variation occurs at the level of government (federal, state, municipal), across cities (Rio de Janeiro, São Paulo, Belo Horizonte), and states (Rio Grande do Sul, Bahia), as well as across policy arenas (health care, education, housing). This book demonstrates how the interaction of these five factors best explains how new democratic institutions may improve ordinary citizens' quality of life, alter state-society interactions, change the distribution of public goods, and deepen the quality of democracy. Some Brazilians have access to a wide range of rights, but many others continue to lack even the most minimal access to constitutional guarantees promised by the 1988 constitution.

The development of multiple democratic institutions has generated a diverse set of incentives to induce Brazil's increasingly heterogeneous civil society to be directly involved in public policymaking. Urban civil society in Brazil today is now characterized by the presence of a broad range of social movements, community-based organizations, nongovernmental organizations (NGOs), service providers, and religious organizations (Dagnino and Tatagiba 2007; Avritzer 2002; Baiocchi 2005; Lavalle, Acharia, and Houtzager 2005; Mische 2008; Arias 2006; Wolford 2010; Lavalle and Isunza Vera 2011). The new participatory architecture permits citizens and CSOs to deliberate in public fora, vote on public policies, monitor public officials, and forge new networks. For decades, Brazilian citizens and CSOs drew from a narrower set of blunt instruments, such as clientelism and contentious politics, when they sought out public officials in search of public resources to solve basic social and infrastructure problems (Holston 2008; Leal 1997; Gay 1994). Today, Brazilian CSOs and citizens continue to use contentious politics (the June 2013 protests as one example), but many CSOs are also directly involved in public policymaking processes in which they express voice and exercise vote.

The participatory citizenship regime generates two sets of incentives that encourage direct citizen participation in public institutions. Citizens and CSOs are induced to participate for narrow, instrumental reasons, thus helping to overcome low mobilization associated with the collective action problem (Olson 1965; Ostrom 1990). Citizens are willing to participate because their involvement greatly increases the likelihood that their community will receive specific public goods. But citizens' participation is not reducible to instrumental issues; citizens and CSOs are also motivated to participate because they are renewing what Jeffrey Alexander terms "bonds of solidarity," whereby they connect to their fellow citizens and contribute to deepening Brazil's democracy (Alexander 2006).

CHALLENGES FACING NEW DEMOCRATIC REGIMES

The establishment of Brazil's participatory citizenship regime is part of a broader political process in which public officials and citizens seek to address three fundamental problems faced by democratic reformers in newly democratizing settings. First, after the euphoria of a transition to democracy has subsided, how can collective action be maintained? Second, in highly unequal societies such as Brazil, how can representative democratic regimes respond to the pent-up demand for basic public goods? Third, how can the state act quickly without trampling on the rights of citizens?

First, after the euphoria of a transition to democracy has subsided, how can collective action be maintained? As has been well documented, it is extremely difficult to maintain robust levels of collective action, especially among poor citizens (Olson 1965; Ostrom 1990; Baiocchi, Heller, and Silva 2011). It was the renewal of civil society in Brazil during the 1970s and 1980s that led democratic reformers to create new institutions that would help CSOs to partially overcome the collective action problem (Avritzer 2002, 2009; Dagnino 1998; Holston 2008; Wampler and Avritzer 2004). The establishment of new democratic institutions induces poor individuals and groups traditionally excluded from formal politics to participate in incremental policymaking processes by creating specific "pro-poor" rules or by focusing on policies (e.g., health care) that are of specific interest to poor communities. The rules induce ongoing mobilization as a means to provide poor citizens with a direct voice in policymaking, but they also generate political support for incumbent government that is necessary to allocate greater levels of public funds to poor communities.

A second challenge faced by democratic reformers, especially those in new democracies in the developing world, is the bias in representative democracy in favor of middle and upper classes, which are better organized and have stronger connections to public officials (Schattschneider 1960; Ross 2006; Verba, Schlozman, and Brady 1995; Schlozman, Verba, and Brady 2012). This bias means that public goods and social services are disproportionally allocated to entrenched economic elites, organized sectors of the middle class, and organizations (unions) that are vital to the government's economic project rather than to the poorer, less well organized sectors of the population. Since the majority of citizens in developing world democracies are poor, and since developing world countries are marked by intense inequality, the bias of representative democracy against the poor is a greater problem in the developing world than in more established, consolidated democracies. Brazil's participatory citizenship regime has a pro-poor, social justice component that includes universal rights based on the 1988 constitution as well as pro-poor incentives embedded in new democratic institutions. This book demonstrates that the expansion of participatory institutions alters the architecture of representative democracy, which then allows citizens to achieve social justice by accessing greater social services that result from the new participatory institutions and the reformed state. New political rights are used to claim social rights. Participatory democracy complements representative democracy, which means that the social rights advanced within the realm of participatory politics affect a broader, more generalized public.

A third challenge faced by democratic reformers is how to more effectively translate citizens' preferences and demands into tangible policy outputs without trampling on the rights of the same citizens (Kohli 2004; Migdal 2001; Cleary 2010; Scott 1998). In new democratic regimes, government officials seek to forge alliances with newly enfranchised voters. Many of these new voters are poor citizens, who have a pent-up demand for public goods and basic services. A key governing problem faced by newly elected governments is that they often inherit states that were designed to meet the needs of authoritarian leaders, which means that existing state bureaucracies and internal processes must be reformed to allow them to work more closely with democratic institutions. The participatory institutions in Brazil now link citizens, CSOs, elected officials, political appointees, and civil servants in intricate webs of preference formation, agenda setting, demand making, and oversight, which are designed to alter how public officials receive and aggregate citizen demand as well as how these same officials mobilize the state to implement new policies (Abers and Keck 2013). CSO activists are brought directly into the state (most often the executive branch), thus establishing the means to allow information to be constantly traded between state and civil society. The challenge for Brazilian reformers has been to harness the transformative power of the state so that it can be used to address problems in poor communities, often favelas, without violating the rights of people living in these communities. Here I argue that the expansion of new democratic institutions has the potential to produce positive-sum improvements in state effectiveness and the quality of democracy.

To show how civil society activists and government officials have addressed these challenges, this book focuses its analytical lens on a single city: Belo Horizonte, Brazil. A comparative analysis at the municipal and submunicipal level is used to demonstrate the extent to which public officials in Belo Horizonte are able to maintain mobilization, address basic social justice issues, and reform the local state. In the context of Brazil and Latin America more broadly, Belo Horizonte is an exemplary case of reform that illuminates the opportunities associated with the new participatory architecture. Sandbrook, Edelman, Heller, and Teichman argue, in *Social Democracy in the Global Periphery*, that "social scientists should also search for *possibilities*—the often hidden opportunities for valued change that lurk in a particular situation" (2007, 3). The city of Belo Horizonte leads the way within Brazil regarding how the municipal state and new democratic institutions can be used to simultaneously improve democratic governance, enhance state capacity, and empower citizens. The relationship between state capacity and democratic outcomes is not a zero-sum game; rather, enhancing state capacity and deepening the quality of democracy can be mutually reinforcing. And yet the pace of change in Belo Horizonte is incremental and bound by numerous constraints, which means that the new participatory citizenship regime is enabling citizens to access rights guaranteed under the 1988 constitution but that these rights are bound by limited state capacity and resources.

VIGNETTES

Alto Vera Cruz

In April 2009, I was spending time in the Alto Vera Cruz favela, a thirty-minute bus ride from the city center (this favela is discussed at length in chapter 7). Four distinct forms of state-society engagement occurred over a two-day span. On a Thursday afternoon, two community leaders took me on a walking tour of the favela. We first walked through the lower part of the favela, where a private construction company, working on a municipal government contract, was removing houses to connect two roads. The community had mobilized itself to work within participatory budgeting (a program discussed in chapter 4) to secure the project as a means to improve public transportation into their community. The homeowners were compensated for the value of their houses, though not the value of the land because the legal ownership was unclear. Another project was going on nearby: construction workers were renovating a school, a project also secured through participatory budgeting. In both projects, the municipal government and community organizations were actively involved.

As we headed back up the hill, a man in his late twenties approached us to discuss the projects. He was very interested in what I was doing there. I subsequently learned that he was a leader in the retail sales of drugs such as marijuana and cocaine that took place in the favela. He was gathering information about my presence. The two community leaders giving me the tour subsequently told me that they act as intermediaries between the municipal state and the local drug traffickers. (See Arias 2006 for a fuller discussion of the relationship between state, society, and illegal criminal networks.) Thus, when the community leaders assured the drug trafficker that I was no threat, he went on his way. I should note that there is a police station roughly two hundred yards from where we had this conversation. A community policing policy initiative was contributing to a reduction in violence in the community, but it was never clear to me if the police were involved in drug trafficking or if they ignored the illegal drug sales on the condition that violence was reduced.

Our walk continued alongside a polluted creek. Two infrastructure projects were being implemented. In a project sponsored by the federal government, workers were cleaning up the headwaters of a creek that ran through the favela. The first step involved the removal of houses built too close to the creek. A housing project, carried out with municipal funds, involved building two apartment buildings with sixty-four new units. The apartments were very small, but they would be provided to families who had been removed from along the creek.

The next day I attended a meeting of the local health council at the local health post. Ten to fifteen people were present, discussing the current challenges to the health clinic. The local administrator explained to the participants that the lack of doctors at the clinic was the principal bottleneck to more efficient service provision. The administrator and the citizens jointly drafted a letter they planned to send to the municipal health council as well as the municipal secretary of health to request full staffing of doctors and nurses. When the meeting ended, several community leaders stayed to discuss different projects that could be proposed in the following week's participatory budgeting meeting. There was general agreement that they would need to narrow their support to two or three of the projects. Community leaders were involved in a series of informal conversations centered on deciding which projects to support in the participatory budgeting program.

Thus, in a single favela, over a two-day period, CSOs, citizens, the federal and municipal state, and private companies were engaged in a series of institutional venues as they sought to build a decent infrastructure in the favela. There was a flurry of state activity in the area, much of it associated with new participatory processes.

Morro de Papagaio

In 2004, a CSO based in Morro de Papagaio led by a local priest organized a well-publicized demonstration against the local government's slow implementation of public work projects selected via participatory budgeting. The demonstration got the attention of the municipal government, which promised to quickly implement the projects (see chapter 4 for a fuller account as well as Wampler 2007, 11–13). In 2010, community leaders continued to debate whether this demonstration helped or hurt the community. Some activists asserted that holding the demonstration created a wedge between the community and public officials, thus making it harder to work together. Other activists asserted that this strategy was successful because it brought pressure on the government, which responded by implementing the projects. Although there are conflicting interpretations among activists regarding the impact, one clear effect of the demonstration was to drive wedges among different community groups, thus making it difficult to develop a unified political approach.

When new democratic institutions and participatory institutions were established in the favela in the early 1990s, community groups initially unified, which allowed them to pursue their common interests in a new democratic institution. However, by 2009–2010, the larger community was divided by conflicting claims regarding how they would make use of these new institutions. In the Morro de Papagaio favela, participatory institutions thus created both "bonds of solidarity" among citizens as well as political competition between different groups (Alexander 2006). Political competition is directly related to instrumental incentives for participation, which include access to public goods as well as specific social services.

Municipal and state governments are actively involved in the Morro de Papagaio favela. Interestingly, state involvement was much greater in areas of the favela that already had better infrastructure; these parts of the community had schools, health care clinics, and a community center built by the municipal state. A virtuous cycle of participation, state-building, and service delivery is now taking place. However, in the poorest, most destitute areas of the favela, residents had the fewest interactions with state officials and received the fewest policy improvements. As I will explain in greater depth in chapter 7, residents from the poorest sectors of the favela were living in "areas of risk," which precluded the state from spending resources in their section of the favela. These families are caught in a bind, as the official "area of risk" designation prohibited the state from spending public resources for much-needed infrastructure improvements, but the state was also unwilling to allocate the resources to move the people out of the area.

In another area of the favela, the municipal government, working in conjunction with the federal government, initiated planning for a major infrastructure project that would dramatically alter the favela. The government proposed tearing down significant sections of the favela and building a series of apartment buildings. Some community members championed this plan because they believed that it would improve the overall quality of life. However, others strongly objected, asserting that the proposed apartments would be too small for multigenerational families to live to-gether. Divisions and limited trust among community leaders as well as vis-à-vis government officials slowed the reform effort.

These vignettes point to the complexity of the new democratic mo-ment in Brazil. The state is being demonopolized, thus allowing activists and citizens to engage government officials and each other in a broader range of activities and conversations. The demonopolization promotes democratic activities, but it doesn't necessarily eliminate the use of politi-cal tactics, such as clientelism, that have long played a central role in Brazilian politics. This book aims to advance our understanding of how participatory governance helps to build new forms of state-society rela-tions, but it also examines how traditional practices are carried into the participatory governance system.

FROM BASKET CASE TO INTERNATIONAL DARLING

Brazil, long recognized as one of the world's most unequal countries, changed significantly in the 1990s and 2000s as a result of economic sta-bility and a subsequent economic boom, extensive state involvement in providing public goods to Brazil's poor, and institutionalization of partici-patory policymaking venues. This book uses the analytical frame of the par-ticipatory citizenship regime to draw attention to shifts in basic state-society relations that are part of Brazil's remarkable transformation in the 2000s. To be clear, I am not asserting that the participatory citizenship regime was the only factor that accounts for the improvements in the quality of democracy and of people's lives. It would be foolhardy to assert that the proliferation of democratic institutions is single-handedly more important than economic transformations, such as Brazil's commodities-led economic boom or the suite of conditional cash transfer programs now provided to Brazilian citi-zens. Rather, I am asserting that the participatory citizenship regime is an integral part of Brazil's social and political transformation that took place during the 1990s and 2000s because Brazilian governments are building the institutional architecture that allows citizens and government officials to re-spond to the pent-up demand for public goods and social services. The eco-nomic boom and the new social programs extended by the federal govern-ment were built on an institutional architecture that alters how citizens, CSOs, and public officials engage each other.

During the 1990s, as Brazil slumbered through a second decade of anemic economic growth, political scientists focused their attention on how Brazil's political system was unable to address key structural and systematic problems. "Deadlocked Democracy," "Democracy without Equity," "Traditional Politics and Patronage," and "The Myth of Civil Society" were just a few of the pessimistic descriptions of Brazil's political and civil society shortcomings (Ames 2001; Weyland 1996; Hagopian 1996; Encarnación 2003). These political scientists sought to explain a series of crises afflicting Brazil: hyperinflation, weak economic growth, deindustrialization, and a major corruption scandal led by the president, Fernando Collor de Mello, which led to his impeachment, were the key political facets of Brazil during the late 1980s and 1990s.

Brazil's reemergence onto the world scene in the 2000s with strong economic growth, a real reduction in extreme poverty, and the adoption of a wide array of new democratic innovations is a striking rebuttal to scholars who have argued that Brazil is unable to reform itself (Kingstone and Power 2008; Montero 2014). Brazil's transformation is unfolding on multiple levels: improvement of its macroeconomic policy outlook, deployment of state authority more effectively to promote economic growth, development of stable multiparty presidentialism, institutionalization of a broad participatory governance system, and allocation of public goods to poor, marginalized Brazilians (Montero 2014). In this book I explore one aspect of this remarkable set of changes: the activation and institutionalization of the participatory citizenship regime as a key factor transforming democratic politics, the local state, and civil society.

POPULAR PARTICIPATION, INTERLOCKING INSTITUTIONS, AND SOCIAL JUSTICE

Brazil's participatory citizenship regime is based on three pillars: popular participation, which includes the direct participation of citizens in participatory venues; interlocking institutions, which includes the development of formal and informal linkages among government agencies, new democratic institutions, CSOs, and citizens; and social justice, which has an explicit focus on the extension of universal rights to all Brazilian citizens. The participatory citizenship regime marks a significant rupture from previous periods because of the emphasis on universal social rights, direct participation, and building state institutions to provide public goods to allow ordinary Brazilians access to social rights.

Popular Participation

The participatory citizenship regime is based on the development of new democratic institutions that directly incorporate citizens into ongoing policymaking processes. Participatory institutions consist of state-sanctioned institutional processes that devolve decision-making authority to venues that are jointly controlled by citizens and government officials. Central to this definition is that these processes are *jointly controlled*, indicating that we must consider the interests and activities of both citizens and government officials. The challenge for researchers is to unravel the degree of authority and influence wielded by citizens and their elected representatives because there are often wide gaps between the formal authority delegated to citizens and the authority citizens actually exercise. Participatory institutions should be analyzed as instrumental policymaking bodies because they produce specific incentives for citizens to participate as well as specific policy outcomes. However, they must also be analyzed as new forms of democracy, since they offer the opportunity to overcome deficiencies with actual existing representative democracy (Bobbio 1993; Fung 2003; Fung and Wright 2001, 2003; Santos 2005).

Three institutionalized forms of participatory governance—public policy management councils (*conselhos*), thematic policy conferences (*conferências*), and participatory budgeting (*orçamento participativo*)—are now jointly controlled participatory venues. Within these venues, citizens exercise *voice* and *vote*. They directly engage each other and government officials in ongoing meetings and public forums. They listen, deliberate, and negotiate with each other and government officials. Citizens typically vote for different policy options, specific projects, and internal citizen-representatives. Of course, there is a wide range in the quality of public deliberations. At moments, well-informed CSO leaders use public fora to reshape broader policy initiatives. At other moments, the debates are dominated by a narrow focus on very specific problems (e.g., drainage problem on a single street), which may help a small number of individuals but doesn't allow the larger group to advance their agenda. The power of the vote varies significantly, as some votes allow citizens to approve or veto projects that will cost hundreds of millions of dollars, whereas other votes are largely symbolic acts.

Government officials administer participatory institutions, providing the necessary logistical support to ensure that the participatory meetings, conferences, workshops, and subcommittees function.[1] Government officials receive policy decisions (binding or recommendations) made by citizens and then mobilize the bureaucracy to implement those policies (Abers and Keck 2009, 2013). Government officials also bring many of their own policy initiatives to these participatory venues, thus asking citizen-participants to ratify decisions already made.

A key fault line in the academic debate on the role of citizen participation in democratic regime is between the "participationistas" versus "elitists" (Saward 2010, 4). At the core of this division is a disagreement regarding why people are motivated to participate in public life, which then leads to alternative prescriptions for how citizens should be incorporated into politics. Elitists are concerned that the active engagement of citizens in democracy would be detrimental to a democratic republic's political health because the passions of an inflamed majority could trample on the rights of minorities (Madison 1787a; Schumpeter 1942; O'Donnell and Schmitter 1986; O'Donnell 1994). The solution is to thus limit direct citizen participation by relying on formal elections and representative democracy. Working within the "elitist" tradition, Bernard Manin argues that "representative democracy is not a system in which the community governs itself, but a system in which public policies and decisions are made subject to the verdict of the people" (Manin 1997, 192). Thus, representative democracy constrains the passions of citizens by reducing their input to biannual votes for elected representatives. Representative democracy becomes a political system in which citizens are exempted from much engagement in political life.

In stark contrast to the elitist theories of democracy, "participationistas" advocate for the direct involvement of citizens in public life, conceptualizing a political environment in which citizens are actively engaged in shaping their lives, their communities, and their governments (Barber 1984; Pateman 1970, 2012; Santos 2005; Saward 2000; Avritzer 2002; Alexander 2006; Tarrow 1998). Jeffrey Alexander's *The Civil Sphere* focuses on the processes through which "bonds of solidarity" can be crafted and is representative of the participationistas. The civil sphere is "a world of values and institutions that generates the capacity for social criticism and democratic integration at the same time" (Alexander 2006, 4). In this approach, civil society creates the possibility of forging connections, addressing seemingly intractable social problems, and providing a counterbalancing authority to existing power holders. This approach advocates for the increased involvement of citizens in public life as a means to make the public sphere and state institutions more democratic.

This book contributes to these theoretical debates on participation by first demonstrating that participatory institutions induce new types of participation by allowing citizens to secure instrumental outcomes (e.g., public works and social services) as well as to forge "bonds of solidarity," build new networks, and deepen the quality of democracy (Alexander 2006; Granovetter 1973; Knoke 1990b; McClurg and Young 2011). Citizens forge bonds, develop trust, and are actively engaged in democratic politics while at the same time pursuing specific policies that will improve the quality of their lives. This book's argument establishes new theoretical ground by demonstrating how specific participatory institutions allow citizens to be inserted into state institutions and state actors into civil society. Although we can analytically distinguish between citizen participation in representative democracy, state bureaucracies, or participatory institutions, the reality is that citizen participation cannot be walled off between these institutions. The local state in Brazil, to paraphrase Migdal, is morphing into a body that now hosts a large number of public venues in which citizens are able to exercise voice and vote (Migdal 2001). Citizens and public officials are working to activate these institutions in ways that will help them to best pursue their short- and medium-term interests. As citizens are inserted into public institutions and as government officials provide support for civil society mobilization, there is now a blurring of the line between state and society This blurring raises difficult theoretical and practical questions associated with co-optation, clientelism, preference formation, and power, as traditional political practices creep into participatory institutions.

I employ a pluralistic and expansive definition of civil society: it is the sphere of social and political associational activity separate from the state, the market, and the family (Cohen and Arato 1992). "Civil society organization" is an umbrella concept that incorporates a wide range of collective groups: social movements, community-based organizations, and "third sector" organizations are prominent within this category. These organizations have diverse sets of interests—organizing communities and potential allies, establishing a coherent political and policy agenda, and working to achieve social change (McAdam, McCarthy, and Zald 1996). The umbrella concept of CSO allows us to recognize the diversity of organizational type and interest.

Fitting unions into this scenario is not a simple analytical task in Brazil because union activists are often times also social movement activists. In one sense, there is a clear division, as social movements and community and neighborhood organizations are commonly referred to as "civil society" (*sociedade civil*), whereas union officials are clearly identified as representing *sindicatos* (unions). Union membership in Brazil is required in most formal job classifications (e.g., civil servant, journalists, teachers), which means that many individuals employed in the formal sector are union members. Although we can formally distinguish between union-related activity and community-based activity, a complicating factor is that many public employees elected to leadership positions within unions are often released from their formal job duties. This permits "union leaders" to organize in both the union sector and the social movement field. Thus, when CSO activists are also union leaders, it is not clear who these CSO activists are representing during ongoing public policy debates.

Brazilian civil society is increasingly heterogeneous: professional NGOs occupying the same policy arenas as small community organizations, national networks of social movements providing support to far-flung affiliates, evangelical churches providing social services, policy-oriented think tanks competing for resources and media attention, social movements mobilizing their followers, political parties and elected officials providing resources to support civil society activities, and, importantly, local governments supporting an extensive infrastructure that allows CSOs to engage in public life (Hochstetler and Keck 2007; Arias 2006; Mische 2008; Lavalle, Acharia, and Houtzager 2005). The heterogeneity of Brazil's civil society expanded in the 1980s, 1990s, and 2000s when a more diversified set of class interests developed as a result of the expansion of Brazil's economy, the rise of evangelical churches, the protection of CSOs by democratic values and institutions, support from international funding agencies, and an increase in institutional venues (Alvarez, Dagnino, and Escobar 1998b; Dagnino and Tatagiba 2007). In addition, I include groups and activity that are not explicitly politicized, such as soccer clubs and cultural associations (Putnam et al. 1993), as well as groups that do not necessarily advocate for democratic values (Bernam 1997). Civil society has an apolitical side (bird-watching clubs) and a dark side (i.e., fascist groups, Ku Klux Klan).

Although some CSOs resist engaging public officials through participatory processes or campaigns and elections, my experience of conducting research over a fifteen-year period in Brazil shows that the vast majority of community leaders are interested in gaining access to government officials (Wampler 2007; Dagnino and Tatagiba 2007). Research by Wendy Wolford shows that the most radical social movement in Brazil today, the Landless Movement (Movimento Sem Terra), regularly works with public officials (Wolford 2010). Evangelical churches deliver social services with the support of public funds and are significant players in electoral campaigns (Burdick 1993). Community-based organizations are actively involved in participatory budgeting programs (Baiocchi 2005). Environmental social movements seek out public defenders as a means to enforce environmental regulations (McAllister 2008).

The initiation of the participatory citizenship regime means that CSOs are now expected to carry out a wide range of duties. Many CSOs engage in several, if not all, of the following activities: developing coherent organizational frames, mobilizing followers, raising funds, delivering social services, launching policy initiatives, monitoring implementation, and working on electoral campaigns. Thus, they have characteristics similar to social movements (mobilizing and setting frames), NGOs (policy initiatives and service provision), and party loyalists (work on campaigns). A problem faced by many poor communities is that small, community-based organizations come and go at a rapid rate because they are unable to secure funding or maintain the mobilization of their followers. Professional NGOs seek funding from national and international sources, often changing their objectives to ensure that they align with the policy goals of funding sources. The diversity of CSOs' interests and organization means that a crucial task in this book is to draw attention to how the participatory citizenship regime induces citizens and CSOs to engage in different political and social activities.

Interlocking Institutions

Many elected governments seek to reform the state so it that can act quickly and effectively without trampling on the rights of ordinary citizens. The participatory citizenship regime is based on the establishment of a multilayer, multichanneled set of participatory institutions that link government officials and citizens. States and governments in the developing world (often marked by high poverty, deep inequalities, poorly performing state) have a long history of violating the rights of poor, politically weak groups, but there is often in these very settings high demand for the state to be actively producing public goods (Scott 1998; Migdal 2001; Kohli 2004). Poor citizens in new democracies hold the reasonable expectation that the new democratic regimes will provide public goods to a wider range of citizens (Sandbrook at al. 2007; Sen 1999). Elected governments in new democracies in the developing world face the difficult task of simultaneously protecting individual rights, strengthening the rule of law, and improving social well-being. State capacity is integral to activating the participatory citizenship regime because state authority and resources are used to build the new participatory architecture, implement citizens' policy choices, and allow citizens to exercise constitutionally guaranteed rights. The concept of interlocking institutions is based on the idea that citizens and governments will use complementary sources of knowledge and information in order to improve the policy performance of the state while also protecting citizens' rights.

In James C. Scott's excellent book *Seeing Like a State* a central concern is that states often violate the rights of citizens as they seek to produce transformative projects. This is especially true in societies that are poor and unequal, both because the government embarks on transformative projects in the hopes of generating new sources of wealth that will improve social well-being (and thus support for the government) and because the poor majorities often lack the rights to counter the government's actions. Scott demonstrates how states and governments use "simplification" projects, whereby they transform the unmanageable and illegible into the manageable and legible, which then allows states to act on and control previously unruly individuals, communities, and "wild" spaces. "State simplifications such as maps, censuses, cadastral lists, and standard units of measurement represent techniques for grasping a large and complex reality; in order for officials to be able to comprehend aspects of the ensemble, that complex reality must be reduced to schematic categories" (Scott 1998, 77). Scott's work demonstrates that many of these transformative projects had disastrous consequences for nature, cities, communities, and individuals as a result of the authoritarian practices employed by states. This is a major issue in many urban favelas in Brazil today because the state wants to transform these communities in order to improve the quality of residents' lives.

Scott then argues "it is typically progressives who have come to power with a comprehensive critique of existing society and a popular mandate (at least initially) to transform it. These progressives have wanted to use that power to bring about enormous changes in people's habits, work, living patterns, moral conduct, and world view" (Scott 1998, 89). This insight is central to Brazilian politics because it is more often leftist, progressive governments that seek to harness state authority to improve the quality of life for poor and marginalized communities. Leftist governments, including the ones in Belo Horizonte and the presidential administrations of Luis Inácio "Lula" da Silva (2003–2010) and Dilma Rousseff (2011–2014), sought to transform Brazil by providing greater public goods that would improve the daily lives of Brazil's excluded classes.

Scott suggests a way to avoid a domineering and authoritarian state: combining expert knowledge with practical, local knowledge. He writes, "Broadly understood, *mētis* represents a wide array of practical skills and acquired intelligence in responding to a constantly changing natural and human environment" (Scott 1998, 313). Although Brazilian civil society activists and government officials designing new participatory institutions may not have been familiar with the Greek concept of *mētis,* "participatory policymaking" captures the spirit of this concept—linking expert and elite knowledge with ordinary citizens' ideas, information, and knowledge. Government officials use scientific knowledge to ground the debate (e.g., civil engineering, budget rules), and they also draw on practical knowledge (*mētis*) from citizens and CSO leaders to guide the process of project selection and urbanization. In the final paragraph of *Seeing Like a State,* Scott argues: "A good many institutions in liberal democracies already take such a form and may serve as exemplars for fashioning new ones. One could say that democracy itself is based on the assumption that the *mētis* of its citizenry should, in mediated form, continually modify the laws and the policies of the land" (1998, 357; italics added). Therefore, it is *mētis*-based popular participation within interlocking institutions that provides an opportunity to increase state authority to carry out transformation projects without violating the rights of citizens.

A conversation I had with a government official in Belo Horizonte illustrates the concept of *mētis.* Waldir and I were talking about the government's interest in building new housing units in the Morro de Papagaio favela (see chapter 7), which would require the removal of existing housing, relocating some families to temporary housing, and permanently relocating others to new neighborhoods. Waldir, the regional director of Participatory Budgeting Center-South Region, made it clear that the process was slow and that every major step took about a year to accomplish. The process was slow because government officials would present each stage of the project to the community at a public meeting. And over the next six to twelve months CSO leaders and citizens would participate in community-based meetings to discuss the proposals. CSO leaders and citizens also engaged in informal conversations as part of their daily lives. After receiving feedback, government officials would modify their plans based on citizen response. Once individuals became accustomed to the idea of the project and voted to approve the final set of plans, the government would be able to initiate the infrastructure projects. Citizens and CSO leaders living in crowded favelas seek state support because they desperately want access to the expert knowledge that might produce better living conditions. Community leaders want access to state authority and resources (public or private) that generate a high quality of physical infrastructure in middle- and upper-class neighborhoods.

Brazil's interlocking institutions are innovative in that they focus on participatory policymaking within the executive branch, which is the most powerful branch of government in Brazil (see chapter 3 for a discussion of the expansive authority of mayors). This is quite different from the horizontal interlocking institutions envisioned by James Madison in *The Federalist Papers*. Madison's checks and balances were designed to limit the potential for a tyrannical government, whereas Brazil's interlocking institutions are designed to harness state authority to allow government officials to accomplish their goals. These new institutions serve the role of linking interested citizens, CSOs, and public officials to each other. What is fundamentally different from Madison's conceptualization of checks and balances is that these councils induce cooperation within the executive branch rather than inducing competition among different branches of government (Mansbridge 2012).

Latin America's and Brazil's strong executives have long overshadowed legislative and judicial branches, which means that Madison's hope of having "ambition counteracting ambition" through the use of a "check and balance" system has been weakly extended (1787a, 1787b). Importantly, the interlocking institutions largely ignore the legislative and judicial branches, and focus on working within the executive branch in order to get things done (Mansbridge 2012). The innovation is that participatory institutions link citizens to the executive branch in new ways; citizens and CSOs now have multiple entry points to influence government officials' political and policy choices. Brazil's interlocking institutions thus represent

Figure 1.1   Interlocking Institutions

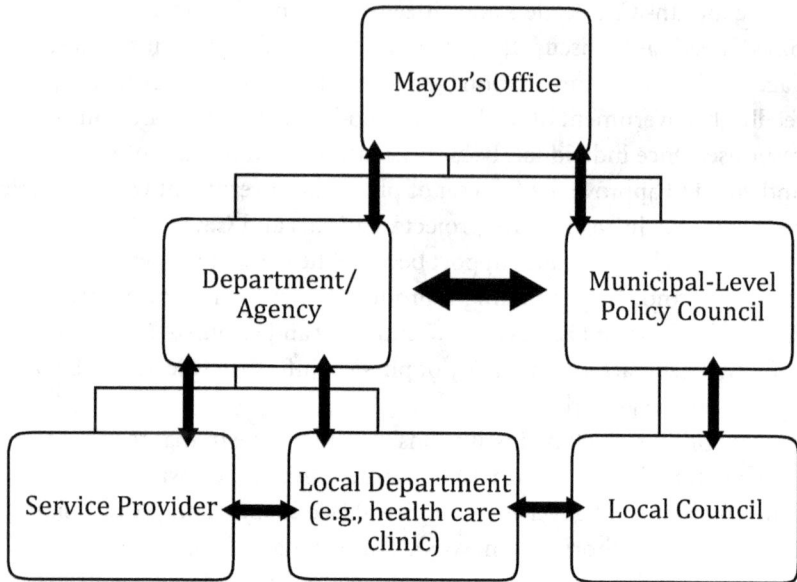

an attempt to work within the traditional authority of the executive branch to extend basic citizenship rights.

There is one significant limitation to this institutional innovation: limited oversight of the executive because citizens are being induced to work within the executive branch. As will be demonstrated in chapters 3 and 4, Brazilian reformers attempted to finesse this point by granting citizens and CSOs the right to engage in oversight practices of the executive, but the problem is that citizens and CSOs now have dueling sets of incentives (policy proposal and oversight), which make it difficult for them to effectively carry out both.

The second main point regarding interlocking institutions rests on the idea that the expansion of state authority isn't in a zero-sum game vis-à-vis civil society. There is an opportunity to generate positive-sum gains for both the state and CSOs. Government officials can now "mobilize the state" through interlocking institutions to promote more coherent public goods provision (Abers and Keck 2009, 2013). By using popular participation and *mētis* within the new democratic process, CSOs may be strengthened because the activists involved gain credibility as legitimate intermediaries between state and society (Touchton and Wampler 2014).

Atul Kohli's work on state formation and late industrialization in the developing world illuminates how variation in state formation had a significant impact on the ability of countries to industrialize. Although Kohli focuses his empirical attention on late industrialization in the developing world, his theoretical insight concerning the central importance of an effective state is useful for understanding the participatory citizenship regime. Regarding economic development, Kohli writes (2004, 418):

> The key theoretical problems of understanding state intervention in developing country economies are thus to identify how effective state power for development is generated and how this power is used to promote economic change.

Kohli's argument can be applied to analyze the role of the state in activating new interlocking institutions and the participatory citizenship regime. In the following sentence, I replaced key words from Kohli's original statement with words related to political development. My changes are in italics:

> The key theoretical problems of understanding state intervention in developing country ~~economies~~ *democracies* are thus to identify how effective state power for ~~development~~ *the expansion of citizenship rights* is generated and how this power is used to promote ~~economic~~ *political and social* change.

An effective state is necessary to promote citizens' access to basic political and social rights because the former require a state to provide the appropriate institutions to encourage participation and deliberation and the latter require a state to provide public goods. The state is a crucial actor proving social rights such as education, health care, public security, and clean water. State agents, such as the police and the judicial branch, are at the center of efforts to build a rule of law in which all citizens have equal access to rights protections. State agencies also organize elections and oversee public demonstrations, which means that citizens' ability to exercise political rights is tied to state action. When the state more effectively delivers public goods, there is going to be a corresponding support for the democratic regime (Putnam, Leonardi, and Nanetti 1994).

State effectiveness is extended in conjunction with an expansion of the breadth and density of civil society (Putnam, Leonardi, and Nanetti 1994; Baiocchi, Heller, and Silva 2011). Francisco Weffort, in his famous article "Why Democracy?," argued that Brazil needed to build a broader civil society so that citizens would be able to control the state (Weffort 1984). Weffort approvingly cites from the work of James Madison, whereby democratic reformers first need to establish an institutional framework in which government officials can control the governed (i.e., establish public authority), which is then followed by a period in which the governed can then control public officials. Participatory institutions, on which the new interlocking institutions are built, are designed to promote civil society organizations as a means to be able to check the state. This book demonstrates the extent to which the new participatory architecture and interlocking institutions generate a broader and denser set of civil society organizations.

Prior to the 1988 constitution, it was very difficult in Brazil to incorporate citizens' practical, local forms of knowledge (*mētis*) in formal decision-making bodies. Executives and policy experts made decisions with minimal public input. The participatory institutions being activated across Brazil now provide an opportunity to produce positive-sum gains among state and civil society actors through the establishment of vertically and horizontally integrated participatory institutions. These institutions are horizontally integrated at each level, linking each participatory institution to the corresponding state agency as well as across policy sectors (e.g., housing council is linked to education council and education department). They are also linked vertically, from the local neighborhood level to municipal and eventually to the federal level. Given the strong incentives for poor individuals and communities to participate and given that expansive state action is needed to physically transform Brazil's shantytowns, the interlocking participatory institution systems directly link poor citizens and public officials to better protect rights, respect the rule of law, and improve social well-being.

Social Justice

Devising institutions in the developing world to address extensive social demands is at the forefront of local reform efforts in democracy's "third wave." Restricted democratic regimes have been politically contested in newly democratizing parts of the developing world because citizens, especially the poor majority, have held the reasonable expectation that democratic institutions would improve the basic social and economic conditions of their lives (Dagnino 1994; Casteñeda 1993; Avritzer 2002; Sen 1999). It is easy to understand why many citizens in developing world democracies are ambivalent about the purported benefits of representative democracy if they don't experience improvements in their quality of life.

In Brazil, social justice concerns are addressed through several complementary routes. One route follows the lead of Nobel Laureate Amartya Sen, who argues for the development of human capabilities as a means to produce the types of citizens capable of more fully engaging with society, market forces, and the state (1999). Participatory institutions have civic and social education components whereby information is provided to citizens to help them gain a better understanding of the state, government, and policymaking (Baiocchi 2005). This aligns with Evelina Dagnino's assertion that a cultural shift involving the "right to have rights" generates new capabilities that allow citizens to activate their rights (see chapter 2 for a fuller discussion).

Second, participatory institutions encourage citizens to forge "bonds of solidarity," which helps them mobilize across traditional cleavages (Alexander 2006; Putnam, Leonardi, and Nanetti 1994). It is hoped that the growing density and heightened mobilization of civil society will create the conditions for civil society to provide a locus of power to counterbalance the concentration of power among elite economic actors (Tarrow 1998). Baiocchi, Heller, and Silva's 2011 book uses a "paired case" comparison; they demonstrate that cities adopting one type of participatory democracy produce more robust and positive change in civil society than comparable cities that did not adopt participatory democracy.

Third, participatory institutions seek to incorporate poor citizens by focusing on policy issues that are of particular interest to the poor or by creating specific rules that provide a preferential bias in favor of the poor (de Jong and Rizvi 2008; Pateman 2012; Wampler 2012). Thus, poor citizens have specific reasons to participate, which help them maintain pressure on governments to allocate resources to poor communities. This moves beyond the liberal conceptualization of individual rights that is often central to representative democracy and allocates resources based on individuals' social and political situation.[2] Participatory institutions seek to promote social justice through accountability and oversight mechanisms, which support more efficient use of public resources and state authority (Wampler 2007).

The institutional design principles of social justice–oriented participatory programs in Table 1.1 were influenced by the work of Ostrom and of Fung and Wright (Ostrom 1990; Fung and Wright 2001, 2003). The design principles build on Fung and Wright, but the principal difference is that social justice concerns are addressed at each stage of the process.

In sum, Brazil's new participatory citizenship regime offers an integrated approach to addressing participation, institutional coordination, and social justice problems that have long bedeviled representative democracy. The 1988 constitution provides the basis to allow different public units (federal, state, municipal governments) to activate the participatory citizenship regime, but there is tremendous variation in how citizens can access the rights formally guaranteed under the constitution. In order to better understand how and why there is such tremendous variation, this book focuses its analytical lens on the city of Belo Horizonte, Brazil.

BELO HORIZONTE

Belo Horizonte is a city of 2.5 million and the state capital of landlocked Minas Gerais, located to the northwest of Rio de Janeiro. Five successive mayoral administrations built a complex participatory architecture that now allows citizens the opportunity to be elected to thousands of political positions as well as participate in multiple formal venues in order to deliberate with their fellow citizens and public officials in public meetings. The research strategy follows the lead of Sandbrook and his coauthors in *Social Democracy in the Global Periphery*. They argue that focusing on places that have achieved significant change helps us to understand the possibilities of change elsewhere (Sandbrook et al. 2007). Thus Belo Horizonte is an exemplary city that offers important insights into how the participatory citizenship regime may unfold across the rest of the country.

The city of Belo Horizonte is an exceptional city for at least three reasons. First, it is Brazil's first planned city (Eakin 2001). Political elites in the state of Minas Gerais, following the founding of Brazil's republic in 1889, moved their state capital to a more centrally located and easily accessible site. The city of Belo Horizonte was based on Paris and Washington, DC. There is an inner core, a ring road, wide avenues, cross-cutting streets, and public parks. The fact that Belo Horizonte is a planned city and that it was a partner to São Paulo during Brazil's early industrialization indicates the

Table 1.1 Participatory Design Principles to Promote Social Justice

Decentralize government	• Allows targeted populations to make decisions on local issues • Links bureaucrats and policy experts at neighborhood level • Distributes resources on a per capita basis with poorer neighborhoods receiving greater levels of funding
Reward mobilization	• Permits citizens to directly vote on policy outcomes • Draws attention to policy issues that have strong relevance to targeted communities (e.g., basic infrastructure, health care clinics) • Allocates resources based on need and population—poorer communities receive greater levels of public resources
Expand deliberative forums	• Encourages citizens to debate each other and government officials • Provides information to citizens to allow them to hold a more substantive debate on government priorities and state responsibilities • Permits citizens to question the (in)actions of government officials and community leaders
Promote new networks and alliances	• Links citizens to government officials, citizens to other citizens, CSOs to CSOs • Fosters growth alliances among poor • Establishes new intermediaries in the absence of strong parties
Engage in oversight	• Allows citizens and CSOs to monitor policy implementation • Helps citizens to gather information about ongoing policy efforts • Promotes more efficient and effective use of state funds.

Source: Adapted from Wampler 2012.

Table 1.2 Basic Social Indicators in Major Brazilian Cities

	Population 2000	*HDI 1991*	*HDI 2000*	*HDI 2010*	*Per Capita Income, 2005*	*Gini 2000*
Belo Horizonte	2.3 million	.602	.726	.810	7,531	.620
Porto Alegre	1.4 million	.660	.744	.805	12,340	.606
Curitiba	1.6 million	.640	.750	.823	10,690	.594
Recife	1.4 million	.576	.660	.772	6,996	.680
Salvador	2.4 million	.563	.654	.759	5,220	.658

Source: Instituto Brasileiro de Geografia e Estatística 2014.

presence of a forward-looking, modernist, and reform-minded political and economic elite (Eakin 2001; Evans 1979).

Second, Belo Horizonte is also exceptional because basic social indicators present very positive results that are not easily explained through a standard economic modernization account. In comparison to other large state capitals, Belo Horizonte's per capita income is lower than that of southern cities such as Porto Alegre and Curitiba and is close to northeastern cities like Recife and Salvador. But Belo Horizonte's Human Development Index score (HDI, a composite of education, longevity, and income) is closer to its wealthier southern neighbors. Thus governments are involved in producing positive social indicators, which gives weight to a political process–oriented argument rather than one based on socioeconomic development.

Third, Belo Horizonte is exceptional because of the five terms won by a center-left political coalition. The Workers' Party and the Brazilian Socialist Party won mayoral elections in 1992, 1996, 2000, 2004, and 2008. The 1992 mayoral election was a critical realignment, beginning twenty years of political control by a center-left political coalition (Key 1964). The municipal government activated the local state to induce appointed and elected officials to be more responsive to the demands and interests of citizens and CSOs. A twenty-year period allows for consolidating administrative processes that provide the necessary support to the participatory citizenship regime. As a result of this long-term hold on political power, the redesign of the local state greatly expanded the number of access points that enable citizens to have formal, public contact with government officials. The government developed new tools and administrative procedures to grapple with the triple challenge: (a) allocating scarce resources to members of a marginalized, poor population in order to help them realize a new body of social rights guaranteed under the 1988 constitution (social justice); (b) incorporating interested citizens into participatory governance venues as a means to expand democratic voice and vote (popular participation); and (c) altering the state to govern with a large number of citizens, helping fulfill the pledge of a sitting government to govern for all citizens while also helping the government select policies to help them win elections (interlocking institutions).

Belo Horizonte is at the crossroads of the southeast, northeast, and center-west and is representative of key sociocultural and political characteristics of urban Brazil. First, there are high levels of inequality. A significant plurality live in favelas with limited access to public infrastructure and employment (Gonçalves 2007). Most favelas are located far from the city center, although several key favelas are in the heart of the city. The spatial segregation that most favela residents experience is thus similar to that of São Paulo, but the insertion of two large favelas into the city core produces a dynamic reminiscent of Rio de Janeiro (Perlman 2010).

Second, Belo Horizonte has long received migrants from the interior of its own state (Minas Gerais) as well as from the northeast of Brazil. The city and metropolitan area grew rapidly during the 1940s and 1950s as a result of this internal migration, comprised of people seeking jobs (Eakin 2001; Hagopian 1996). Rural to urban migration is a feature of Brazilian cities. Third, the state of Minas Gerais is heavily involved in agriculture and mining. The financial service sector is located in Belo Horizonte and has strong ties to these primary products. Fourth, Belo Horizonte's metropolitan area has a strong industrial presence, although it is clearly secondary to São Paulo. Industrialization created a strong union presence, the development of a middle class, and a working class. The traditional political oligarchy that dominated the state for much of the twentieth century remains strong, although its influence has waned in the larger urban areas.

RESEARCH METHODOLOGY AND CASE SELECTION

This book is a subnational comparative analysis of multiple institutions in a single city in Brazil (Snyder 2001; Dahl 1961). This book shows how a new political coalition activated the participatory citizenship regime. Participatory institutions are now an integral part of agenda setting and policymaking in Brazil, from local health districts to national policy conferences. Political scientists and sociologists have made great headway in understanding the opportunities and limitations for change produced by these new institutions (Abers 2000; Avritzer 2002, 2009; Baiocchi 2005; Baiocchi, Heller, and Silva 2011; Fung 2003, 2006; Fung and Wright 2003; Goldfrank 2007, 2011; Heller 2000, 2001; Wampler 2007, 2008; McNulty 2011; Van Cott 2008; Pateman 1970, 2012). Researchers in the development field have been much less sanguine about the potential impact that these institutions may have on improving social well-being, empowerment, and human capabilities (Mansuri and Rao 2004, 2012; Navarro 2003; Grindle 2007).

The first generation of research on participatory institutions in Brazil and Latin America tended to focus on a single institution, such as health care councils or participatory budgeting, in a single city (Abers 2000; Tatagiba 2002). The second generation compared the same institutional type across multiple cities (e.g., analyzing participatory budgeting in multiple cities; Nylen 2002; Wampler 2007; Goldfrank 2011) or used paired comparisons of cities with and without one type of institution (Baiocchi, Heller, and Silva 2011). The third generation of reforms focuses on the policy and political impact of these institutions in longitudinal, national, and cross-national studies (Wampler and McNulty 2011; Pogrebinschi and Samuels 2014; Touchton and Wampler 2014).

What is missing from this debate is long-term comparative analysis demonstrating how participatory institutions contribute to the activation of the participatory citizenship regime. This book fills this void by demonstrating the different patterns of political and social behaviors produced by the participatory citizenship regime. I employ a comparative analysis within the city of Belo Horizonte to show how institutionalizing participatory governance is now transforming state-society relations. In this case, citizens and government officials work closely together to produce policy and political solutions to seemingly intractable problems, like property rights issues in favelas, access to good quality housing and health care, and the urbanization of favelas.

My comparative analysis draws on six different participatory governance institutions as well as the mayoral administration and legislative branch in Belo Horizonte. This book employs a mixed-methods approach that I developed and refined between 1995 and 2009 as I conducted research on subnational and participatory politics in Brazil; throughout this period, my research focused on civil society, new democratic institutions, and state reform. I am particularly interested in how the interaction of new rules, actors, and interests promotes social and political change. This interest led me to conduct research in multiple political institutions. Included for analysis are the municipal executive branch (mayoral administration), the municipal legislative branch, three public policy management councils, and three participatory budgeting programs in the city over an eighteen-year period.

Between 1995 and 2010, I lived in Brazil for more than four years in major cities (São Paulo, Belo Horizonte, Porto Alegre, Recife). Over this fifteen-year period I attended more than 150 public participatory meetings, conducted more than two hundred elite interviews (with politicians and civil society leaders), attended dozens of meetings held by social movements and community organizations, and spent time in favelas (mostly doing research but also hanging out with friends).

My first book, *Participatory Budgeting in Brazil: Contestation, Cooperation, and Accountability*, used a mixed-method, subnational comparative approach to analyze a single institution in eight Brazilian municipalities. It was the first comparative analysis that documented and then accounted for the wide variation in the functioning and impact of participatory budgeting programs. The idea for the current book was seeded while I was conducting research for the first book in Porto Alegre. I became aware that many civil society leaders participated in multiple venues as they sought to gain access to scarce public resources. My methodological approach in the first book captured what these activists did in participatory budgeting, but I wasn't able to analyze their political activities in other institutions. I observed that government officials and civil society activists sought each other out prior to and after formal deliberative sessions to discuss problems and projects that didn't fit within the scope of PB. Thus, while I was working on the eight-case analysis, I realized that a major gap in our understanding of civil society, new democratic institution, and state building was a deep analysis of a single case.

In order to conduct a detailed analysis of a single case, I draw on evidence from multiple sources: participant observation, elite interviews, original surveys, and budgetary and legislative documents. With regard to participant observation, I attended a wide range of meetings in Belo Horizonte. I first attended participatory meetings in 2000, followed by six weeks of research in 2004, followed by ten months in 2009–2010.

During 2009–2010 I attended dozens of meetings that ranged from large PB meetings attended by more than one thousand citizens to public policy management council meetings with twenty to thirty attendees. I attended meetings across four policy arenas—housing, health, social services, and participatory budgeting—in two different favelas.

Attending multiple meetings over a ten-year period allowed me to develop the necessary trust to conduct meaningful elite interviews. Brazil continues to be beset by low levels of trust, which means that researchers conducting interviews must know someone who knows someone so that the interview will be fruitful. In Belo Horizonte, over the ten-year period, I interviewed over fifty CSO activists and government officials, with more than thirty interviews taking place in 2009–2010. Throughout the book I try to bring the argument to life by illustrating my findings with quotations and vignettes that are representative of the evidence I collected. This approach differs from a richly detailed ethnography in that I draw from a wider spectrum of political and social positions to illustrate key points.

Finally, this book incorporates evidence from two surveys I administered in Belo Horizonte. One survey was administered to 300 civil society activists. My research agenda has demonstrated the vital importance of using surveys to complement elite interviews and participant observation of meetings. For example, in the 2007 book, my survey findings confirmed many of the insights gleaned from elite interviews and participant observation. In addition, my research team also administered a similar survey to 328 residents in two different favelas. I also conducted additional interviews in the favelas and spent time attending different events. The data presented doesn't have the rich ethnographic detail of work by Desmond Arias, Robert Gay, or Javier Auyero, but it is designed to help the reader understand how the participatory citizenship regime is unfolding in two important favelas.

PLAN OF BOOK

Chapter 2 provides a historical overview of changing citizenship regimes, arguing that the current participatory citizenship regime follows "conceded" (1889–1930) and "regulated" (1930–1988) citizenship regimes. Chapter 3 examines how the local state was reengineered in the 1990s and 2000s. A new political coalition *activated* the local state by allowing new ideas, new interests, and new actors into the decision-making process; there was an institutionalization of the venues through which citizens and CSO leaders participate. Chapter 3 analyzes the process of state formation and local political conflict during the 1990s and 2000s. Chapters 4 and 5 shift the focus to six distinct forms of participatory governance—three public policy management councils and three types of participatory budgeting. A core issue is how these new institutional processes affect the broader polity as well as specific public policy arenas.

The last two substantive chapters focus attention on how citizens and CSOs are engaging in the new participatory architecture. Chapter 6 closely examines the ways in which civil society leaders have responded to this new state and to the new participatory architecture. I draw from an original survey of three hundred community leaders to better explain how they are using the new strategies. Chapter 7 turns the focus to two favelas, Morro de Papagaio and Alto Vera Cruz. This chapter shows how citizens are now interacting with CSO leaders and broader participatory institutions in pursuit of their common interests. The focus on two favelas gives readers a better sense of the complexity of social and political change. The book's final chapter moves beyond Belo Horizonte to illuminate how democracy is being activated across Brazil. Belo Horizonte provides an excellent lens through which we could examine the challenges facing Brazilians as they seek access to the rights formally guaranteed by the constitution.

CHAPTER TWO

Establishing the Participatory Citizenship Regime

Citizenship regimes define who has political membership, which rights they possess, and how interest intermediation with the state is structured.
—Deborah Yashar, *Contesting Citizenship in Latin America*

The mobilization of civil society in Brazil during the 1970s and 1980s revolved around efforts to broaden who was eligible to access rights, which rights would be available to the larger public, and the institutions that would mediate political contestation among public officials and citizens. The promotion of citizenship rights (*cidadania*) was a politically contentious idea because it was based on the premise that all Brazilians should have access to the same basic set of constitutional rights (Dagnino 1994, 1998). By asserting equality among citizens, citizenship activists were confronting an extremely unequal political and social system. The mobilization of civil society during the 1970s and 1980s sought to empower citizens, expand public goods provision to poor communities, and create new institutions that would allow Brazilians to move beyond the confines of representative democracy. Although the promulgation of the 1988 constitution formally initiated the participatory citizenship regime, it was the renewal of civil society during the 1970s and 1980s under the authoritarian military regime (1964–1985) that pushed the expansion of democratic institutions and social rights.

Brazil experienced three distinct citizenship regimes after the establishment of the First Republic in 1889: conceded (1889–1930), regulated (1930–1988), and participatory (1988–). The conceded citizenship regime was dominated by Brazil's infamous *coreneis*—land-owning oligarchs who governed through a combination of direct force and clientelistic exchanges (Carvalho 1987 and 2002). The regulated citizenship regime, formally initiated with the Revolution of 1930, marks the expansion of social rights to members of the professional classes and organized labor, both sectors vital to Brazil's industrialization project (Santos 1979). The participatory citizenship regime represents the expansion of political and social rights as well as new democratic institutions, thereby formally guaranteeing all citizens a set of civil, political, and social rights formally enshrined in the 1988 constitution. Since the promulgation of that constitution, political contestation continues to revolve around who should access which rights and which institutions should address citizens' demands.

The introduction of a new citizenship regime does not cleanly supplant the previous citizenship regime, since each regime is slowly built and extended over time. There is not a sharp, complete break between one regime and the next. For example, the Revolution of 1930 initiated the regulated citizenship regime, but rights were extended to only a small minority of the population, which meant that most Brazilian citizens continued to be trapped under the violent and clientelistic control of the *coreneis*, which is associated with the conceded citizenship regime. In the twenty-first century we see the existence of three different rights regimes within Brazil: some citizens remained trapped in the conceded citizenship regime, others have access to the rights afforded by the regulated citizenship regime, and yet others are now gaining access to a wide range of rights under the participatory citizenship regime.

This chapter first develops the concept of the citizenship regime to illustrate how individuals, organizations, elected officials, and state officials interact to extend rights. The second part of this chapter shows how and to whom civil, social, and political rights are extended within the conceded, regulated, and participatory citizenship regimes. Within each type of regime we can see the fruits of the next period, which means that there are not clear ruptures between the regimes, but political and cultural activities cut across periods.

The final part of this chapter links the participatory citizenship regime to broader debates on the quality of democracy. At the core of democratic societies and political regimes is the ability of citizens to effectively use rights formally established under constitutional law (O'Donnell 1994, 1998; Marshall 1950; Dahl 1971). When citizens lack access to rights, especially political rights, there is an obvious weakening of the quality of democracy. The participatory citizenship regime is grounded in an effort to expand both political and social rights, with a much weaker focus on civil rights. After twenty-five years of Brazil's democratic regime, it is clear that where people live—which state, which city, which neighborhood— tremendously affects their ability to access rights guaranteed by the 1988 constitution. Guillermo O'Donnell's use of "brown" and "green" spaces (similar to a topographical map) captures the differential access that citizens have to rights (O'Donnell 1994). In this vein, citizens living in "green" spaces have access to a wide selection of constitutionally guaranteed rights, whereas citizens living in "brown" spaces don't have access to these same rights.

CITIZENSHIP REGIMES

Citizenship rights—analytically distinguishable as civil, political, social, and collective rights—are exercised by citizens and guaranteed through state and societal protections (Marshall 1950; Yashar 2005). The legal basis of citizenship rights most commonly occurs at the individual level, based on how individuals are treated by state officials (e.g., judges, police officers, teachers), private corporations, and other citizens. The legal basis can also be collective, as constitutions and state policies recognize rights for different groups of citizens (based on categories such as gender, race, and ethnic identity). In addition, state officials, private corporations, and citizens often treat individuals based on their social identifiers, such as gender, class, or race. Thus the ability of individuals to access their constitutionally guaranteed civil, political, and social rights is often based on others' perceptions of which rights they should be afforded. This difference is captured by de jure and de facto legal interpretations, whereby individuals' ability to exercise law is based on public officials' interpretation of the law. The infamous phase in Brazil "For my friends, everything; for my enemies, the law" captures the difference between a rule of law based on universal application and a legal system based on the political interests of public officials. (See Carvalho 1987 and 2002 for excellent discussion of this topic.)

T. H. Marshall's seminal work demonstrates that the extension of citizenship rights to English citizens was uneven, contested, and occurred over several centuries (Marshall 1950; see Thompson 1996; Somers 1993). In the case of England, civil rights (e.g., protection in courts, habeas corpus, private property) were extended over several hundred years, first to land-owning property classes and then slowly spreading to a greater share of the population (Marshall 1950). Likewise, political rights (e.g., the right to vote, free speech, organization) were first extended to the nobility and propertied classes and later expanded to the middle and working classes during the nineteenth and twentieth centuries. Finally, social rights (e.g., education, health care, retirement) provided by the state were primarily established after the end of World War II. A key insight is that rights are established unevenly and over a long time; individuals' social position profoundly affects how they are able to access rights. The stratification of Brazilian society allows us to conceptualize the presence of multiple citizenship regimes. Citizens have access to different citizenship regimes based on where they live, their formal or informal work status, and their socioeconomic class.

Although Marshall argues that civil rights in England were expanded in the eighteenth century, political rights in the nineteenth, and social (welfare-state) rights in the twentieth, he never asserts that this was the necessary order or the only way that rights can be extended. The sequence of expanding rights has been quite different in Brazil, since some citizens gained access to civil and political rights at the republic's founding in 1889, whereas other citizens didn't gain access to these rights until the 1988 constitution. Some citizens, such as unionized workers, gained access to social rights prior to civil or political rights.

Deborah Yashar introduces the concept of "citizenship regime" as a means to capture a broader, more comprehensive understanding of rights. "Citizenship regimes define *who* has political membership, *which* rights they possess, and *how* interest intermediation with the state is structured" (Yashar 2004, 6; italics in original; see also the preliminary discussion in chapter 1 of this book). The first and second parts of this definition draw attention to the variation in political access (*who* holds rights) and *which* rights individuals and groups may be able to formally exercise. This definition is based on the assumption that individuals and groups have differential access to rights and that access to these rights shifts over time. There is no fixed set of rights, but ongoing political and social struggles and conflicts shape the type of rights citizens will be able to access.

The challenge in Brazil and Latin America is that the state has played a very uneven role in providing access to civil and political rights. In Brazil, people have profoundly different access to the state, based on where they live, their socioeconomic status, their type of employment, and their personal networks. The Brazilian state is notoriously violent (Arias 2006; Perlman 2010), especially toward poor young men, many of whom are black and living in favelas. The state has long provided poor public education to its citizens, thereby encouraging the middle and upper classes to turn to the private market for expensive K-12 education. However, the state is also effective and efficient in other areas. For example, the state launches satellites, successfully developed and administers a public company that produces mid-sized aircraft (Embraer), and built an infrastructure that permitted extensive industrialization (as seen in the Itapúa Dam). The demand for social rights is done in the context of a state already providing public goods and infrastructure to targeted sectors.

CITIZENSHIP REGIMES IN BRAZIL

Since the founding of Brazil's Republic in 1889, there are three important historical periods when citizenship rights were extended to the population: conceded (1889–1930), regulated (1930–1988), and participatory (1988–).

Conceded Citizenship: "O Brasil não tem povo"[1]

The First Republic was founded in 1889 with a limited set of citizenship rights. The republic was based on the rule of rural oligarchies, strong governors, a liberal economic orthodoxy in which the state had limited involvement in economic affairs, and the dominance of the state of São Paulo and Minas Gerais (Carvalho 2002, 45–64; Fausto 1999, 158). Although the Brazilian monarchy (1822–1889) established the formal framework of modern representative democracy (three branches of government; voting for representatives at federal, state, and municipal levels), the founding of the First Republic marks the formal establishment of Brazilians as citizens rather than as subjects of Brazil's emperor.

The transition to the republic from Brazil's monarchy was based on elite negotiations with little direct involvement from the broader public (Carvalho 2002; Fausto 1999). As a result, there was not a significant rupture in how Brazilian political and civil societies were organized. Civil society organizations were scarce, which limited the ability of nonelite actors to influence the founding of the republic (Carvalho 2002). The absence of meaningful political contestation during the founding meant that the primary political relationships that sustained Brazil's monarchy were carried into the republic. The lack of a broad-based movement precluded the development of a strong national identity.

Teresa Sales conceptualizes the type of rights extended during this period as "conceded citizenship, or *cidadania concedida* (Sales 1994). Brazilian political bosses, the infamous local *coreneis*, "gave" or "conceded" rights to the masses, thereby extending a "culture of donation" into the realm of liberal rights. "This culture of donation outlived the private domination of the colonial estates and sugar plantations, it outlived the abolition of slavery, and it expressed itself in a particular way in the commitment of the colonel" (Sales 1994, 26; see also Leal 1997). As a result, individuals who received the "donation" of rights were dependent on more powerful actors, which meant that those rights could be withdrawn based on the needs of the more powerful actors. Weaker, dependent individuals did, of course, receive some value from the clientelistic exchanges, but these clientelistic relationships are based on sharp divisions of political and social power. The important implication of Sales's argument is that key political culture relationships developed during Portuguese colonialism and Brazil's monarchy (1822 to 1889) and thus formed the foundations of elite-mass relationships during the First Republic.

Brazil was the last country in the Western Hemisphere to abolish slavery, which meant that the most basic of civil rights—an individual's right to personal freedom, to power over their own life—was established in 1888, the year prior to the establishment of the First Republic. Pressure to end slavery was largely driven by Great Britain, although there was a small and growing abolition movement within Brazil (Carvalho 2002; Marx 1998). The lack of significant social or political upheaval leading to the end of slavery meant that former slaves did not conceive of themselves as rights-bearing members of the polity (Marx 1998). Furthermore, the entrenched political and economic elite of the country did not view former slaves as citizens, which reinforced the use of an elite-dominated citizenship regime.

Following the end of slavery, the Brazilian elite promoted the immigration of Europeans (mainly Italian and Germans) as a way to lessen the potential conflicts between state and society. By "whitening" the country, the Brazilian elite hoped to limit the racial conflicts that affected other countries with large Afro-Descendent populations (see Marx 1998).

Civil Rights

Brazil had a judicial system and a military police that was responsible, in theory, for ensuring the extension of the rule of law. A legalistic, bureaucratic state was inherited from Portugal and from Brazil's monarchy. Although the institutional structure was in place, laws and state institutions were used by the infamous *coreneis* to promote their interests. José Murilo de Carvalho cites a famous phrase from this period: "For my friends, everything; for my enemies, the law" (2002, 57). Behind this popular saying is the idea that state officials can use the power of a legalistic, bureaucratic state to promote their personal interests. As a result, most Brazilians didn't have access to basic civil rights during the First Republic (1889–1930).

Wealthier and more politically powerful groups did have access to property rights protections and were able to seek redress for their grievances through the judicial branch. But only a small minority of people who were allied with the *coreneis* could access their civil rights. Manipulation of the legal system undermines the concept of a fair and just rule of law because individuals' social and political positions determined their ability to use civil rights. The type of individuals who might assert, "*Você sabe com quem esta falando?*" ("Do you know with whom you are speaking?"), were able to secure rights protections, but ordinary citizens were unable to access basic civil rights (Matta 1979). Thus local political bosses extended civil rights to those individuals and groups with whom they had strong political connections.

Political Rights

Political rights under the First Republic were limited to wealthier, well-connected individuals. Ironically, voting rights became more restrictive in the First Republic than they had been during the 1860s and 1870s. Under the Brazilian monarchy (1822–1889), the percentage of male citizens who could vote was relatively high, indicating that Brazil was using features of a modern political system (representative democracy) with traditional hereditary rule. "According to the calculations of the historian

Richard Graham, around 50 percent of the adult male [nonslave] population voted prior to 1881" (Carvalho 2002, 31). Voting was required for all
males above twenty-five who met very low property qualifications. The
percentage of Brazilian men who voted was higher than in England, the
United States, and Italy during the same period (Carvalho 2002, 31). According to the analytical framework developed by Larry Diamond, Brazil
was developing a "prototype" democracy that would lay the groundwork
for representative democracy (see Diamond, Linz, and Lipset 1988).

Although elections were relatively well attended during the 1860s and
1870s, they did not promote open political competition. The infamous
coreneis used elections to reward allies, establish loyalty, and punish rivals
(Leal 1997). Traditional political families used elections to consolidate
their political positions within their home area (similar to Ames's use of
the term "bailiwicks" to describe Brazilian elections in the 1990s; see Ames
2001). With the low property qualifications for voting, clientelistic ties
were used to extend the oligarchy's control over poor Brazilians. The political control established through elections was important because of
mayors' and governors' use of state authority to violate—or respect—
citizens' civil and political rights.

In 1881, prior to the end of slavery and the establishment of the First
Republic, Brazil's lower chamber added a literacy requirement, raising the
property qualifications and making the vote optional rather than mandatory. The percentage of Brazilian males who voted dramatically declined:
from 50 percent in the 1870s to less than 1 percent of the population in
1886 (Carvalho 2002, 39). The decreased formal participation was extended into the First Republic, which meant that elections counted on
very small turnouts. The First Republic thus limited the potential impact
of representative democracy because the rules limited the number of voters. Vertical, or electoral, accountability, was not established (Cleary 2010).
Beyond voting, the right to organize was tightly controlled by the state governments, which were in the domain of the *coreneis*. This was particularly
true in rural areas, where workers fell under the control of the local *coreneis*. The right to strike was outlawed, so workers in the newly industrial-
izing areas had limited legal ways to advance their interests (Wolfe 1993;
French 1992). Thus Brazil's First Republic was an illiberal, restricted democracy (Fausto 1999; O'Donnell 1994).

Although public officials sought to control public demonstrations
and strikes, and although the *coreneis* "gave" rights to a limited number of
citizens, there were multiple armed conflicts between 1889 and 1930. The

causes of each conflict are varied, ranging from messianic movements to anarchist organizations to Communist Party mobilization. The regularity of the armed conflicts suggests that "intermediation" institutions didn't exist or failed to meet the most basic demands of the organized citizens. The lack of any meaningful citizen vote in elections and the direct control exerted by the state over organized groups did not induce individuals or groups to work within formal state institutions. Thus the idea of "ambition to counteract ambition," envisioned by James Madison (in the context of the US Constitution) as a means to draw organized groups into formal political institutions and dampen the likelihood of violent political conflict, was not present in Brazil.

Social Rights

The First Republic established a very limited set of social rights. Carvalho argues that "there was even a recession of what we refer to as social rights" (Carvalho 1987, 45). Former slaves were formally included in the national community at this time (slavery was abolished in 1888) but were unable to seek redress for violations of their rights (Carvalho 2002, 52). Political elites did little to ensure that these individuals could access basic social rights (Marx 1994).

There was a very limited state during the First Republic, which meant that public officials had little authority or resources to provide public goods. The state did not provide public education, which helps to explain the abysmally low levels of literacy: just 24 percent of the population was literate in the 1920s (Carvalho 2002, 65). University education was also limited, in part because the Portuguese colonial government had not established universities in Brazil. The state did not provide access to health care. Health care for the poor was provided by the *santa casas*, which were administered by the Catholic Church.

However, during the First Republic, the state-level governments in São Paulo and Minas Gerais began to promote industrialization (Evans 1979; Eakin 2001). These state-level elites in Minas Gerais and São Paulo initiated urbanization and public health campaigns in the major cities—an attempt to provide public goods to a larger public. Political elites also used public resources to encourage the immigration of Europeans and Japanese to Brazil at the end of the nineteenth and twentieth centuries. The impetus behind the immigrant push was racial in nature; elites didn't believe that former slaves had the cultural and intellectual traits necessary to participate in the industrialization project (Marx 1998).

In sum, Brazil's conceded citizenship regime began with the start of the First Republic, whereby a small elite "gave" a minimal set of rights to the population. Rights were thus weakly extended and were not "won" through protracted struggle or through the construction of a strong national identity. The limited extension of rights encouraged the use of clientelistic politics, which would mark local politics in Brazil throughout the twentieth century. Government officials and politicians were able to "donate" minimal goods to poor individuals and communities in exchange for their support at the ballot box or their attendance at a campaign rally.

Returning to Yashar's definition of citizenship regime, we can confirm that political membership in Brazil's new republic was limited to a small minority of the population: the landed elite, the entrepreneurs attempting to set up an industrialized economy, and the small but slightly growing professional classes. Individuals from these political and economic classes had access to a limited set of civil, political, and social rights. Interest intermediation with the federal state was managed through the politics of *café com leite* (coffee with milk), whereby the political elites from the states of Minas Gerais (dairy-based agricultural) and São Paulo (coffee-based agricultural) governed the country. Political competition outside of urban areas was control by the traditional *coreneis*, who governed with a heavy hand. Thus, the majority of the population did not have access to basic citizenship rights; citizens didn't have civil rights protections, and they couldn't vote or easily express voice in public demonstrations. Interest intermediation was largely regulated through private, clientelistic exchanges (Roniger 1994). The political and economic elites, especially the powerful *coreneis*, used political clientelism and the cultural practice of "conceded citizenship" in order to manage their control over the state.

However, the roots of change in a new citizenship regime—regulated—can already be seen in the conceded citizenship regime. Brazil's economy and civil society were changing. Brazilian political elites, especially those in São Paulo and Minas Gerais, supported the shift toward a new pattern of industrialization, which eventually led to the regulated citizenship regime.

Regulated Citizenship

The industrialization of Brazil, which began at the end of nineteenth century, was led by political and economic elites from the states of São Paulo and Minas Gerais (Evans 1979; Eakin 2001). The industrialization project set in motion a series of changes that would lead to the second citizenship regime. Industrialization generated more wealth and a broader set of economic interests, principally enabling the growing professional and middle classes to access a broader array of civil and political rights (Carvalho 2002; Putnam, Leonardi, and Nanetti 1994).

The federal government's first broad extension of social rights to the working classes came during the first half of the 1930s (Santos 1979, 74–79). The formal rupture that led to the end of the First Republic was the Revolution of 1930, whereby political and military leaders from three states (Minas Gerais, Rio Grande do Sul, and Paraíba) sought to block the political aspirations of São Paulo's increasingly powerful economic and political elite. The successful revolution, or military coup, brought a new governing coalition to power.

> A new type of state was born after 1930. It differed from the oligarchical state not only owing to its centralization and its greater degree of autonomy, but also because of other factors: (1) economic policy slowly turned toward the promotion of industrialization; (2) social policy tended to provide some sort of protection for urban workers, who were soon gathered into a working-class alliance supported by the state; (3) the armed forces, in particular the army, was given a central role in support of the creation of an industrial base and in maintaining internal order. (Fausto 1999, 196)

The regulated citizenship regime (*cidadania regulada*) extended social rights to specific categories of workers while simultaneously denying any new rights to the majority of the population (see Santos 1979). "By regulated citizenship, I refer to its roots found not in the 'code' of political values but in the system of occupational stratification . . . a system of stratification defined by legal norms" (Santos 1979, 75). Social rights were extended to specific sectors of the Brazilian working class, but political and civil rights were not extended. Social rights were extended to public sector employees (e.g., members of the military, university professors, bureaucrats) and private sector employees (e.g., assembly line workers, machinists, dock workers) who were vital to the industrialization efforts.

The partial extension of citizenship rights created a perverse set of incentives. Individuals had strong incentives to organize within their specific job category (e.g., metal worker, teacher, doctor) to secure specific benefits from the state. Rights were extended based on individuals' positions within the formal job market, which meant that there was a disincentive to provide public goods to the broader public. Not only did this increase the distance between those in the formal and informal wage markets, but it also exacerbated already low levels of trust (Chaui 1989; Carvalho 2002; Putnam, Leonardi, and Nanetti 1994).

The dominant feature of the 1930–1988 period was the establishment of a corporatist governing model in which social rights were extended on the basis of individuals' occupation and the limited ability of citizens to press for their rights outside of the corporatist governing structure (Schmitter 1974). There were three national political regimes during the "regulated citizenship" period. From 1930 to 1945, President Getúlio Vargas dominated national politics. Vargas came to power in 1930 and formally founded the Estado Novo in 1937, which curtailed the limited political and civil rights that had been extended to the working class. Second, a democratic period (1945–1964) expanded some basic rights, including the right to vote, which was available to a minority of citizens. Vargas was elected president in 1951, and he served until he died by suicide in 1954. Third, the military returned in 1964 and governed until 1985. Although these were obviously distinct political regimes, corporatist forms of interest intermediation institutions marked which groups of citizens would be able to access social rights.

Social Rights

The Brazilian state expanded under President Getúlio Vargas during the 1930s and 1940s. The governing system employed by Vargas was corporatist, involving the direct incorporation of labor, business, and state officials into policymaking venues (Wolfe 1993; French 1992; Santos 1979; Kohli 2004). Workers included in the formal labor market enjoyed access to public services (e.g., housing, education, and health care) that were not provided to most Brazilians, the majority of whom could also not afford market prices for decent services. Vargas was following the corporatist governance system first developed in Europe: government officials formally incorporate labor and private corporations into governing institutions, thus increasing direct government control. Vargas was also responding to the successful organizing efforts of communist and anarchist labor unions during the 1920s, 1930s, and 1940s; Vargas extended rights to hundreds of thousands of workers, which provided a base of loyalty for the regime (French 1992; Wolf 1993). These efforts were part of an effort to siphon away potential support for socialist and communist parties. The corporatist system isolated the more radical unions from playing a central role in labor organization.

This extension of social rights to unionized workers was based on a top-down logic, similar to the conceded citizenship regime, with the government extending rights to a select group of citizens. The rights were used to reward loyal labor unions but could be withdrawn or modified through the government-dominated corporatist system (Schmitter 1974). However, a key difference between the regulated and conceded citizenship regimes is that the mobilization of a growing, skilled union class pushed the government to expand the terrain of social rights. Thus, rights were much stickier than those extended in the conceded citizenship regime as a result of prior mobilization and the institutionalization of corporatist rule.

Civil Rights

Civil rights were partially expanded to the growing professional classes and to some sectors of the organized working classes. Access to the judicial branch continued to be heavily dependent on citizens' ability to hire lawyers to work within the legalistic and bureaucratic system. Unionized workers increasingly had access to lawyers, thus allowing them to protect their individual interests vis-à-vis the state. Access to lawyers was a social right provide by the corporatist state, which enabled unionized workers to seek to use the courts to protect their civil rights Although professionals and unionized workers slowly expanded their access to civil rights, most Brazilians did not have access to basic civil rights. State-level public officials, through their control over the police, often violated the rights of ordinary citizens. The poor majority suffered at the hands of a repressive police force (Holston 2008; Perlman 2010).

The ability of the professional classes to access civil rights varied significantly across the three national political regimes types. During the 1930–1945 period, President Vargas sharply restricted political organizing, free speech, and other basic civil rights (Carvalho 2002; Fausto 1999). During the democratic regime (1945–1964), there was a broadening of civil rights protections, but these were distributed unevenly. Access to civil rights was more likely among urban workers and the growing middle, professional classes.

In 1964, a military coup ushered in more than two decades of authoritarian military rule. Initially, the military government was initially a caretaker government and did not have a transformation project, which distinguishes the 1964 coup leaders from their counterparts in Chile,

Argentina, and Uruguay (Garreton 1994; Alves 2014). In 1968, Brazil's military dictatorship radicalized its governing strategy by issuing the draconian Institutional Act #5, which effectively eliminated the political and civil rights that had been exercised by the middle and professional classes. Institutional Act #5 greatly increased the power and authority of the state security apparatus, helping the military government to successfully defeat a number of small guerilla movements. This period was marked by the most extensive withdrawal of civil rights. Citizens, including the growing middle classes, lost access to the basic rights that had been slowly been extended to them.

Political Rights

Political rights were repeatedly extended and withdrawn between 1930 and 1988. The establishment of corporatist rule meant that unionized workers had very limited autonomy to organize themselves politically. Government officials controlled unions and thus made it very difficult for unionized workers to mobilize or to carry out strikes. During this period, Brazil experienced military rule (1930–1945), representative democracy (1945–1964), and military rule (1964–1985). Across all three regimes, citizens maintained the right to vote; Congress was allowed to function even under the military governments. The number of citizens who could vote was expanded. Women gained the right to vote in 1934, but the implementation of the Estado Novo in 1937 meant that women would not effectively exercise the vote until 1945. Property qualifications were eliminated, opening the vote to the working classes. However, literacy qualifications were maintained, effectively meaning that well over half the adult population didn't have the right to vote.

The limited impact of the vote on elite decision making is best illustrated by the fact that the military dictatorship (1964–1985) maintained the vote for federal and state legislators (lower and upper houses) as well as for mayors in cities with fewer than a hundred thousand residents.[2] By allowing citizens to continue to vote, the military government was able to gain a basic sense of citizens' attitudes, although it also opened the military regime to criticism because the elections had no clear impact on elite decision making.

From the 1930s through the 1980s, the regulated citizenship regime extended rights to specific members of organized labor as well as the professional classes. Brazil developed a citizenship regime in which specific individuals and categories of workers had access to an expanded set of rights. The key political problem for the corporatist system was that the conceded citizenship regime existed alongside the regulated citizenship regime. The regulated citizenship regime included unionized workers formally incorporated into the labor markets, and the conceded citizenship regime continued to dominate the lives of citizens living in rural areas as well as in urban favelas. Citizens with access to the formal economy who were considered valuable members of industrialization had access to an intricate system providing social and civil benefits to unionized workers from both private and public sectors. These workers' access to rights contrasted with that of the majority of Brazilians, rural and urban, who were not formally incorporated into the regulated citizenship regime but who remained embedded in the conceded citizenship regime.

In sum, from the 1930s through the 1980s, Brazil was marked by two citizenship regimes that incorporated individuals differently, based on their formal connection to the labor market. Urban workers incorporated into the formal labor market and professional classes had access to an expansive set of social, political, and civil rights. They lived under the confines of the regulated citizenship regimes. Most importantly, social rights created a base of support by citizens for corporatist governance.

RENEWAL AND EXTENSION OF CIVIL SOCIETY

The roots of the participatory citizenship regime are located in the civil society mobilization during the military dictatorship, just as the roots for the regulated citizenship regime were first extended under the conceded citizenship regime. The slow withdrawal of the military government (1964–1985) during the 1970s and 1980s created the necessary political and associational space in which opposition groups could organize; the expansion of social movement and union activity throughout the 1980s created an energized civil society (Keck 1992; Jacobi 1989; Alvarez 1990; Mainwaring 1986; Dagnino 1994, 1998; Baierle 1998).

The renewal of civil society during the 1970s and 1980s is the primary factor that explains the establishment of the participatory citizenship regime. There are three complementary lines of analysis that help us to understand the renewal and extension of civil society. First, Evelina Dagnino uses a Gramscian approach to illuminate that there was a shift toward "the right to have rights," thus changing the political cultural basis of citizenship (1998). Second, James Holston captures the contested process through which citizens and CSOs struggle to claim rights; Holston coins the phrase "insurgent citizenship" to illuminate that gaining access to rights requires contestation from those groups who are long denied access to rights (2008). Finally, Leonardo Avritzer introduces the concept of "participatory publics" to show that new forms of political organizing were developing (2002).

Cidadania is a broad term that came to represent the ability of Brazilian citizens to gain access to civil, political, social, and collective rights (e.g., right to health care, right to food). Evelina Dagnino argues that the promotion of the "right to have rights" inculcated a belief among ordinary citizens in their right and responsibility to engage in public life (Dagnino 1998; Arendt 1958). There was a deliberate effort by political reformers and political outsiders to work with poor individuals and communities to educate them on their rights (Weffort 1984; Jacobi 1989; Villas Boas 1994; Villas-Boas and Telles 1995; Holston 2008). The focus on empowerment was supported by the expansion of a "critical pedagogy" associated with the educator Paulo Freire. In addition, the progressive wing of Brazil's Catholic Church, most strongly associated with liberation theology, led a movement that mobilized extensive sectors of the population and helped to refine the moral and political basis for rights (Mainwaring 1986; Dagnino 1994; Burdick 1993).

James Holston employs the concept of "insurgent citizenship" as a means to illuminate the broad field of demands and activities that emerged from Brazil's poor majority. Citizens sought to advance their interests by organizing themselves into collective associations in an attempt to force the state to protect their rights. Holston demonstrates how citizens used a wide variety of tactics to ensure that their rights to property and housing were protected by the state. In Holston's account, citizens used the judicial system, reached out to the mayor's office, worked with city council members, connected with university groups, and engaged in contentious politics. The frame of citizenship rights, whereby citizens organize their political strategies around the "right to have rights," links the diverse tactics. This allowed individuals to directly contest the conceded citizenship regime. By demanding rights, many citizens were able to move beyond the limited set of rights extended to them through clientelistic relationships. It also allowed union employees to contest the political control exerted over their unions by government officials. Thus the insurgent citizenship regime began to break down the conceded and regulated citizenship regimes. Holston's excellent book shows how citizens' use of political rights (e.g., demonstrations, petition drives) allowed them to gain protection of civil and social rights. However, Holston's conceptualization of "insurgent citizenship" doesn't address the institutionalization of participatory institutions and the direct incorporation of these "insurgent citizens" into incremental policymaking processes.

The concept of "participatory publics," first developed by Avritzer in his 2002 book and later refined by Wampler and Avritzer in 2004, complement's Holston's insurgent citizenship. The concept draws attention to how the development of new strategies in civil society led to the creation of new institutional arrangements. In other words, the emphasis on citizenship rights in civil society led activists to reimagine the shape and role of the state and democratic institutions. Local CSOs—often neighborhood associations—partnered with reformist politicians, nongovernmental organizations, and international funding agencies to work with ordinary Brazilians to broaden their expectations of the government's role in providing access to decision-making venues. Leonardo Avritzer and I identified three stages that allowed for the development of new practices:

First stage: Proliferation of new voluntary associations.

> The renovation of public life in the urban centers fostered new forms of participation, rooted in face-to-face deliberation and association. Contentious issues were placed in the public sphere and deliberated in public forums. Face-to-face deliberation is a process through which social actors move issues from the private to the public level to raise new themes, express new identities, and promote new values. (Wampler and Avritzer 2004, 295)

Second stage: Introduction of new practices.

> Social movements and voluntary associations raise contentious issues by introducing alternative practices. The second stage of the development of participatory publics recognizes that voluntary associations serve as an alternative locale that allows for the innovation of new democratic institutions. The new values and institutions promoted by social movements may create vibrant and inclusive public institutions. Existing forms of political organization, such as mass political parties, do not exhaust all possible forms of political organization. Instead, voluntary associations invent new democratic practices and institutional formats that confront social and political exclusion. (Wampler and Avritzer 2004, 297)

Third stage: Development of new policymaking institutions.

> The third stage of the development of the participatory publics is the implementation of institutions that allow for binding deliberations to be made by citizens. The third stage emphasizes the need for civil society organizations and citizens to propose political designs in conjunction with elected municipal administrations. This stage of development is the empirical link that bridges the theoretical divide between institutional and civil society theorists. (Wampler and Avritzer 2004, 298)

The concept of "participatory publics" embodies the process leading to the creation of new institutional arrangements that incorporated moral and political values embedded in the *cidadania* concept. Civil society, with a broad focus on citizenship and democratic values, served as an incubator for a new citizenship regime.

In sum, research and analysis by scholars such as Evelina Dagnino (using the concept the "right to have rights"), Wampler and Avritzer ("participatory publics"), and Holston ("insurgent citizenship") highlight the renewal of civil society and the creation of new repertories of action during the 1970s and 1980s. Dagnino captures how CSOs focus on changing people's consciousness. Avritzer and Wampler analyze the experimental use of democratic practices within CSOs, which transformed not only their internal workings but also their ideas for how public venues should function. Holston identifies the third part of civil society renewal by looking at the process of claiming rights within a variety of different state institutions. These approaches capture different facets of the broader renewal within civil society, as CSOs fought for the expansion of democratic rights as well as social and civil rights long denied to Brazil's majority. The roots of Brazil's current participatory citizenship regime were firmly planted during the 1970s and 1980s, when CSOs developed new political strategies in pursuit of their political, social, and economic interests.

FOUNDING MOMENT: 1988 CONSTITUTION

The 1988 constitution produced three significant institutional changes that are pertinent to how the participatory citizenship regime is being activated today: municipalization of authority and resources, expansion of participatory venues, and formal guarantee of universal social rights. Following the promulgation of the 1988 constitution, the Brazilian state was restructured so that different levels of the state could begin the process of addressing the massive socioeconomic, political, and cultural problems faced by the majority of its citizens. We must always remember that Brazil is one of the most unequal countries in the world: parts of São Paulo appear to be like Manhattan, but other Brazilians live in conditions more similar to the poorer parts of Central America. Following the 1988 constitution, local states were rebuilt with considerable variation. Some municipalities chose to rebuild with an elite decision-making model (Curitiba), others a clientelistic model (Rio de Janeiro), and yet others a participatory model (Belo Horizonte, Porto Alegre). One of the clear tensions in the participatory citizenship regime is that rights are inscribed into the 1988 constitution (federal level), but local governments must act to ensure that individuals can exercise their constitutionally guaranteed set of rights.

The 1986–1987 Constitutional Assembly, charged with drafting a new constitution, was comprised of individuals elected to the lower house of Congress in 1985. The Constitutional Assembly permitted introducing "popular amendments" if groups were able to collect thirty-five thousand signatures. This mechanism helped to expand the political debate within the Constitutional Assembly. The 1988 constitution is a broad document that represents numerous political victories for both conservative and leftist groups. Both favored decentralization and municipalization, albeit for different reasons. Conservative groups wanted municipalization because it would put greater resources in the hands of the local political bosses (*coreneis*), who sought to maintain the conceded citizenship regime. Leftist groups sought to municipalize as a way to improve service delivery, expand citizens' voice, and gain power via local elections.

Municipalization

The new federal arrangement was decentralized and municipalized, with states and municipal governments having greater control over resources and social service provision. Municipalities follow federal and state guidelines to ensure the transfer of resources, but they also have considerable flexibility to develop their own agendas and complete their own projects. They are now responsible for a wide range of social policies, including the public health care system (Sistema Unica de Saúde), education (often shared responsibility with state government), housing, infrastructure, some local policing, and social services. Municipal governments control 15 percent of all public expenditures (Montero and Samuels 2004).

Municipalities are responsible for providing public services that would help citizens gain access to their constitutionally guaranteed social rights. The 1988 constitution formally guaranteed Brazilians a wide range of social rights, but it is the lower tiers of the federal system that are now responsible for ensuring that individuals' constitutional rights are protected. Thus, it is impossible to discuss the social rights that "all Brazilians" are able to exercise. Rather, citizens' access to rights depend, in great measure, on their municipal and state-level governments.

Although the 1988 constitution delegated significant authority to municipal governments, a recentralization process occurred during the late 1990s and throughout the 2000s. The law of fiscal responsibility set specific limits on how municipal governments must spend resources transferred from the federal government. Most municipalities depend on direct transfers from the federal government. Wealthier municipalities, often in the south and southeast parts of the country, have access to extensive property and sales taxes, but even in a wealthy city such as Belo Horizonte, tax revenue contributes only 25 percent of the total available budget. Federal legislation now requires that municipal governments spend at least 25 percent of the total budget on education and 25 percent on health care.

In sum, municipalities are important actors in the new federal compact: they spend nearly 15 percent of all public funds on public policies such as health care, housing, and social services. The federal government provides general guidelines for municipal spending, but considerable discretion exists for how mayors and governors design and implement programs.

Participatory Venues

Under the 1988 constitution, direct participation of citizens in policy-making processes is now explicitly permitted. In Elinor Ostrom's Nobel Prize–winning work, she employs the concepts of "requires," "permits," and "forbids" to illuminate the different types of authority that may be extended to the local level by national or federal governments (Ostrom 1990, 91). The 1988 constitution now *permits* federal, state, and municipal governments to include direct participation of citizens in policymaking processes, thereby providing greater flexibility for government officials to innovate (Ostrom 1990). State and municipal governments, then, can choose to hold public meetings, reach out to different constituencies without having to draft legislation, or write rules for new programs. Activating democracy, as the title of this book suggests, is the process through which new ideas, new practices, and new political actors expand democracy's reach.

Federal legislation takes an additional step to *require* that state and municipal governments adopt specific types of participatory venues. In public policy arenas of vital importance (such as education, health care, and social services), public policy management councils are now required at the federal, state, and municipal levels. This ensures vertical integration of the public policy arena and also that citizens and CSO leaders will be able to participate in the policymaking process at three distinct levels.

In sum, the 1988 constitution marks a shift in how the Brazilian state allows citizens to be engaged in public venues. It was not clear during the 1986–1987 Constitutional Assembly that Brazilian subnational governments would emerge to become laboratories of democratic innovations. The 1988 constitution created an opportunity for the reorganization to local states; the evidence now shows that new coalitions of civil society actors and political reformers were able to alter local states' functions.

Social Rights

The 1988 constitution also expanded the number of collective social rights (e.g., right to education, housing, and health care). Although the Brazilian state has been unable to meet its constitutional obligation to guarantee that all Brazilians have access to a broad range of rights (such as health care, housing, education, and a decent retirement), including these rights in the 1988 constitution is understood by many political activists to be a significant advance because it crafted a clear set of rights that they would work to activate. Citizens and their collective organizations are now operating within a new set of institutions to pressure governments to act to ensure that ever-growing numbers of citizens can gain access to social rights. Because these rights are legally guaranteed, the state finds itself subject to an ongoing number of lawsuits because people have been unable to access their rights (Couto and Arantes 2006). The quality and breadth of social programs produced by local governments has a significant impact on the extent to which individuals can access their social rights. In other words, an individual's local jurisdiction matters greatly in terms of how they will be able to use their constitutional rights.

Municipal governments are now responsible for the provision of public policies such as housing and health care, as required by the 1988 constitution. But they lack the resources, infrastructure, and technical competencies to carry it out, resulting in unfunded mandates. However, the devolution of authority through municipalization has produced the opportunity for innovations and new ways of developing and implementing public policies. The opportunity to initiate new programs and institutions has occurred most significantly at the municipal level. Mayoral administrations in particular have used the authority afforded to them under the 1988 constitution to devise new ways to address chronic social and political problems.

In sum, it is the combination of three constitutional reforms that created the opportunity for local governments to emerge as the incubator of change: (1) the municipalization of service delivery, authority, and resources; (2) explicit permission for governments to experiment with new program and institution types; and (3) the expansion of social rights that induced policy experts, citizens, and government officials to produce a clear set of policy goals.

DEEPENING DEMOCRACY

The deepening of the quality of democracy by expanding access to civil, social, and political rights has been a central part of the political debate in Brazil since the 1980s (Weffort 1984; Alvarez 1994; Avritzer 2002; Wampler 2008). The political and academic debate within Brazil stands in sharp contrast with the academic debate in the United States and Europe, where a procedural definition of democracy initially dominated academic discussions during the transition and consolidation debates, as well as Samuel Huntington's work on the Third Wave of democratization. Huntington argues that the 1974 establishment of a democratic regime in Portugal marks the beginning of a twenty-year expansion of democratic regimes (Huntington 1993; Diamond, Linz, and Lipset 1988). The procedural characteristics of democracy emphasized limiting citizen participation to biannual votes, establishing checks and balances across three branches of government, and establishing civilian control over the military.

Scholars and democratic reformers promoted a Madisonian version of representative democracy whereby the new democratic regimes would avoid the harsh punitive features of authoritarian military regimes (tyranny) as well as the populist impulse to appeal to the passions of the people (Diamond, Linz, and Lipset 1988). The procedural approach provides regime stability in the short to medium term because restricted democracy seeks to draw key political elites into a "grand bargain" based on creating a pro-business investment climate and placing limitations on poor citizens' political demands for short-term improvements in their standard of living.

However, the Madisonian version of representative democracy was contested across Latin America and Brazil: politicians, CSOs, academics, and citizens advocated for institutions that would continue to encourage direct citizenship in public life as well as improve the quality of citizens' lives. In Brazil, the 1988 constitution and the subsequent participatory citizenship regime moved beyond the procedural definition of representative democracy. The direct engagement of citizens in policymaking processes devolves and decenters decision-making authority.

The concepts of "participation," "representation," and "deliberation" illuminate how citizens and CSOs are able to use new political rights. These three concepts allow us to assess the varying configurations of the participatory citizenship regime across the city of Belo Horizonte.

Participation

The participatory citizenship regime expands the terrain of representative democracy by broadening the access points, venues, and institutions through which elites, CSOs, and citizens engage each other. When citizens directly interact with state institutions and use their political rights on a regular basis, there is a deepening of democracy: the political and policy preferences of these citizens are more likely to be translated into specific public policies. That is, participatory citizenship regimes provide the institutional means to allow citizens to overcome the difficulty of organizing (the problem of collective action) in order to pressure the state, which increases the likelihood that citizens' interests and demands will be translated into specific public policies. An institutionalized process now filters citizens' preferences into government or state action.

The direct participation of citizens has the potential to deepen the quality of democracy in two specific ways. First, there is the expansion of *who* has access to decision-making processes. The participatory citizenship regime is designed to incorporate a wide range of socioeconomic backgrounds into the policymaking process. As discussed in chapter 1, representative democracy has a middle- and upper-class bias. The participatory citizenship regime expands the terrain of the state (access points) as well as who participates , thus improving the quality of democracy because of the different interests these citizens bring to the public policy-making process.

The second key issue is the extent to which citizens and CSOs are able to exercise political rights to secure social rights. Most citizens are not participating for the sake of participating, but because their efforts will translate into specific improvements in the quality of their lives. Throughout this book, then, there will be a close examination of the extent to which participants' decisions become part of official state policy. When citizen participation has measurable and meaningful impacts on public policies, on how state authority and resources are deployed, and on the composition of civil society, we can assert that the quality of democracy is deepening.

Representation

> The opposite of representation is not participation. The opposite of representation is exclusion. And the opposite of participation is abstention. Rather than opposing participation to representation, we should try to improve representative practices and forms to make them more open, effective and fair. Representation is not an unfortunate compromise between an ideal of direct democracy and messy modern realities. Representation is crucial in constituting democratic practices. (Plotke 1997, 19)

Brazilian citizens, especially CSO leaders, are now involved in a variety of democratic and state institutions in which they are simultaneously participants as well as representatives. Plotke captures the complementary nature of participation and representation: (a) citizens are *participants* in participatory governance venues (e.g., attending meetings, listening, debates) as (b) *representatives* of those who are unable to attend (e.g., time or financial cost, work, caring for young children) and (c) as the *represented*, by CSO leaders and party officials who claim to be acting on their behalf during deliberations and negotiations. Citizens thus play three distinct roles within participatory governance, combining the roles of "partici-pant," "representative," and the "represented" (Saward 2010).

For example, when there are large mobilizations (e.g., participatory budgeting meetings, policy conferences), individual citizens are partici-pants promoting their interests, but they also claim to be the representa-tive of friends, family members, and neighbors who were unable to attend. During these large meetings, citizens also play the role of the represented as they often listen to deliberations led by a CSO leader, their representa-tive, who advocates for their shared interests. CSO leaders claim to speak on the behalf of their followers but are also careful to show that they are part of a larger political movement in which they are participants, repre-sentatives, and represented.

In 2010 in Belo Horizonte, during the first round of participatory bud-geting meetings, this process was evident. CSO leaders from the Alto Vera Cruz favela organized community members to attend a region-wide meet-ing. The city government provided several large buses to take people to the event, but community leaders needed to organize citizens to attend. The presence of hundreds of ordinary citizens sent clear signals to government officials regarding their respective communities' capacity to mobilize and the strength of their commitment. During the meeting CSO leaders en-gaged in public deliberation, spoke with other CSO leaders as well as with government officials, and picked up the necessary paperwork to allow them to register their demands. The CSO leaders were participants, but perhaps more importantly they were also representatives.

Thus institutionalization of a participatory governance citizenship regime now means that we have to look for how citizens are simultaneously acting as participants, as representatives, and as the represented. Hanna Pitkin argues: "Political representation is primarily a public, institutional-ized arrangement involving many people and groups, and operating in the complex ways of large-scale social arrangements. What makes it represen-tation is not any single action by any one participant, but the over-all structure and functioning of the system, the patterns emerging from the multiple activities of many people" (1967, 221–22). This approach helps us to imagine how citizens and government officials constantly engage each other in ongoing processes of participation and representation. Pitkin's broader conceptualization of representation illuminates the fact that our theoretical understanding of democracy cannot only focus on campaigns or civil society, but needs to account for the myriad of ways through which contact and connections occur. In sum, political representation has been significantly expanded as a result of the use of representative democracy and a new participatory architecture. Participatory institutions are now altering how citizens are represented inside the state and in new democratic institutions. Democracy will be deepened if citizens' preferences are more clearly expressed in these venues and, importantly, if there is an identifiable, tangible impact on social policy.

Deliberation

> Public deliberation, not simply voting, characterizes democracy. . . . In a democracy, a plurality of opinions makes speech the main instrument for reaching decisions. (Urbinati 2000, 765)

Public deliberation is central to participatory institutions because it is based on an ongoing dialogue among public officials (elected, appointed, and technical experts), community leaders, and ordinary citizens. Public deliberation occurs at specific moments during formal meetings, but it also occurs in preparatory meetings—informal exchanges prior to, during, and after the formal meetings. When I started attending participatory meetings in Brazil in 1995 as well as through 2004, I was surprised to learn that most meetings started twenty to forty minutes late, even through a quorum was established. (Porto Alegre's participatory budgeting is an exception because the meetings always seemed to start on time.) Meeting organizers and participants were involved in conversations with no apparent rush to begin the meetings. For years, I interpreted this chronic lateness as a sign of disrespect to the participants. Government officials started the meetings according to their own time frame because they weren't concerned about a backlash from less powerful participants. However, during my 2009–2010 research year, I started to realize that starting meetings late was a specific strategy by government officials and CSO leaders to allow CSO leaders to connect with each other as well as to allow government officials and CSO leaders to have informal conversations. These informal deliberative sessions establish and maintain the bonds of solidarity that are vital to the political success of civil society activists.

Participatory governance creates opportunities for people from traditionally excluded sectors to have their voice heard in the public arena. If the 1980s and 1990s experienced the formal expansion of the public sphere through debate and dialogue, the first decades of the twenty-first century mark an effort to institutionalize the public sphere, since citizens' voices are now central to formal policy and political process. Within Brazilian participatory governance institutions, public debate occurs prior to voting on policy outcomes. Given time limitations, generally a small number of participants speak. During the 1990s and 2000s, citizens commonly made specific references to social justice and the value of democracy. "Thanks to deliberation, the common good can be seen as a cooperative construction of the whole community and as the outcome of ongoing persuasion and compromise that never ends in a permanent verdict" (Urbinati 2000, 772). Speakers seek to reach out to other citizens by making social justice claims, in an attempt to forge bonds of solidarity among individuals who face similar socioeconomic situations. This aspect of public deliberation is strongly associated with the broader set of incentives that induce citizens and activists to be involved because they are seeking to improve their communities, their cities, and their democracy.

A second key feature of the new deliberative venues is the emphasis on information exchange. Meetings typically begin with a leader providing basic information about upcoming events (e.g. street fair on Saturday, demonstration on Friday), ongoing muckraking research projects (e.g., "we visited three health care clinics, and we found . . ."), or specific problems faced by their community (e.g., busted sewage lines, flooding caused by improperly maintained drainage systems). Information exchange also occurs during the meeting, as government officials provide updates to ongoing policy projects or when subcommittees report on their findings.

Participatory governance remains a far cry from an idealized form of deliberative democracy, whereby all participants actively deliberate on the most pressing policy issues of the day (Fishkin 1993). Issues of scale, policy knowledge, and policy complexity make it difficult for ordinary citizens to influence major policy decisions. However, while participatory governance allows citizens to express voice on a broad set of issues, they primarily vote on smaller-scale issues. Crucial to the process associated with participatory governance is that CSO leaders and citizens (especially the former) seek to represent their interests within and parallel to the new institutional structures. CSO leaders engage in multiple participatory meetings, and they also have community meetings in which they report on the participatory meetings. This suggests that the public sphere is being expanded as a result of the continual deliberation among citizens, CSO leaders, and government officials.

In sum, the participatory citizenship regime expands the scope of where and how citizens and community leaders publicly deliberate with each other and with public officials. Public deliberations take place in formal institutional venues and during informal conversations. Citizens are provided the opportunity to participate in regularly scheduled meetings (weekly, monthly, annual) where they listen to and engage in public deliberations about government actions (*controle social*) and what the government should do (*co-gestão*). Participation induces dialogue among citizens within and parallel to formal deliberative sessions.

In sum, these three conceptual areas—participation, representation, and deliberation—are used throughout the rest of the book to shed light on how the participatory citizenship regime is changing the way citizens, CSO leaders, and public officials engage one another. The quality of democracy can be deepened when citizens have the ability to use new forms of participation, representation, and deliberation as they pursue their interests in the public sphere.

The 1988 constitution initiated a participatory citizenship regime, thus allowing citizens and CSOs to work within and parallel to a complex participatory architecture. The renewal of civil society during the 1970s and 1980s expanded the terrain of political and social rights that citizens sought to exercise in the new democratic regime. The new participatory citizenship regime was built on top of two overlapping citizenship regimes, the conceded and the regulated. The participatory citizenship regime is distinct in three ways.

First, the participatory citizenship is based on the expansion of social rights based on universal access to public goods. Rights are not "donated" to individuals or communities, nor are rights extended based on individuals' insertions into the formal labor market. Rather, the 1988 constitution extended a formal set of social rights to which all Brazilians are formally guaranteed access. As noted in chapter 1, access to these rights is politically contested. The remaining chapters in this book explain the contours of rights access.

Second, the participatory citizenship regime allows citizens to engage with the state and policymaking venues in a wide range of institutions. The state has been demonopolized, thus permitting citizens to express voice and vote in a wide range of public institutions. Much of the political debate revolves around the types of social rights that will be extended. The proliferation of democratic institutions now revolves around how scarce public goods will be used.

Finally, the participatory citizenship regime enables citizens to use political rights to claim access to social rights. Although social rights are universal and formally guaranteed by the 1988 constitution, there continues to be considerable variation in how citizens access them.

CHAPTER THREE

Rebuilding the Local State

The state . . . is the vexed institution that is the ground of both our freedoms and our unfreedoms.

—James C. Scott, *Seeing Like a State*

Differences in patterns of state building produced differences in the opportunity structures of social movements. . . . Tocqueville's underlying message was that state building creates an opportunity structure for collective action of which ordinary people take advantage.

— Sidney Tarrow, *Power in Movement*

In 1992 the Workers' Party (PT) won the mayor's office in Belo Horizonte, the capital of the state of Minas Gerais and Brazil's third largest city. The election, based on a coalition of the PT and the Brazilian Socialist Party (PSB), was a critical realignment that shifted power to a group of political outsiders who had deep ties to Brazil's new civil society and party system. Belo Horizonte's municipal government, led by the PT, has been at the forefront of innovative reform efforts, working to expand social justice, incorporate citizens into participatory venues, and establish interlocking institutions. The new government activated the participatory citizenship regime, ushering in a twenty-year period of political reforms. By reorienting the priorities of the local state, by incorporating citizens into policymaking venues, and by reforming internal policymaking processes, the local state in Belo Horizonte has significantly changed how public services are provided to poor and marginalized communities.

To activate the participatory citizenship regime, Mayor Patrus Ananias's PT government in 1993 institutionalized participatory budgeting, expanded the public policy management councils (*conselhos*) and thematic policy conferences, and developed "techniques of access" that permitted the state to promote participatory policymaking in order to link local forms of knowledge (*mētis*) with bureaucratic and legal forms of knowledge (see Scott 1998 and chapter 2 for a discussion of *mētis*).

This chapter demonstrates how the local state was reengineered to allow the PT government to extend political and social rights into poor and underserved communities. These benefits are material, as greater levels of resources are spent in low-income communities, but also sociocultural and political, as evidenced by noteworthy changes in how citizens engage each other and public officials. A larger number of citizens now have greater access to their constitutionally mandated social and political rights.

This chapter begins with a brief overview of the founding of Belo Horizonte in the 1890s and its expansion during the twentieth century. The second section focuses on electoral politics from the 1992 realigning election through the 2008 election. The electoral politics of representative democracy strongly affects how participatory institutions will be employed and how the local state will be rebuilt. This section also presents the type and degree of authority granted to mayoral executive and legislative branches. Importantly, the legislative branch remains very weak in relationship to the executive branch. The third section details the participatory institutions established through 2010 and illuminates the steps taken over a twenty-year period to activate the participatory citizenship regime.

PLANNING AHEAD: BELO HORIZONTE

The city of Belo Horizonte is Brazil's first planned city. It became the capital of the state of Minas Gerais in 1897, when the *mineiro* political establishment moved the capital to a large valley located in a more convenient location to take advantage of incipient industrialization. The previous state capital, the colonial gold city of Ouro Preto, no longer offered the economic advantages that the new capital had to offer. Belo Horizonte was modeled on Washington, DC, and Paris, with public parks and wide sweeping boulevards that radiate out from a downtown core and crosscut residential neighborhoods (Eakin 2001). This city, much like the building of Brasilia in the 1950s and early 1960s, was built by labor imported from surrounding regions. Urban planners in Belo Horizonte, just as in Brasilia in the 1950s, did not include housing or public infrastructure for the poor, working-class population, which meant that the first informal housing settlements, favelas, were established within the urban core as well as in the surrounding areas at the time of the city's founding.

Belo Horizonte thus was "born unequal" (Ananias interview). Belo Horizonte was built based on the social and political dynamics of the conceded citizenship regime, but the local elites laid the foundations for industrialization, which would lead to the regulated citizenship regime. The political and economic elite of Minas Gerais developed a capital city that met the needs of a wealthy agricultural class ready to transition toward incipient industrialization (Eakin 2001; Kohli 2004). The development of Belo Horizonte focused on industrialization and the provision of public goods to the professional and unionized working classes living in the downtown core, but provided few benefits for workers living in new, informal settlements.

The state of Minas Gerais was an integral part of Brazil's early industrialization drive at the beginning of the twentieth century. Peter Evans persuasively argues that there was a "triple alliance" of the federal government, the Brazilian private sector, and multinational corporations promoting economic development (Evans 1979). Marshall Eakin builds on the work of Evans to show that there was a fourth partner in Minas Gerais: the state government (Eakin 2001, 89). The political and economic elite of Minas Gerais crafted an activist state that could directly intervene to promote industrialization, leading to the development of a regulated citizenship regime in the city of Belo Horizonte. Unions comprised of public sector bureaucrats, along with employees working for private companies, were extended a series of social benefits, which included access to public education, health care, and housing. Individuals living within Belo Horizonte's central core had access to good infrastructure, such as well-maintained roads, a public trolley system, public parks, and public theaters. The growing middle and organized labor classes thus directly benefited from the economic wealth generated by industrialization as well as from rights extended through the regulated citizenship regime.

However, the majority of the population remained trapped in the conceded citizenship regime. For these individuals and communities, they had limited access to public services and infrastructure. As migrants poured into Belo Horizonte from the rural regions of the state, their housing options were limited. Many moved into favelas, where they built their own housing and neighborhoods. These communities were generally not served by the state, which meant that favela communities didn't receive state-sponsored benefits (Perlman 2010; Gonçalves 2007). Belo Horizonte, during most of the twentieth century, experienced two distinct citizenship regimes: public sector employees, unionized workers, and the growing professional classes had access to the regulated citizenship regime, whereas those trapped in informal and/or low-paying jobs (e.g., construction workers, maids, service employees) were embedded in the conceded citizenship regime.

Belo Horizonte is at the crossroads of Brazil: located between the industrialized southern part of the country, the agricultural development of the center-west, and the economically poor northeast. As noted in Table 1.2 in chapter 1, the per capita income of Belo Horizonte is more similar to the northeastern cities of Recife and Salvador, which is due to a large migrant population and a limited number of high-paying jobs. However, the social indicators are closer to those of the wealthier cities in the southern part of the country.

Belo Horizonte was the political home of one of Brazil's most important post–World War II politicians: Juscelino Kubitsheck. Appointed mayor of Belo Horizonte in 1940, Kubitsheck worked with a young architect, Oscar Niemeyer, to design Pampulha, a major residential area with a lake, in the northern part of the city. Mayor Kubitsheck was part of a long line of reformist mayors who sought to develop the city economically and socially. The success of Kubitsheck as mayor and the importance of Minas Gerais as a key state in national politics led to Kubitsheck's election to Brazil's presidency. Kubitsheck served as Brazil's president from 1956 to 1961 and helped to realize a longtime dream of Brazilian elites: building a new capital in the center-west of the country—Brasília.

Belo Horizonte continued its economic growth under the 1964–1985 military dictatorship, cementing its position as the most important industrial center outside of São Paulo (Eakin 2001). The industrialization was accompanied by the growth of unions, a substantial middle class, and a broad state sector. The regulated citizenship regime permitted government officials to selectively reward specific sectors of the economy.

Under the military regime, the extensive mobilization of social movements and unions helped to produce a renewal in Belo Horizonte's civil society (Somarriba, Valadares, and Afonso 1984; Avritzer 2002). Unions in
Belo Horizonte and in the larger metropolitan region participated in a series of strikes led by the new labor movements in São Paulo (Somarriba,
Valadares, and Afonso 1984; Keck 1992). Social movements in the health
care and housing sectors organized in pursuit of universal access to health
services and access to dignified housing. Community organizations focused
on basic infrastructure issues such as paving, electricity, and sewage; these
would later expand to other public goods like education and health care.
The renewal of civil society developed based on combined mobilizing by
unions, social movements, and community-based organizations. Social
justice, the extension of citizenship, access to public goods, and expanded
political participation were key themes that linked disparate movements.
During the renewal of civil society, groups made material demands (e.g.,
better infrastructure), political demands (e.g., the right to participate) and
cultural demands (e.g., the right to equality and inclusion). The 1980s in
Belo Horizonte were a transitional period, as the development of the insurgent citizenship regime allowed citizens and CSO activists to move beyond
the confines of the conceded and regulated citizenship regimes.

The city of Belo Horizonte and the state of Minas Gerais experienced
two distinct types of political mobilization by opposition forces. One track,
mentioned above, was the mobilization of civil society. Unions engaged in
strikes and work slowdowns, while social movements and community organizations carried out demonstrations, land occupations, and incipient
party building. A second important track was the use of political opposition to military rule through the auspices of a legalized opposition party,
the Brazilian Democratic Movement (MDB), and, its immediate succes-
sor, the Brazilian Democratic Movement Party (PMDB). A powerful politician from Minas Gerais, Tancredo Neves, was a strong advocate for return
to democratic rule. In 1984, millions of Brazilians organized around the
banner "Direct elections now," demanding that Brazil's president be elected
by a direct vote. The movement was unsuccessful—it did not establish direct elections in 1985—but it did succeed in placing tremendous pressure
on federal legislators, who responded by electing Tancredo Neves as Brazil's first civilian president after more than twenty years of military rule.
Neves died just prior to taking office, and Jose Sarney became the first
civilian president.

In sum, Belo Horizonte was at the heart of the renewal of Brazil's civil society and party system during the 1980s. Belo Horizonte's experience is most similar to the cities of São Paulo, Recife, and Porto Alegre, all of which also experienced significant civil society mobilization as well as the entrance of new political parties that would alter the party system. In other cities, Rio de Janeiro most notably, there was a renewal of civil society, but the entrenchment of traditional political parties led long-term politicians, such as Leonel Brizola, to reinstitute clientelistic politics (Gay 1994). Finally, in cities like Curitiba, there was elite renewal within the party system but no reconfiguration of civil society.

Municipal Elections

In Belo Horizonte, the 1992 mayoral election was a realigning election that initiated twenty years of control by a center-left coalition of the municipal government (Key 1964; Burnham 1970). In Belo Horizonte's first round of the 1992 election, the PT mayoral candidate received the largest plurality, at just over a third of the vote in the first round of voting. This was similar to Olivia Dutra's share of the mayoral vote in 1988 in Porto Alegre as well as Luiza Erundina's vote share in 1988 in São Paulo. The small margin of victory provided a clear incentive for the PT government to increase its share of the vote. The 1992 election was a critical realignment because it ushered in a new coalition of forces that would govern for 20 years.

Mayors in large Brazilian municipalities have been directly elected since 1985. To elect mayors, Brazil uses a presidential system whereby voters select a single candidate. Beginning with the 1992 elections, there are two rounds of voting for executives (president, governors, mayors).[1] If a candidate wins 50 percent plus one of valid ballots, he or she wins the election. If no candidate wins more than 50 percent of the valid ballots, a second election occurs between the first round's top two vote getters. Table 3.1 below details the percentage of votes received for the principal parties in Belo Horizonte's mayoral elections.

A second observation is that the PFL (Partido de Frente Liberal) (which renamed itself the Democratas in the 2000s), a conservative political party representing the interests of the traditional oligarchy and conservative sectors, had their last successful election outcome in 1992, when they captured 21 percent in the first round and 40 percent in the second round.

Table 3.1 Mayoral Vote: First Round, 1992–2008

| | % of valid votes | | | | |
	1992	1996	2000	2004	2008
PT		22		69	
PSB/PT	37*		44*		44*
PSB		41*		22	
PMDB	14		17		41
PSDB	15	26	31		
PFL/DEM	21	2		6	1
All others	12.21	8.741	8	2	12

*Eventual winner in second round
Source: Tribunal Superior Eleitoral 2013.

Table 3.2 Mayoral Vote: Second Round, 1992–2008

| | % of valid votes | | | | |
	1992	1996	2000	2004	2008
PT	**50**	-	**55**	n/a	**59**
PSB		**77**			
PMDB					35
PSDB		23	45		
PFL/DEM	41				

Note: Winner in bold.
Source: Tribunal Superior Eleitoral 2013.

Table 3.2 demonstrates that the PT and the PSB, working together, have support from a solid majority. Neither party, by itself, is able to consistently capture 50 percent of the vote, but their alliance helps them to maintain control of the mayor's office.

Tables 3.2 and 3.3 demonstrate that the PT and the PSB were able to turn their 1992 electoral victory into a long-term hold on the authority of

Table 3.3 Party Affiliation of Mayor and Vice Mayor

	Mayor	Vice Mayor
1993–1996	Workers' Party	Brazilian Socialist Party
1997–2000	Brazilian Socialist Party	Workers' Party
2001–2002	Brazilian Socialist Party	Workers' Party
2003–2004	Workers' Party*	
2005–2008	Workers' Party	Brazilian Socialist Party
2008–2012	Brazilian Socialist Party	Workers' Party

* In 2003, the Workers' Party vice mayor became mayor after the mayor's resignation (as a result of poor health).
Source: Tribunal Superior Eleitoral 2013.

the mayor's office. The renewal of civil society that promoted widespread mobilization in the 1970s and 1980s helped to establish a broad base of support for leftist and centrist mayoral candidates.

However, the PT and PSB mayoral candidates did not translate into a greater share of the vote for leftist candidates in the municipal legislature. Municipal legislators are elected from a municipal-wide district and are notorious for relying on clientelistic exchanges to ensure voter support. The forty-one seats in Belo Horizonte's legislature are distributed according to the percentage of valid votes won by an electoral coalition. The candidate list and the coalitions are decided by party elites. In Belo Horizonte, there is high party fragmentation because candidates are elected from a large number of parties.

Figure 3.1 shows a highly fragmented party system, which makes it difficult for legislators to organize themselves and craft coherent policy proposals. Thus, municipal legislators are isolated from each other and unable to form alliances that might allow them to exercise oversight on government policies or to propose new policies. The left and center-left routinely secure 30 percent of the seats, but they are unable to move much beyond that vote share. As a result of the fragmentation, the power of the mayoral administration increases because it is easier for the executive to offer small payouts to municipal legislators as mayors attempt to build a stable voting coalition. The fragmentation of the legislation is one rea-

Figure 3.1   Distribution of Seats on Belo Horizonte's Municipal Council, 1997–2012

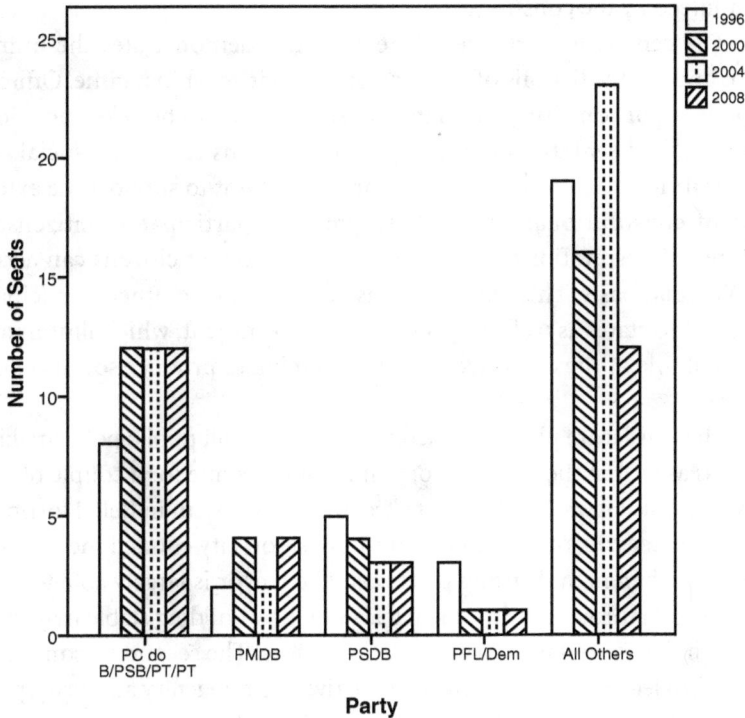

Source: Tribunal Superior Eleitoral 2013.

son that it was the mayoral administration in Belo Horizonte that led the efforts to activate the participatory citizenship regime.

Executive-Legislative Relations

The 1988 constitution devolved considerable authority, resources, and responsibilities from the federal government to municipal governments. This increased the authority of local government officials to select and implement their preferred policy outcomes. However, the municipal executive— the mayor—continues to be the dominant political actor at the local level, which means that legislators' power is often dependent on the political and policy interests of mayors (Couto 1995; Wampler 2007; Abruçio and Couto 1996). One of the key factors that explains the variation in the participatory citizenship regime is the presence of a mayor, a governor, or a president interested in promoting the extension of political, social, and civil rights guaranteed by the constitution.

The central importance of the executive demonstrates the limitations and contradictions of the participatory citizenship regime. Officials supportive of constitutional rights must be elected to hold key positions through representative democracy so that citizens can access social and political rights. If mayors or governors choose not to support the extension of constitutionally protected rights, the participatory citizenship will remain aspirational rather than something that citizens can access on a regular basis. This observation is generalizable to other municipalities, and to states as well as to the federal government, which illuminates the vital role of the executive branch in helping to produce social change in Brazil.

The legislature plays a limited role in the overall public policymaking process as well in the participatory citizenship regime for a couple of reasons. First, as Figure 3.1 demonstrated, the party system in Belo Horizonte is fragmented, making it difficult for opposition city council members to develop coherent and strong positions. The mayor is largely able to push their agenda through the municipal legislator by building stable majorities through the use of targeted goods to legislators. The second reason is that municipal legislators have limited legislative and budgetary authority, placing them in weak negotiating positions vis-à-vis the mayor.

The basic powers of the mayor and executive branch are the following:

- Propose annual budget
- Implement budget with limited oversight from legislative branch
- Designate political appointees with no vote or oversight from legislature
- Administer bureaucracy

A key resource of a mayoral administration is its control over financial resources. The budget data in Figure 3.2 demonstrate that the municipality of Belo Horizonte has considerable resources at its disposal to spend on personnel, social services, and infrastructure. The figures are in Brazilian reais, but the exchange rate in 2010, when the table was put together, was US $1 = 1.75 BRL. In 2007, the municipality's 3.5 billion BRL budget was equivalent to $2 billion. Given that the population is around 2.5 million inhabitants, this corresponds to $800 per inhabitant per year.

Figure 3.2   Belo Horizonte's Municipal Budget, 1999–2008

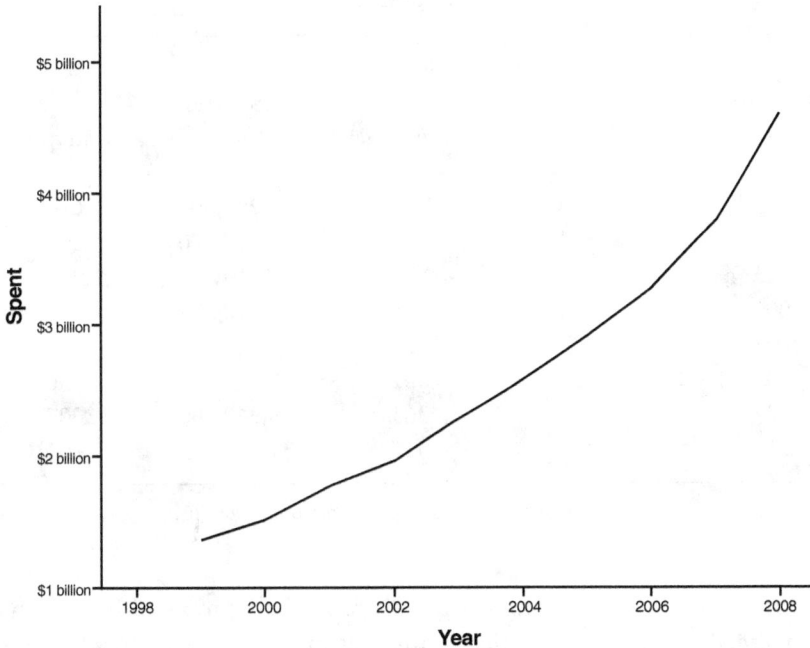

Currency in Brazilian reais.
Source: Instituto Brasiliero de Geografia e Estatística 2014.

Key powers of the legislature include the following:

- Modify mayor's proposed budget
- Hold public hearings
- Have a small staff to perform constituency service
- Approve or reject legislation proposed by mayor

One of the legislature's principal powers is to amend the mayor's proposed budget. Each September, the mayor must present a budget to the municipal legislature, which has until December 31 to approve it. If the budget is not passed, then the current year's budget is adopted. As Table 3.4 demonstrates, municipal legislators approved amendments that reallocated only a tiny fraction of the overall budget.

The table above demonstrates that municipal legislators (*vereadores*) make little use of their limited authority. The first reason is that the budgetary rules require that any budget amendment must transfer resources

Table 3.4 Budget Amendments Presented by Belo Horizonte City Council Members, 2003–2010 (amounts in Brazilian reais)

Budget Year	Budget Amendments Rejected	Budget Amendments Approved	Total Resources Altered	% of Budget Changed
2003	N/A	N/A	39,295,308	.016
2004	N/A	N/A	24,527,470	.008
2005	N/A	N/A	N/A	N/A
2006	230	355	19,290,288	.005
2007	137	393	23,327,182	.005
2008	122	301	32,334,245	.006
2009	118	363	49,940,000	.007
2010	185	317	31,224,277	.004

Sources: Câmara Municipal de Vereadores de Belo Horizonte 2004, 2010.

away from an existing budget line to fund their proposed budget increase. This produces political conflict as municipal legislators take resources away from one department to fund another department; their budget transfer has the potential to alienate an executive-branch department. A second reason is that the mayoral administration doesn't have to implement any of the budget amendments because the Brazilian budgetary system permits them to carry out policies and programs included in the budget but doesn't require them to do so. Thus, municipal legislators have a weak incentive to draft amendments whose implementation is at the discretion of the mayor. Third, the mayor can legally alter any budget line by 10 percent, which means that transferring money away from a program will have limited impact because the mayor can merely add additional resources to that budget line. Taken together, these rules produce few incentives for legislators to be active participants in the policymaking process.

Legislators do, however, influence the distribution of municipal resources through an informal process. Each legislator is able to allocate 150,000 Brazilian reais (about $90,000 in 2010) to social service programs or small infrastructure projects of their choosing.[2] This is a rather paltry figure that is further confounded by the mayoral administration's unwillingness to fund budgetary requests. Municipal legislator Adriano Ventura

(PT) stated to me in an interview: "The majority of the amendments are never done. . . . The power here in the legislature is so limited that a person ends up feeling deceived. . . . Our power is almost nothing." As municipal legislator Silivinho Rezende (PT) told me, "There is no real opposition to the mayor. The majority trade favors for votes [*troca de favores*]." The money is allocated from a "rainy day" fund, and implementation decisions are completely at the discretion of the mayor. No information is published regarding whether these budget amendments are implemented.

The municipal legislature continues to have authority to act as a veto point, but their ability to secure constituency service is based on their willingness to work closely with the executive branch (Tsebelis 2002). Municipal legislators have little formal authority but seek to represent the interests of their constituents. Legislators continue to be key conduits for citizens wanting direct access to the state. Legislative staff (eight to twelve people per legislator) spend most of their time on constituency service, similar to legislators in other countries (Mayhew 1974). Municipal legislator Paulo Motorista, a former bus driver, elected in 2008 with the second highest individual vote total (just over five thousand votes), told me that his primary responsibility as a municipal legislator is to secure transportation to the hospital for his constituents. His votes came from the largest favela in the downtown area of Belo Horizonte. Motorista asserted that his work is no different from the well-known federal program Bolsa Família because both involved using public resources to help individuals: "People criticize me because I arrange for cars, for buses, to take people to the hospital. They say that this isn't how politics should be done. But isn't this what Lula does with Bolsa Família? He throws Bolsa Família out there and goes fishing for votes. What is the difference?" Of course, the key difference between this legislator's work and that of Bolsa Família is that the federal program has a standardized list of criteria that determines eligibility, whereas Paolo Motorista helps those people he knows.

Municipal legislators in Belo Horizonte mobilize citizens and provide transportation to participatory meetings, especially participatory budgeting (Gonçalves 2007). This allows them to engage in "credit claiming" for helping to strengthen democracy, but it also helps to direct resources to their "bailiwick," which is their primary source of votes (Mayhew 1974; Ames 2001). Municipal legislators seek to develop ties to participatory venues because they are potential recruiting grounds for supporters as well as a way for the legislators to assess the most important demands emerging from civil society.

Thus the limited authority granted to the municipal legislature, in conjunction with a highly fragmented party system, results in a weak legislature. Such fragmentation makes it difficult for the political opposition to sustain any substantial investigations into the executive branch (mayor's office). The municipal legislature has not promoted new forms of participation. Clientelism and constituency service are now both key attributes of legislative action. The extreme fragmentation of political parties has weakened the possibility of producing new forms of representation through the legislative branch. No clear signals are being sent from the population to legislators and to the mayor's office through legislative elections. The municipal legislature is attempting to carve out a broader voice, using a greater number of public hearings, but legislators dominate these hearings. Citizen-participants are spectators rather than active participants. Quite simply, the municipal legislative branch has been outside the institutional innovations that mark local governance in Brazil during the 1985–2010 period.

Mayors remain dominant political players in municipal politics. The establishment of the 1988 constitution didn't alter the basic authority inscribed in this office. Thus, any analysis of how local political authority is employed in Brazil must begin with a careful assessment of mayoral interests and power. As the subsequent section and chapters make clear, the institutional redesign of the participatory citizenship regime led to a broadening of an executive-dominated state and the extension of rights based on executive action.

MAYOR ANANIAS: ACTIVATING THE PARTICIPATORY CITIZENSHIP REGIME

The 1992 election of Patrus Ananias launched a transformative project at the local level. In the early 1990s, Brazil was experiencing hyperinflation, anemic economic growth, a major corruption scandal that led to President Collor de Mello's resignation, and a mobilized civil society. The realignment in Belo Horizonte was driven by the same forces that led to the changes in the 1988 constitution: mobilization of leftist social movements and labor unions, extensive participation by a Catholic Church hierarchy associated with liberation theology, an engaged university community (faculty and students), and neighborhood-based organizations seeking to improve their communities. Patrus Ananias stated (Ananias interview):

My 1992 election was the division of the waters in the city. We carried out a revolution—quietly, calmly, and in a democratic fashion. . . . We surprised the city, especially the more conservative sectors, because we were so capable of managing conflict in a democratic fashion, because we were capable of administering the city in an honest and efficient manner, because we were able to accomplish so many of our objectives.[3]

The electoral victory of Mayor Patrus Ananias marks a significant shift in the local state's policy interests; the PT administration focused on popular participation, social justice, and interlocking institutions. His victory was unexpected because he was a member of the Workers' Party, which was still attempting to carve out political support in local and national elections. In 1989, the PT won important mayoral races in São Paulo, Santo Andre, and Porto Alegre, but in 1992, the PT was Brazil's fourth or fifth most important party at the municipal level in 1992 (following the PSDB, PFL, PMDB, and PDT).

Patrus Ananias was a two-term municipal legislator and university professor when he ran for the mayor's office in 1992. During the 1989–1992 term, he served as the president of the municipal legislature. His primary accomplishment was to draft a new municipal master plan, which led him to work extensively with housing social movements, community-based organizations, urban planners, university faculty, and the business community. Patrus Ananias had long-standing and deep ties to the progressive wing of the Catholic Church, working to build Christian base communities. The liberation theology sector of the Catholic Church was very influential, socially and politically, in the state of Minas Gerais.

Navarro has described the PT political project this way: "Their campaign document, 'A Democratic and Popular Agenda,' was the basis for the political coalition. The point of departure is the implementation of the municipality's new charter and there are several references to the establishment of a 'democratizing project' in the administration of the city and its urban policies" (Navarro n.d., 85). The vice mayor, Célio de Castro, was from the Socialist Party of Brazil (PSB), a center-left political party, but he also had long-term ties to the Communist Party of Brazil (PC do B), which had a much more radical political agenda. Thus the governing coalition led by Mayor Patrus Ananias and Vice Mayor Célio de Castro was comprised of political outsiders. As one housing movement leader explained in an interview in 2009, "We organized before Patrus's government, but Patrus was important because he opened doors. . . . He assumed the politics of 'inversion of priorities.' He worked to ensure the inversion of priorities" (Padua interview).

Popular Participation

The central institutional reform of the new governing coalition in Belo Horizonte involved rebuilding the local state by creating a wide range of participatory institutions that permit the direct incorporation of citizens. As noted in the previous chapter, the 1988 constitution permits governments to experiment with different institutional designs; federal legislation passed in the 1990s and 2000s required governments to implement specific public policy management councils (e.g., health care, education) in order to receive funds. Beginning under Mayor Patrus Ananias (1993–1996), the government voluntarily established a series of new institutional venues that would increase citizens' access to transparent information about government revenues and budgets and allow citizens to directly connect with government officials and directly intervene in the policymaking process. Mayor Ananias's government adopted participatory budgeting (PB) in 1994, PB Housing in 1996, and the creation of nine public policy management councils (Azevedo and Fernandes 2005; Azevedo and Nabuco 2008; Avritzer 2002; Wampler 2007; Martins 2007, 88–89). As Mayor Patrus argued, "PB and the councils are powerful instruments that contribute to people's ability to engage and confront the bureaucracy. . . . When the government is committed to these processes, the individual participant becomes a subject in the process. This raises the issue of citizenship. . . . People become active participants in their own lives" (Ananias interview). Thus these processes promote new ways of engaging the state and new ways of connecting people to each other, and they contribute to social justice by enabling people to empower themselves.

By 2010, 571 different public policy management councils (*conselhos*) had more than four thousand positions to which citizens could be elected. The municipal state, broadened in this way, is now open for direct and consistent negotiations with citizens at municipal, regional, and local levels. This is remarkable in the context of Brazil's long history of social and political exclusion. The expansion of the number of participatory seats indicates that the local government has consolidated a broad participatory infrastructure.

Table 3.5 Public Policy Management Councils: Venues and Formal Representation for Citizens, Government Officials, and Unions in 2009–2010

	Municipal	Regional*	Local**	Total
Participatory Venues	41	52	479	571
Government Officials	325	124	1406	1855
Citizens/CSOs	309	377	2725	3411
Union Officials	35	132	141	308
Service Providers	64	N/A	N/A	64
Total	733	633	4272	

*Regional venues are councils in the areas of health care (9 venues, 183 citizens, 75 government officials, 92 government workers); social services (9 venues, 54 citizens, 9 government officials); *conselho titular* (9 venues, 45 elected and paid citizens); BH Transports (10 venues, 50 citizens, 40 government officials, 40 union officials); public parks (15 venues, 45 citizens).

** Local venues include an urbanization program Vila Viva (25 venues, 276 citizens, 10 government officials); local health posts (141 venues, 141 citizens, 141 government officials, and 141 union representatives); schools (186 schools, 1,700 citizens, 1,116 school officials), social services (54 schools, 108 citizens, 54 government officials); BH Cidadania (25 venues, 50 citizens, and 75 government officials, civil defense (48 teams, 400 citizens, and 10 government officials).

Sources: Martins 2007, 64; Ana Flavia Martins, personal communication, April 14, 2010; Flávia Julião, personal communication, April 19, 2010; Savio Araújo, personal communication, April 16, 2010; Marcus Annibal Rego, personal communication, April 23, 2010; Magalhes and Ferreira interviews.

At the regional level, there are different types of participatory venues: planning units, hospitals, social service centers, day care centers, and so forth. These bring together a broader cross-section of residents than the participatory venues at the local level. Table 3.5 also shows that most of the "offices" for citizens are at the local level, generally in the fields of education and health care. Poor and lower-middle-class citizens rely on public education and health care, so they have a stronger interest in the local and regional councils because they depend on the state for the provision of these public goods. We should note that middle- and upper-class individuals and families tend not to rely on the public provision of health care or education because they have the financial resources to rely on privately funded, market-based services. This means that the middle class has few incentives to be involved in the public policy management council system, unless they are technical experts or policy advocates for a specific issue.

Table 3.6 Participatory Budgeting, 2008–2009

	Institutional Venues	*Numbers of Participants, 2008–2009**	*PB Delegates***
PB Regional	9 regions	40,967	1,200
PB Housing	6 regions	13,000	599
PB Digital	Online	113,383	N/A

* Participation numbers are taken from the municipality's website, http://portalpbh.pbh .gov.br/pbh/ecp/comunidade.do?app=portaldoop (accessed 2014). See chapter 4 for a fuller discussion of participation in PB.

** The number of PB delegates fluctuates from year to year. Every two years, a small number of citizens are elected to the Comforça, which is responsible for project oversight. Over the past several PB cycles, roughly 850 Comforça members are elected during the biannual electoral cycle. However, the rules of the Comforça state that the mandate of the members continues until all projects from that region's project list are completed. Thus, in 2009, there were still Comforça members from the 1999 PB cycle in some regions as a result of slow implementation.

The government drew from the successful case of Porto Alegre's participatory budgeting (PB) to initiate its own program, adapting the process to meet local needs and demands (Abers 2000; Baiocchi 2005; Fedozzi 1998, 2000; for an important discussion of local innovation and adaption, see Baiocchi, Heller, and Silva 2011). The two most important innovations of the Belo Horizonte government include the Quality of Life Index (IQVU), which became the basis for the distribution of resources, and the PB Housing program, which channels housing-related issues into a separate venue.

As shown in Table 3.6, participatory budgeting now has three separate components: regional, housing, and digital. They have different means and ends (described in greater detail in chapter 4). What links the three PB programs together is an effort to keep a direct link between citizens' active participation in a state-sanctioned institution and the distribution of public goods.

Participatory budgeting is the focus of chapter 4, so the analysis of how it works and its effects will be left until later. The municipal government consistently sought to reform participatory budgeting to better align it with citizens' demands and government capabilities. For example, when it became obvious in 1994 and 1995 that demands from the housing movements might overwhelm the participatory budgeting process, the government creatively established the PB Housing program, which incorporates the movement's demands.

The final major participatory institutions are the policy conferences that incorporate citizens and community leaders into daylong or weekend-long workshops that focus on specific policy arenas (e.g., health care, housing, education). In 2009, at least nineteen distinct policy conferences mobilized nine thousand or more citizens.[4] The purpose of the policy conferences is to allow citizens to share ideas and connect with each other, to demonstrate their policy preferences to government officials, to permit ordinary citizens to show their solidarity with their leaders and movements, and to establish general policy recommendations. Policy conferences do not make binding decisions but are part of a consultative process that contributes to agenda setting and the exchange of information (Pogrebinschi and Samuels 2014). Conferences are first held at the municipal level but are then linked to state and federal policy conferences.

Social Justice

The second pillar of the reforms begun under Mayor Ananias was social justice, characterized by preferential bias in favor of individuals from communities traditionally excluded from access to public good provisions. The strong emphasis on social justice led the municipal government to develop policies and programs that would help citizens access their social rights guaranteed by the 1988 constitution. The PT-led government worked on the assumption that previous state activities dedicated too few public goods to poor favelas and the majority of citizens, who were living in favelas and *vilas* (in the context of Belo Horizonte, *vilas* are smaller communities consisting of informal housing). The PT government sought to mobilize local state resources and authority in a redistributive effort to increase public goods provision to communities that had limited public investment in basic infrastructure, health, education, and other social services.

To achieve state-sponsored social justice, the government in Belo Horizonte created "techniques of access," which link different forms of knowledge (local, *mētis*, legal, technical) with a moral commitment to allocated resources to communities and individuals underserved by the state. The techniques of access allow governments to transform the amorphous qualities associated with social justice into specific, concrete improvements in social well-being. The municipal government in Belo Horizonte, in conjunction with it civil society allies, created new rules based on principles associated with social justice. The techniques of access allowed the government to move from a broad claim—"the right to food"—to a real reduction in malnutrition, from the broad claim "the right to voice" to allowing citizens to select specific infrastructure projects to be built in shantytowns. Mayor Ananias argued in November 2011, "Public offices are not venues for friends; they are venues to make things happen. Technically competent and ethically committed individuals are needed to make this happen" (Ananais interview). The local state became an instrument through which the new governing coalition sought to extend social justice and activate social rights.

Technique of Access 1: Index of the Quality of Urban Life (1995)

The Workers' Party government developed a Quality of Life Index (Índice de Qualidade de Vida Urbana—IQVU) as a means of providing a clear rationale for how resources are allocated to poor neighborhoods within participatory budgeting. Communities with a lower quality of life receive a greater per capita share of resources. The IQVU provides the technical rules allowing the government to legitimize (politically, morally, and technically) the allocation of resources to poor communities. The IQVU represents a fusion of the amorphous qualities of social justice with technical, expert knowledge made available through a fairly capable state and high-quality university system. The index is part of an explicit attempt to reimage the use of state authority.

The technical logic behind the IQVU is to establish a clear map of public and private infrastructure in eighty-one planning units (roughly nine per region). It was originally devised to guide the discussion on the 1995 master plan but later became an integral part of the participatory budgeting process.

> The IQVU is comprised of 75 separate components that seek to measure local service delivery and public infrastructure in the following areas: Food security, social services, culture, education, sports, housing, infrastructure, health care, public security, and urban services. Based on these objective criteria, the IQVU allows us to identify those planning units were there is a lower access to services. Those planning units should receive priority in the distribution of available resources

as well as those government departments that need to expand services to increase the IQVU in the planning unit. (Nahas et al. n.d., 7; my translation)

The seventy-five components do not require new data collection but allow the government to use data already collected by federal, state, and municipal agencies in ways that help them achieve their goal of social justice. Importantly, the criteria for what should be included in the IQVU as well as the weight of different indicators are created in conjunction with "street-level" bureaucrats who have an intimate understanding of the diversity of problems within each favela as well as across favelas (Nahas et al. 2000; Nahas et al. n.d.,14; Lipsky 1980). These street-level bureaucrats have local and practical knowledge but no systemic means to measure these differences. The IQVU allows their knowledge to be accumulated in a much more systematic way, which gives the government a much better understanding of the problems faced by favela residents.

This is an excellent example of how state interest and local knowledge can be combined to produce successful policy outcomes, providing an excellent counter to James Scott's warning about how simplification projects often lead to negative outcomes. Local knowledge first included that of street-level bureaucrats but was expanded to include citizens' knowledge, which is included through popular participation, the second pillar of the Workers' Party government. The IQVU, originally developed for the 1995 Master Plan, became part of an official component of the participatory budgeting process in 1996. The IQVU was thus linked to participatory governance institutions to allow citizens to decide how they would spend resources allocated to their region or micro-region. In sum, the role of this tool is to link demands and needs to the technical and professional expertise of the local state.

Technique of Access 2: Food Security

In the area of food security, Mayor Ananias argued for a moral and political right to a nutritious and healthy diet (Machado, Menicucci, and de Souza 2009). Again, this amorphous right is much easier for government officials to declare than it is for them to create the policies and programs to get decent food into poor households and public schools. To achieve this goal, Ananias reorganized the local state. Successful programs include the establishment of municipal-run popular restaurants in poor neighborhoods (in 2010, breakfast was 35 US cents and lunch 70 cents), the creation of a farm-to-market program delivering food to schools and to public markets located near favelas, and the establishment in 1993 of the Secretaria Municipal de Abastecimento and in 1994 the food security public policy management council (Machado, Menicucci, and de Souza 2009).

By 2009, the municipality of Belo Horizonte had twenty-nine different social programs that focused on food security and nutritional issues (Machado, Menicucci, and de Souza 2009, 96–98). Thus we can assert that the strong emphasis on food security by Mayor Ananias led to the institutionalization of social programs that successfully improved low-income families' access to inexpensive food. By bringing a diversity of voices to a single institutional venue, the government developed better programs and, importantly, created a common language among public opinion makers in this area (Sousa Júnior and Lott interviews).[5]

The most significant change produced by the PT and PSB mayoral administrations was the creation of specific rules and programs that institutionalized the process through which broad moral and political claims were translated into specific policies. Public officials and their civil society allies activated the participatory citizenship regime by creating new programs that were inserted within the broader constitutional and legal framework.

INTERLOCKING INSTITUTIONS

A third pillar of the reform project was the development of interlocking institutions in the hopes of improving coordination among different government agencies as well as linking citizens to different policy arenas. The municipal government in Belo Horizonte initiated a series of interlocking institutions to improve policy coordination so that different agencies could respond more comprehensively to intense social and political problems.

For example, in the area of housing policy, the government adopted policies promoted by the national urban reform movement. A key problem addressed by the national housing movement was that new housing units were often located in isolated areas that lacked basic infrastructure such as schools and public transportation. When the Workers' Party began planning new housing units, they brought together the departments of housing, education, transportation, health, and so forth to consider issues such as the location of hospitals, health care clinics, schools, and public transportation networks. Comprehensive planning was established through the internal redesign of the administration, thus allowing for horizontal interlocking institutions internal to the municipal state (Bedê 2005, 163).

The interlocking institutions were also built through the participatory system—the councils, the conferences, and the participatory budgeting programs are the institutional linkages among different agencies (see chapters 4 and 5 for a more complete analysis). In some councils, seats are allocated to members of other councils, which promotes the spread of information. This allows for information sharing between relevant councils as well as learning from the individual council member. Similarly, councils in the fields of health care and social services were also vertically linked, from the local level to the regional to the municipal (see chapter 5). This vertical linkage allows information to move quickly upward and downward. When government officials propose a new idea at the municipal level, citizens take the information from the municipal meeting to the regional meeting and then to the local meeting. Conversely, when there is a problem at the local level, the information can quickly find its way into the municipal council and then into the offices of key policy experts.

Finally, government officials established internal decision-making bodies that were designed to link elite decision making to the participatory processes. As will be explained in greater detail below, the government consolidated different departments in 2000 in the hopes of providing a more coherent response to the myriad pressing demands placed on the government.

SHIFTING SUPPORT FOR THE PARTICIPATORY CITIZENSHIP REGIME

In Belo Horizonte, as in Brazil more broadly, citizens have differential access to the participatory citizenship regime because of the interaction of five variables: state formation, support from the executive branch for voice and vote, the local configuration of civil society, available resources, and the specific rules that regulate participation, representation, and deliberation. In Belo Horizonte, mayoral support shifted over two decades as four successive mayors emphasized different institutional arrangements to promote citizens' access to the participatory citizenship regime. In an earlier book (2007) and article (2008), I identified the incentives that would induce mayors to delegate authority to citizens. At the core of this delegation of authority is the individual mayor's electoral and governing strategy, which is most strongly affected by a mayor's need to directly incorporate their political base into participatory venues; the usefulness of participatory institutions to draw political bystanders into their electoral coalition; the ability to use the new policymaking processes to "brand" the government as inclusive, pro-poor, and participatory; and, finally, the government's need to legitimize a reallocation of scarce resources to poor communities. Belo Horizonte's four mayors (1992–2012) confronted a changing political and social landscape, which altered how they would use participatory institutions to advance their agenda.

FOUNDING MOMENT: MAYOR PATRUS ANANIAS (1993–1996)

Under Mayor Patrus Ananias, the municipal government initiated a comprehensive approach to incorporating the three pillars of popular participation, social justice, and interlocking institutions. The techniques of access used by the state were informed by commitments to social justice and popular participation, allowing the state to act on civil society, communities, and individuals in fundamentally different ways. Government officials expanded who could participate in public meetings and changed the basic criteria by which the government's activities were oriented. Policy experts and community leaders learned the language and "frame" of social justice that formed the foundation of the new policy community. The state was mobilized to organize relevant information to ensure that social justice principles would guide policymaking.

At the municipal level, the creation of nine new councils allowed civil society activists to transcend the physical barriers that had often made their communication difficult as they established the types of alliances necessary to maintain the vitality of civil society mobilization. Participatory budgeting was established in 1994, followed by the PB Housing program in 1996; the new councils and conferences provided new opportunities for activists to forge interregional and intrapolicy arena alliances across multiple policy arena and different public agencies. Finally, the Workers' Party made significant inroads, expanding and solidifying their ties to organized social movements and community associations. Thus, the activists working with the political community to support the PT and PSB government gained information and knowledge in the council and participatory spaces.

Mayor Célio de Castro (1997–2002)

In 1996, direct election of mayors was not permitted, and Patrus Ananias left office. Célio de Castro (PSB) was elected mayor in 1996 without the support of the Workers' Party. The Workers' Party broke an agreement they made in 1992 to support Célio de Castro for mayor in 1996. After Castro's victory, he brought the PT into the government to craft a stable governing coalition as well as to ensure that the two parties could work together to address major social problems. Mayor Castro deepened the political project initiated by Mayor Ananias, which had the effect of strengthening the three pillars of popular participation, social justice, and interlocking institutions.

Castro's first term in office is thus an extension and refinement of the policies created during the Patrus administration. For example, Castro's government created nineteen additional public policy management councils, which shows his interest in popular participation, and he also maintained the emphasis on social justice (Martins, 2007, 89). Castro was a medical doctor and former member of the then-clandestine Communist Party of Brazil. His government invested heavily in the medical system, which meant that he was involved in designing the municipal health care system, which would later produce strong results. Thus, Castro's first term in office was a consolidation of the reforms initiated by Mayor Patrus Ananias in 1993.

The 1988 constitution was amended in 1996 to allow for direct reelection of incumbent presidents, governors, and mayors. President Fernando Henrique Cardoso led the effort to pass a constitutional amendment that would allow all executives to be directly elected. In Belo Horizonte, Castro was reelected to office in 2000. Mayor Castro's second term in office marks a significant shift within the left-leaning progressive coalition that governed Belo Horizonte. The emphasis on social justice and popular participation gave way to a stronger focus on centralized administrative control, major infrastructure projects, and a decrease in the funds available for participatory budgeting.

The most important administrative reforms occurred at the start of Castro's second term (Martins 2007, 74–79). The mayor's office created two large departments (*SuperSecretarias*). One was for urban affairs (housing and sanitation), and the other was for social policy (education, health care, human rights, social services, etc.). The purpose was twofold. First, the concentration of decision-making authority increased the control the mayor and his team had over resource allocations and public

goods provision. Second, the government established an Interdepartmen-
tal Council on Social Policies (Câmara Intersetorial de Politicas Socias), a
collaborative policymaking space whereby seven department heads met
on a weekly basis to discuss policy problems. This is an excellent example
of the horizontal interlocking institutions initiated by the government.
These department heads were in constant contact with regional administrators responsible for policy provision and participatory governance venues (an example of vertical interlocking institutions), which allowed for
the consistent and direct flows of communication between community
leaders and government officials.

The reason for consolidating control in the executive branch is that the
government wanted to more carefully manage its response to the demands
emerging from a wide array of participatory institutions. The demands, of
course, were much greater than the government's capacity to respond. The
response was both policy oriented and politically oriented. From a policy
perspective, it was vital for the government to ensure that the allocation of
resources based on citizens' votes in participatory institutions was an effective use of public resources. But the government also wanted to make sure
that they implemented projects because elected officials' political support
was now associated with citizens' and activists' impressions of the results
being generated by the participatory programs.

A second important change was the creation of a financial coordinating body that would green-light policy projects prior to project implementation. This body consisted of the department heads of finance, planning,
and the two *SuperSecretarias*. From an administrative policy perspective, by
concentrating authority in the hands of four municipal department leaders, the government sought to address policy problems in a more comprehensive fashion. These two institutions thus allowed government officials
to better identify which projects and new programs should receive public
investment. Importantly, the department heads met on a biweekly or
monthly basis (depending on department) with mid-level bureaucrats in
order to better understand the key demands coming from civil society.

Mayor Castro's municipal government built a vertically integrated
policymaking process, transforming popular participation into a filtering
mechanism while simultaneously concentrating authority at the highest
levels of government to streamline the policymaking processes. What this
means is that citizens' voice in the policymaking processes is maintained,
but the power of the vote became much more limited. Thus, the first government of Mayor Castro was marked by the extension and deepening of

the political project initiated in 1993 by Mayor Patrus. However, Mayor Castro suffered from major medical problems and was forced to resign in 2002. Castro's vice mayor and department head of the powerful planning department came to power.

Centralizing Power Under Mayor Pimental (2003–2008)

Fernando Pimental was a professor of economics who had participated in the armed struggle in the 1960s against the military government. Pimental is associated with the majoritarian faction of the Workers' Party, which includes Brazilian presidents Lula (2003–2010) and Dilma Rousseff (2011–2014). This faction of the party, beginning after Lula's defeat in 1994, concentrated authority within the PT leaders and focused on electing Lula as Brazil's president (Hunter 2010).

During Pimental's two administrations (2002–2008), three noteworthy changes took place. First, the government began to invest in long-overdue major infrastructure projects, such as transportation arteries connecting downtown to the distant suburbs. The municipal government worked closely with the state government to invest in the expansion of roads to improve transportation in Belo Horizonte. The emphasis on social justice was no longer a principal concern of the government, but it was interested in building major infrastructure projects to help Belo Horizonte's economic and social environment.

Second, the Pimental government froze the level of resources dedicated to participatory budgeting, thereby decreasing the relative influence of citizens in the decision-making process, since the budget continued to grow each year (see chapter 4 for more detail). Although Mayor Pimental was not a strong advocate for participatory governance, these programs were sufficiently well institutionalized that the government was forced by CSOs and some factions of the PT to maintain the direct incorporation of citizens into participatory programs. Pimental was a leader of the party, which branded itself as being participatory and inclusive, so that Pimental had to continue to formally support the program even though he was slowly moving resources away from it.

Although Mayor Pimental's administration moved away from participatory governance, they did seek to create one significant change to the participatory budgeting process, which was the introduction of "PB Digital." PB Digital was implemented in 2006, and it functioned again in 2008, 2010, and 2012. This new form of participation was designed to achieve three goals: induce a larger number of citizens to participate, include larger infrastructure projects in the process, and appeal to middle-class and youth sectors. PB Digital is thus representative of the changes that Mayor Pimental sought to produce; it remains within the initial project initiated by Mayors Patrus and Castro because PB Digital seeks to legitimatize itself through references to popular participation, but the program also seeks to limit direct citizen participation in decision making. PB Digital will be discussed in greater detail in chapter 4.

During Fernando Pimental's second term in office, he established a political alliance with the governor of the state of Minas Gerais, Aécio Neves. Neves is the grandson of a key figure, Tancredo Neves, representing prodemocratic forces during the transition to democratic rule in the mid-1980s. Mayor Pimental and Governor Aécio Neves established an important agreement between the Workers' Party and the PSDB; these two parties have held Brazil's presidency since 1995 and are intense rivals that rarely cooperate. One part of their agreement was that Mario Lacerda of the PSB would have the support of the PT and the PSDB in the 2008 election.

Methods and Results: Mayor Lacerda (2009–2012)

Mayor Lacerda was elected in 2008 in a competitive election in which he only won 44 percent of the vote in the first round of the election, although he did secure 59 percent of the vote in the second round. Civil society organizations provided only lukewarm support to Lacerda in the first round of the election but were willing to support him in the second round because the PT would occupy the vice mayor's office. In several interviews, community leaders asserted that they did not support candidate Lacerda in the first round but only worked for his campaign in the second round because he was a much better candidate than his opponent, who was from the centrist PMDB.[6] The 2008 election illustrates how the first round can be used by organized coalitions of voters to punish candidates who are straying from their political agreements. Mayor Pimental and candidate Lacerda were far less invested in the participatory elements of reform than the previous two mayors.

The last major reform of the twenty-year governing project was initiated in 2009 by Mayor Mario Lacerda: "BH: Methods and Results." There was a specific effort to consolidate the basic advances and reforms of the previous administrations, to focus on the types of social policies that the new mayor wanted to implement, and, finally, to show to the growing middle class that the government could identify and accomplish a series of goals. The methods and results governance approach is a technocratic approach to governing, being inspired by the new public management programs. Mayor Lacerda's prior business success in the telecommunications field led him to focus on developing specific metrics to evaluate the quality of public policies provided by the government. As one high-ranking government official stated, "In sixteen years, we never had such a strong focus on the outputs of our programs" (Sousa Júnior interview). Lacerda sent a clear message that if the government was providing a service to the public, then the quality of the service could be measured.

The focus on methods and results marks a shift away from a previous focus on popular participation and social justice, but these principles are sufficiently well-institutionalized that the government has been unable to divorce themselves from the process. During the ten months I was in Belo Horizonte, Lacerda made a concerted effort to reach out to the participatory programs. I was at multiple events in which he sat for hours listening to citizens and CSO leaders discuss their problems, propose solutions, and demand action. Lacerda is not a charismatic politician. His speeches at these events were short; he always ended with saying something along the lines of "I am now going to listen to what you have to say." Lacerda lacks the personal charm and charisma of many politicians, but he sought to overcome this deficit by his willingness to sit and listen.

Lacerda continued the basic policy direction initiated by Mayor Patrus in 1993, thus indicating that the institutional changes are sufficiently "sticky" that political actors involved in policy, associational, and political communities now accept that social justice and popular participation must be part of social policymaking. And yet the evidence also indicates that Lacerda is following the agenda established by Mayor Pimental, whereby the government seeks to limit citizens' voice and vote. Although Lacerda governed in a fashion much more similar to that of Fernando Pimental, the Ananias and Castro governments' emphasis on social justice and popular participation continues to be the organizing principle around which the government operates.

This chapter demonstrates how the Workers' Party government took advantage of a window of opportunity created by the transition to democratic rule, the 1988 constitution, and their 1992 mayoral election to initiate a reformist project that would activate the participatory citizenship regime in Belo Horizonte. Four successive left-of-center and centrist governments restructured the local state to alter the access points through which individual citizens and community leaders engage the state as well as government officials deliver public goods and social services. In the context of a structurally weak and constrained legislative branch and a fragmented party system (forty-one city council members come from twenty-seven political parties), participatory governance venues are now key spaces that link citizens, community leaders, and government officials. The three pillars of the PT's reform project—popular participation, social justice, and interlocking institutions—expand access to social and political rights.

With regard to the participatory citizenship regime, this chapter demonstrates the primacy of the municipal executive branch elections and, therefore, of representative democracy. The individual and the party elected to the mayor's office have extensive flexibility to initiate new political projects. Thus, this analysis of participatory institutions is grounded in the broader macro-historical context of representative democratic institutions as well as of state formation that set the parameters of what the municipal government can accomplish.

There are now nearly 5,000 positions to which citizens are elected (3,400 in the public policy management councils and more than 1,500 in participatory budgeting). Direct citizen engagement allows for new forms of deliberation to develop. Belo Horizonte is on the leading edge of change in Brazil because a mobilized civil society and a programmatic political party gained control of a capable local state. This control allowed the Workers' Party to devise new institutions and programs that initiated the participatory citizenship regime.

CHAPTER FOUR

Innovation and Renewal of Participatory Budgeting

We built this party; we built this council; we built this government.
> —community activist Gina, December 2, 2009

Without our ongoing support, participation would not exist in Belo Horizonte.
> —government administrator in Belo Horizonte, May 5, 2010

In 2009, I attended a participatory budgeting meeting after a five-year absence from Belo Horizonte. The monthly meeting, held in downtown, allowed government officials to provide information about the current status of projects and for elected PB delegates to ask questions about these and other projects. The most significant change I noticed since the last time I had attended a meeting was the participants' multiple references to other participatory venues, such as policy conferences and councils. The activists were making use of interlocking institutions, which allowed them to be involved in a broader discussion of policy reform and the institutional pathways needed to promote change. An elderly man spoke first to complain about the poor quality of services provided to people living in a homeless

shelter. He demanded that the government implement specific projects selected through participatory budgeting—in this case, the refurbishing of a
homeless shelter. As soon as he finished speaking, two other participants
stood up to explain that the man was presenting his case in the wrong
venue; one speaker pointed him in the direction of the social service public policy management council, and the other suggested a visit to the municipal and state offices of the social services department. The participants
were well-versed in the intricate institutional policymaking bodies that
had developed over the previous fifteen years.

The next speaker provided information he had obtained from the
health care council. It concerned a health care clinic approved in participatory budgeting for the area around the Morro de Papagaio favela (the
focus of chapter 7). Resources to pay for medical personnel staff had been
approved, he reported, which meant that when the building was completed in 2010, the local population could immediately begin receiving
services at the clinic. He couched his report in terms of the successful
struggle (*luta*) that led to the community's ability to secure their rights
(*conquista*), as guaranteed under the 1988 constitution. Thus, the speaker's
brief talk returned to the social justice theme of rights, which is so vital to
explaining why poor citizens are engaging the state in these participatory
institutions. After a half dozen additional speakers, the government administrator in charge of the central region took the microphone to respond to numerous questions and to provide information. This ongoing
exchange among citizens and government officials was not merely "top
down" or "bottom up" but involved the sharing of information among citizens and between citizens and governments officials. Citizens informed
each other as well as government officials of how and where to engage the
state in order to activate their rights. Government officials received information, and they strategized with activists regarding where their demands should be placed.

At a subsequent participatory budgeting meeting, there was a fascinat-
ing debate in which a community leader demanded that the government
implement a pedestrian footbridge that would connect her community to a
well-established shopping and business area. This leader explained in considerable detail how she had visited different government departments; she
claimed that the overpass was ready to be built and the government was
needlessly dragging its feet and thus endangering people's lives. The government administrator first argued that more pedestrians are killed near

footbridges because cars don't slow down and because people ignore the footbridge and run through traffic to cross the street. The administrator then asserted that the technical rules of building a footbridge made it nearly impossible to place the bridge in the location citizens had selected. This exchange lasted for ten to fifteen minutes, but it was reenacted at several different meetings. After gaining the trust of those involved in this debate, I learned that the community leaders didn't want the pedestrian bridge because they feared that local drug traffickers would use the bridge to increase their retail sales (because of the prime location of the favela near a shopping mall). Thus, PB administrators and CSO leaders privately agreed that CSO leaders would continue to demand the overpass and the government would never implement it. This would protect the leaders from negative repercussions in their community.

This example illuminates the complexity of deliberative exchanges. It's an extreme case in which people's real interests were the complete opposite of what they were claiming in public: it illuminates the fact that public deliberations may involve people staking out positions that do not adequately reflect their preferences. Rather, public deliberation can be used to score political points, to establish a more extreme position in order to establish a better negotiating position, or to send a signal to other groups that they are willing to negotiate.

Since its inception in 1993, participatory budgeting has been the most visible institutional format for the direct engagement of citizens, community leaders, and government officials in Belo Horizonte. Four successive governments of Belo Horizonte invested significant resources (financial, personnel, political capital) in the participatory budgeting process. The support provided by government officials fluctuated significantly between 1993 and 2012 as a result of the changing political coalitions that governed the city (see the end of chapter 3 for a description of the different governing coalitions). Government officials and their allies in civil society experimented with how they could activate state authority and civil society mobilization to take advantage of the formal initiation of the participatory citizenship regime. This chapter demonstrates how state formation, civil society development, the rules specific to each participatory budgeting program, the level of resources available to the program, and government support best account for how the participatory citizenship regime would unfold across Belo Horizonte's three programs. The institutionalization of participatory budgeting is an integral part of how the municipal government sought to activate the participatory citizen regime based on popular participation, social justice, and interlocking institutions.

In this chapter, I demonstrate that participatory budgeting is a key institutional mechanism that activated the local participatory citizenship regime. The PB Regional program remains the site of the most active and involved direct participation. On a biannual basis, tens of thousands of citizens participate in meetings sponsored by the municipal government. Participation serves an instrumental purpose—picking specific public goods—but it also serves the broader purpose of the "bonds of solidarity" (Alexander 2006). Such involvement allows participants to demonstrate to government officials and their fellow citizens the worthiness of their cause and the strength of their commitment (McAdam, Tarrow, and Tilly 2001).

WHAT IS PARTICIPATORY BUDGETING?

Participatory budgeting is a yearlong decision-making process through which citizens negotiate among themselves and with government officials in organized meetings over the allocation of new capital investment spending on public works projects, such as health care clinics, schools, and street paving. Belo Horizonte's participatory budgeting program has had a significant and enduring impact on the lives of low-income communities and social organizations over a twenty-year period. Participatory budgeting is now at the center of the policymaking process for the allocation of small to medium-sized public goods. It is routinized, which constrains the capacity for dynamic change but allows citizens and CSOs to use their understanding of the formal and informal political rules of the policymaking process to contribute to policy formation.

The first section in this chapter explains the basic rules of participatory budgeting as it evolved from 1993 to 2012. The second section examines the impact of the program. By 2012, over 1,200 projects had been implemented, and the municipal government had spent over $500 million on these projects.[1] Over the twenty-year period, successive mayoral administrations slowly withdrew their political and financial support, which has led to a political conundrum in Belo Horizonte: community leaders are often the staunchest defenders and harshest critics of PB. As one leader from the Serra Favela stated in a meeting, "Things are not great in OP [*orçamento participativo*, or participatory budgeting], but it would be much, much, much worse without OP" (PB Regional 2009).

Although the PB experience in Belo Horizonte is not as famous as the one in the southern Brazilian city of Porto Alegre, this chapter demonstrates how government officials in Belo Horizonte managed to overcome some of the basic limitations associated with other PB programs. Because the city's program was outside the national and international limelight, government officials had greater opportunities for ongoing innovation.[2]

THE HISTORY OF PARTICIPATORY BUDGETING IN BELO HORIZONTE

Participatory budgeting was initiated in 1993 by a political coalition that united the Workers' Party (PT) and the Brazilian Socialist Party (PSB); as argued in chapter 3, the new governing coalition forged a long-term electoral realignment that produced twenty years of political change.[3] The PT government, led by Mayor Patrus Ananias, drew from Porto Alegre's PB program, which had been founded in 1989 (Verde and Ananias interviews). The government "sought to stimulate, create, and invigorate diverse participatory channels. . . . The challenge was to democratize the municipal administration through popular participation and create a new relationship between the mayoral administration and society" (Azevedo 2003, 23). The PT-led government in Belo Horizonte produced two significant innovations, both of which were later adopted by other cities. One innovation was the Quality of Life Index (discussed in chapter 3 as a technique of access), which established how the PB program would allocate a higher level of resources to poorer neighborhoods. This innovation ties together the ideas of popular participation, social justice, and interlocking institutions because it requires citizen participation at the local level, allocates greater resources to poor communities, and uses data provided by different government agencies. At its core, PB was infused with "pro-poor" principles that are part of an effort to bring greater public goods into poor communities.

The second main innovation was PB Housing, which developed as a parallel process to the territory-based PB Regional programs. PB Housing created an alternative policymaking process, permitting public officials and CSO activists to negotiate over housing-related issues in a separate format. Providing good-quality public housing is one of the most difficult social problems in Brazil; the state and the market have been unable to supply decent housing to tens of millions of citizens.

PB Regional

Belo Horizonte's PB Regional, founded in 1993, induces citizens to focus on very local issues—their street, their neighborhood, and their residential community (most often favelas and *vilas*). The city is divided into nine administrative regions, which are the sites for voting on resource allocation. Citizens organize themselves at the local level first and then come to region-wide meetings in which they negotiate with other CSOs to select public works for the following two years. Government officials harness existing local state capacity to implement the infrastructure projects selected by citizens through the PB program. An important part of the success of PB is based on government officials being able to redirect existing state capacity toward poor communities. The government doesn't have to generate new state authority, but the focus on small infrastructure helps the government achieve its goals of incorporating citizens into the policymaking process and then providing public works to address pressing problems.

Figure 4.1 shows how citizens are organized within PB Regional. Citizens begin their participation at the neighborhood level, in meetings organized by local CSOs. These meetings help citizens assess their numerical strength, document their needs, and devise strategies to increase the likelihood they will win a public works projects. This step reinforces the bonds of solidarity among community members and also prepares them for the intense political competition that will take place within PB.

Each of the nine regions is divided into three to six subregions. The subregions are grouped according to similar characteristics and needs (e.g.,

Figure 4.1 Participation Flow with Participatory Budgeting

Neighborhood level (organized by CSOs)

↓

Local level (42 regions) (organized by government)

↓

Regional level (9 subregions) (organized by government)

↓

Municipal level (organized by government)

number of inhabitants, socioeconomic characteristics, physical barriers, occupation pattern, proximity). This process links very local concerns (my street) to community (my neighborhood, my favela) to broader regional (the west, the northeast) issues to municipal issues. CSO leaders must develop a unified strategy at the local and community level prior to moving to the regional level. Citizens are induced first to participate in their local communities, among their neighbors. This direct participation can have an empowering effect, as citizens gather information and learn to engage in policymaking. In addition, citizens can renew their bonds of solidarity at local and regional levels by attending local meetings that encourage ongoing discussions regarding community issues.

Belo Horizonte's PB process is divided into nine phases:[4]

1. Opening ceremonies at municipal and regional levels. Government officials present PB regulations, guidelines, and public works applications to participants. Citizens are informed about the current budgetary policies and the investments undertaken within the previous two years. The opening ceremony feels like a political rally, with speeches by government officials and carefully selected citizens who extol the virtues of the program, mention the challenges, and discuss how the challenges will be overcome. CSO leaders pick up the public works application that their community must fill out.

   At the regional openings there is a narrower focus on the specific steps citizens *must* take to secure public works projects; CSO leaders and citizens have the opportunity to address other participants. There is little deliberation at this stage, although a few activists may be invited to speak. The audience in attendance mainly listens (or not); citizen presence is crucial to demonstrate a community's ability to mobilize itself.

2. Neighborhood-level meetings. Citizens discuss the projects they want implemented in their neighborhood. Citizens and CSOs organize the meetings. Meeting organizers must show that a minimum of ten people attended to be eligible to submit a preliminary policy proposal. After the meetings the project proposals can be submitted to the municipal administration. The deadline to submit project proposals ends one month after the respective regional meeting. Deliberation is likely to be the most robust at this stage of the process, with citizens and CSO leaders deliberating among themselves.

3. First approval of submitted project applications. The corresponding municipal agency department reviews the project applications (e.g., the demand for a health care clinic is evaluated by the Health Department). If proposed projects do not meet basic rules or if the technical and financial feasibility is questioned, the group proposing the project will be informed and have an opportunity to revise the application. Technical experts must provide timely and relevant information to allow CSOs to develop policy proposals that can be implemented.

4. Forums at subregional level (forty-two subregions). Participants in each subregion deliberate over the projects submitted for their subregions. Government officials inform the participants of their budget for their subregion—participants can only select projects that fit within the proposed budget. Prior to the meetings, community leaders negotiate with each other to obtain support for different projects. The projects are presented to the general public during open deliberative forums, thereby giving citizens the opportunity to convince others to support their projects. In these meetings, CSO leaders are the most likely to engage in deliberations. They appeal to their base and to other groups to generate the necessary support for their programs.

    At the end of the subregional forums, participants elect delegates to the regional forum. In 2010, 1,700 delegates were elected from the forty-two subregions to represent their subregions' interests at the regional level (nine regions). The number of delegates for each subregion depends on how many people participate in the forums. Delegates need to be at least sixteen years old to be elected to the regional forum.

5. Second approval of submitted project applications. After a region's projects have been identified, city officials visit all project sites to develop a technical appraisal of the viability of the proposals. This is a vital technical step: knowing the cost of a proposed project helps to ground the debate in the technical realities of the government.

6. Caravan of priorities. The municipality provides the delegates elected in phase 4 with information on the background and costs associated with every project proposal. The delegates then visit the sites of the twenty-five preselected public works in their region to gain a broader vision of the region's needs. The purpose of the caravan is to increase knowledge as well as to promote solidarity among the delegates before they vote on which projects are to be funded in their region. The cara-

van of priorities takes place on weekends. Buses are provided to the delegates to visit the sites. Each delegate gets an opportunity to advocate on behalf of his or her project or projects.

7.   Forums at regional levels. Regional forums take place one week after the caravan of priorities. The PB delegates select up to fourteen public works per region. In 2009–2010, 109 projects were approved via the regional PB process. After project selection, the delegates elect representatives for a municipal council and nine regional commissions. The role of the representatives is to follow up on the implementation of the projects. The number of representatives for each region depends on the number of inhabitants of the respective region.

8.   Official closing of the process at the municipal level. The regional PB process is officially closed at the municipal level where the selected public works projects are presented.

9.   Implementation and monitoring. The PB delegates will monitor the contracting and constructing of the selected projects over the next several years. The PB delegates meet monthly at each of the nine regions. The ongoing oversight enables citizens to monitor how public officials and private companies are using public resources to implement the selected projects.

The budget available for each of the nine regions is determined by two factors. Resources for the Participatory Budget are based on the Quality of Life Index (IQVU) and the number of residents. Thus, the lower the quality of life (measured by IQVU) and the higher the population in a particular planning unit, the more resources the region will receive. (See chapter 3 for a description of how the IQVU functions.) The second factor affecting the size of the budget is the level of participation. The budget for a region will be decreased if not enough people participate in the subregional forums. The population of the subregion determines the minimum number of participants in each subregion. However, regions cannot increase their allotted budgets by mobilizing greater numbers of participants.

PB Regional Adaptations

Following its founding in 1993, PB Regional was continually modified through 2012, which is the period that marks the end of this study. The most significant change was the switch to a biannual cycle from an annual meeting cycle. This change happened in 1999 for two basic reasons. The municipal administration hoped that a two-year planning cycle would improve planning and internal coordination and allow them to make more efficient use of scarce resources (interlocking institutions). It was difficult for CSOs to maintain citizens' enthusiasm to participate every year; by mobilizing every other year, CSO leaders could more easily mobilize their followers (popular participation). Thus, this adaptation was undertaken to address long-term collective action fatigue as well as the technical, legal, and financial constraints placed on the state, demonstrating that public officials were responding to public and state pressures.

A second significant change was to require all favelas to have urban planners complete a "community blueprint," which provides a long-term plan for the type and phasing of infrastructure projects (interlocking institutions). Beginning in 2000, projects selected via PB had to first be included in a community blueprint. The community blueprint is an example of a technique of access: the government sought to marry technical expertise, local community knowledge (*mētis*), and a commitment to improving the quality of life among the city's poorest communities.

To operationalize citizens' voices in long-term planning, there are now three phases.

Phase 1: A community blueprint is selected by citizens in PB. Communities must first organize themselves within PB Regional to secure the funding resources for drafting a community blueprint. This means that community leaders must convince citizens to forgo public works projects in the short-term in the hopes that they can secure larger-scale projects.

Phase 2: Urban planners prepare the community blueprint, allowing for a long-term development plan. Citizens and community leaders then have meetings with urban planners to discuss the main issues confronting the community. After urban planners complete the community blueprint, they present their plan to the community, which has the opportunity to request revisions. The community blueprint is only officially completed when community members vote to accept the proposal.

Phase 3: Preapproved public works projects included in the community blueprint can be selected via PB. Citizens and CSOs must then organize themselves to determine which of the preapproved public works projects they would like to have implemented in the short-term. The negotiations can be acrimonious as citizens debate the impact of different policy proposals, but they can also generate community building as citizens are forced to discussion community priorities and needs.

The community blueprint is an excellent example of how government officials craft policies that implement the core principles of the participatory citizenship regime. Citizens participate, and their local knowledge (*mētis*) is used to craft urbanization projects. Following a series of meetings and public deliberations, state officials incorporate citizens' knowledge and preferences into their plans, thus decreasing future conflict and, it is hoped, improving the quality of the public good produced. Of course, the broad transformation of the community will produce local winners and losers. Some citizens will undoubtedly feel as though their voices were not heard in the process and that the final outcome did not meet their policy preferences. We must therefore be cognizant that participatory processes and representative democracy have many similarities: the rules are designed to promote the interests of the majority. There are broader constitutional mechanisms within participatory processes to protect minority rights, but these are not directly incorporated into the program.

The community blueprint illustrates James Scott's "simplification process," whereby states make favelas and *vilas* more manageable (Scott 1988, 77; see the section "Interlocking Institutions" in chapter 1). But the community blueprint is not part of an authoritarian policymaking process whereby the government decides how to redesign a community. Rather, *mētis* (local knowledge) is directly incorporated into the policymaking process.

The inclusion of specific technical information in the urban development plan produces an incremental policymaking process. The scope of deliberation narrows as citizens working within PB are constrained by the technical language and requirements. Citizens had to learn to cast their claims based on a combination of need (social justice) and feasibility (technical/financial). There are two clear benefits to the increased focus on technical issues. First, there is less wasted effort determining what the municipality could afford to implement. Participants learn that their community will have access to a limited set of resources, which means that they must deliberate among themselves to determine their key priorities. Second, ordinary citizens learn to conceptualize the different steps necessary to transform their communities. The creation of the community blueprint allows citizens and CSOs leaders to prioritize their strategies as they work through a complex policy process.

However, this technocratic process removes some of the vitality from the process. Citizens and community leaders are forced to work within their favela to figure out the sequencing of projects: Should we first pave roads? Improve the soccer field? Provide sewage hookups to the poorest part of the community? Establishing priorities within the community places an enormous burden on citizens and CSO leaders because their decisions will have a substantial impact on their community members' lives. This authority creates the opportunity to generate bonds of solidarity but can also be divisive, pitting community members against one another. CSO leaders must also spend hours and hours mastering the technical language and procedures to ensure that their public works are implemented.

A third important change to PB Regional was the establishment of micro-regions, each of which have specific resources available. Small and very poor communities, which are often unable to compete with CSOs representing larger favelas, are able to secure funding through the micro-regions. PB Regional was designed to overcome the class bias associated with representative democracy (the Quality of Life Index creates a preferential bias for the poor), but there remain important differences among poor citizens and communities that PB Regional was unable to address. When small, poor communities organize themselves within the micro-region, their communities are eligible for funding. This was a significant limitation to Porto Alegre's PB program, which never figured out how to incorporate very small groups.[5] In contrast, the political leadership in Belo Horizonte was not tied to any single model of participation and thus was able to transform the rules to overcome a new type of participation bias. PB programs often reward the best-organized groups; the micro-region approach recognizes that the very poor have the most difficult time organizing and are thus provided with a specific set of rules to help them do well.

In 2001, the government created a second index, based on the results of the 2000 census, that allowed them to assess health risks. The Social Vulnerability Index (Índice de Vulnerabilidade Social, or IVS) offers a more refined indicator of risk and social problems than the original Quality of Life Index because it measures social conditions on a smaller scale—the local neighborhood rather than the larger eighty-one planning units. By using a greater number of local units, it became possible to capture the diversity of social conditions within the larger regions, which is especially important in Belo Horizonte because of the presence of many small (and very poor) *vilas* inside larger lower-income neighborhoods. Thus, by 2001, the government was in a much better position to target small *vilas* as well as to identify what was occurring in larger favelas. The municipal government thus allocated resources to these micro-regions through the simplification process.

Another group that benefits from micro-regions are residents from middle- and upper-income communities. Organizations from these communities have a difficult time mobilizing themselves in PB Regional because the rules don't encourage allocating resources to upper-income communities; hence there is no incentive for residents from wealthy neighborhoods to attend PB meetings. The micro-region approach provides wealthy citizens a direct incentive to participate, although it is important to note that the level of resources these citizens have to allocate is much lower in both absolute and per capita terms than the level of resources made available to poor citizens. Middle-class groups are thus incorporated in ways that require less organizational efforts on their part.

The micro-region innovation addresses the social justice component of the participatory citizenship regime by explicitly recognizing the power differentials among competing favelas and organized groups. PB programs have the potential to reproduce the collective action biases associated with representative democracy—the best-organized communities received the greatest benefits because they are able to mobilize themselves to take advantage of the rules. By establishing micro-regions, public officials created specific opportunities for the smallest and often poorest communities to gain access to limited resources. As with participatory institutions more broadly, the establishment of micro-regions provides a way to address the problems associated with societal power differentials but doesn't solve them.

The final innovation, in 2010, was the creation of a municipal-wide council within PB Regional. In my 2007 book, *Participatory Budgeting in Brazil,* I wrote the following about Belo Horizonte's PB program (243):

> The absence of a "PB council" was intended to prevent the emergence of new intermediaries who would represent the interests of delegates during negotiations with government officials. . . . However, the lack of a centralized forum for delegates has had the effect of fragmenting participation. There was no institutional venue in which participants

could gather to compare notes and devise strategies to counter the government's claims. Delegates are often of low income, with limited resources, which meant that it is not possible for them to easily meet in the city center. Decentralization of all decision-making to the district level precluded the development of a consistent block of delegates and activists who might choose to contest the policies of the government. The lack of a unified, centralized institutional venue (e.g., PB council) for PB delegates limits the delegates' ability to form a collective, unified response to the government. Instead, the delegates were a "captured audience," with each group or region believing that their struggles and difficulties with PB and the government were unique to their district rather than understanding that their problems were likely representative of a larger municipal-wide trend.

In 2010, PB participants finally achieved their goal of a municipal-wide PB Council, which they hoped would enable them to better forge the bonds of solidarity so vital to sustaining mobilization. However, the PB Council is a "consultative" body and thus lacks a clear set of responsibilities and authority. This body allows information to be passed among participants, but the lack of any specific authority minimizes its impact on the policy-making process.

In sum, the basic rules of Belo Horizonte's PB were initially adopted from the pioneering case of Porto Alegre, but government, citizens, and CSOs worked together in Belo Horizonte to adapt PB Regional's rules to better tackle pressing social and political problems. The institutional rules were never frozen but rather made significantly flexible to allow for change. The ongoing innovations illuminate that the participatory citizenship regime can be activated in different ways to address citizens' and government officials' policy and political goals. There is no set formula for how rights will be activated, but it is necessary to have strong support from government officials to harness state authority to implement social policies beneficial to poor individuals and communities.

PB Housing

PB Housing, established in 1996, was the second major innovation in Belo Horizonte (the first being the Quality of Life Index). The impetus to implement PB Housing was the presence of a well-organized housing movement as well as the complexity of building public housing units. Housing is a particularly difficult policy issue to address because of unclear property titles in favelas and *vilas*, the financial cost of purchasing land, and the cost associated with building new housing stock (Holston 2008; Gonçalves 2007). Given the long time required to build new housing units, government officials created PB Housing to ensure that the broader PB process would not be impeded by problems specific to this policy area. Government officials also worried that the mobilization strength of the housing movement would overwhelm the incipient PB Regional program.

To be eligible for housing via PB Housing, community organizations need to be formally registered as a housing *núcleo*. Each *núcleo* must register one hundred families, all of whom have lived in the Belo Horizonte area for at least two years and all of whom must have a family income of less than three minimum salaries.[6] Every two years community organizations must reregister their housing *núcleo*. The purpose behind these rules is to create a regulated process through which citizens can gain access to housing while also ensuring that individuals with great need will be able to secure housing. Government officials were concerned that without a universal set of criteria, it was more likely that more politically astute activists would gain access to the units.

New government-built housing units are distributed to the housing *núcleo*. Given high demand and the low number of apartments, PB Housing distributes the apartment units to registered housing *núcleos* using a waiting list as well as a lottery. When a *núcleo* is awarded housing units, its leadership is free to allocate the housing unit to someone from within their hundred registered families. This means that housing *núcleos* control a public resource that they distribute to a few of their registered families. The housing *núcleo* requires ongoing participation by multiple families as well as the continual representation of these families' interests by a small number of leaders. The housing *núcleo* thus institutionalizes direct and ongoing participation.

PB Housing fits within the governing coalition's initial efforts to activate the participatory citizenship regime. They forged new forms of participation by allowing organized groups (housing *núcleos*) to be directly involved in shaping housing policy. The rules sought to promote social justice by creating specific income qualifications. PB housing legitimized the leadership of housing movements by granting these organizations formal representation within the new policymaking venues. Overall, PB

Housing represents an innovative, local response to incorporating citizens into a process that attempts to address a policy arena resistant to change.

PB Digital[7]

PB Digital was established in 2006 and functions every other year (2008, 2010, 2012). It is not designed to address social justice issues. Rather, this new form of participation seeks to encourage middle-class and youth sectors to participate by lowering the time costs associated with participation and by focusing on medium-scale infrastructure projects that will affect greater numbers of people. The Pimental administration (2003–2008) worried that the middle class and youth were not participating in PB Regional (the data on PB participation in Belo Horizonte confirm that middle-class and youth sector participate at lower rates). The PB Digital marks a shift in how citizens participate and deliberate over public goods provisions.

Government officials first select medium-sized public works projects located in areas of general public use. Through a website (http://opdigital.pbh.gov.br) citizens can access information about each project and then vote on which they would like the government to implement. Any citizen with a valid voter identification card from the city of Belo Horizonte can vote for a project.[8] To minimize problems related to the digital divide, the municipal government installed about 170 information kiosks in schools, the central market, and shopping centers throughout the city. The PB Digital website presents basic information about each project, such as costs, location, and pictures. Online participation tools, such as e-mail and discussion forums, are also offered. It is not mandatory to engage in deliberations before voting. After the voting process starts, citizens have forty-five days to gather information about the projects, present questions to the government, and confer with other people online and offline before voting.

PB Digital was revised after its inception in 2006 in order to improve the process. A major improvement was the use of online maps to identify the projects' locations and the public access points for using the Internet. Another innovation was the inclusion of photographs showing the current roads before and after reconstruction. The 2008 PB Digital website provided details on each of the projects, pointing out the impact, costs, benefits, and beneficiaries. Finally, participatory tools were expanded. Besides the reactivation of the discussion forum, two new features were implemented. The first one was the possibility of posting comments online. For each project, there was an option to leave a message without having to register. The second feature was a chat-room discussion that could be used at prescheduled dates. Representatives from the Planning, Budget, and Information Office received questions, suggestions, and criticism from the citizens in the chat room; four sessions took place in 2010. After the vote, the forum and chat room were shut down, but the comments on the website can still be accessed. PB Regional delegates monitor the implementation of the selected projects via PB Digital (an example of interlocking institutions). Information on the process of implementation is provided via a bimonthly newspaper and the Internet.

In sum, PB Digital is an attempt to expand the number of participants who vote for specific public works projects. It limits deliberation by not inducing citizens to engage each other; instead, citizens vote on projects from a range of options selected by the government. PB Digital takes advantage of new information technologies, but in a way that limits rather than expands the new forms of engagement. The program is representative of the changes Mayor Pimental sought to produce. There is little effort in PB Digital to directly empower or educate citizens. Government officials decide which projects citizens will vote on, thus promoting a consolidation of decision-making authority in the mayor's office. Mayor Pimental used the brand of the popular PB program in order to legitimize new policy initiatives. This demonstrates that the reforms initiated in 1993 were sufficiently institutionalized politically that the government needed to justify a shift in their priorities based on the principles of popular participation. Overall, PT and PSB governments made continual efforts to improve PB by modifying the rules that govern it. The willingness to alter the rules demonstrates an intense government commitment to identifying a new rule set that would best achieve its goals.

IMPACT: PB REGIONAL

There have been robust levels of participation since PB's founding in 1994. There were a high number of participants in 1994, especially when comparing Belo Horizonte's first year of PB to Porto Alegre's PB, which had under a thousand participants in its first year (Abers 2000; Wampler 2007). Belo Horizonte government officials implementing their PB program had the benefit of learning from the Porto Alegre experience, thus allowing

Table 4.1 Number of Participants in Participatory Budgeting

Year	Number of Participants
1994	15,216
1995	26,823
1996	38,508
1997	33,695
1998	20,678
1999–2000*	22,238
2001–2002	43,350
2003–2004	30,479
2005–2006	38,302
2007–2008	34,693
2009–2010	40,967
2011–2012	25,871

* PB switched to a biannual process in 1999.
Source: Prefeitura Municipal de Belo Horizonte 2013a.

government officials and community leaders to develop plans regarding how citizens could be mobilized.

Tens of thousands of citizens participate in PB on a biannual basis, as shown in Table 4.1. The population of Belo Horizonte is just over 2 million residents, which means that a minority of the population participates. However, in terms of the distribution of poverty and social inequality in Belo Horizonte, there are roughly 700,000 residents living in communities with high levels of social vulnerability and another 800,000 residents living in communities with medium levels of social vulnerability. Of these 1.5 million residents, one-third are under the age of sixteen. Thus, of the 1 million targeted citizens, the participation of 40,000 residents in 2009 means that roughly 4 percent of the targeted population directly participated.

The number of participants matters insofar as larger or smaller numbers affect the legitimacy of the program. Although 3 to 4 percent of the targeted population is a distinct minority, the participants now assume the role of ligatures between ordinary citizens and the state. Chapter 7 discusses a survey showing that nearly 50 percent of a randomly selected

Table 4.2 Demographic Profile of Participatory Budgeting Delegates

	Percentage Responding	
	2003 (n = 60)	*2009 (n = 100)*
Monthly household income less than $400 in 2003 and less than $500 in 2009	61	27
Less than high school diploma	51	58
Women	48	60

Sources: Wampler 2007, 2009.

group of ordinary citizens received information from community leaders on elections. Communities and groups that previously struggled to have any sort of formal representation inside state institutions are now able to consistently have their issues discussed in public venues.

Data from two surveys—one administered in 2003 and the second in 2009—demonstrate that citizens elected as PB delegates are from low-income communities. Elected PB delegates randomly selected to participate in the surveys are from poor communities. The principal actors in PB Regional are thus representative of the low-income communities they are elected to represent (for similar findings see Azevedo and Nabuco 2008; Azevedo and Fernandes 2005; Marquettti et al. 2008). The most significant difference in the two surveyed populations is the significant drop in the number of very poor respondents. This is attributable, in part, to the economic boom that was creating a lower middle class, many of whom were living in favelas. In addition, we can also surmise that the class bias associated with representative democracy is now being replicated in Belo Horizonte's PB; families that are better off financially are mobilizing themselves to influence the distribution of public goods.

Overall, we see that poor residents are the principal political actors in a policymaking institution that has helped to build basic infrastructure in favelas and *vilas* across the city. Although the number of participants is noteworthy, the socioeconomic profile of the participants is even more significant. The elected leadership within PB is drawn from the poor communities that PB targets. This has an empowering effect at the individual level, as specific leaders exercise authority on behalf of their community. But it also has an empowering effect for the broader community because they have a representative who has a mandate from their community to negotiate with government officials. This mandate does not stop at the formal boundaries of PB but extends into different policymaking spheres. PB delegates are then able to bring local knowledge (*mētis*) on a host of issues to the broader public debate.

Advancing Social Justice: Redistribution of Resources

Overall, citizens selected over $700 million in public infrastructure projects between 1993 and 2010. The high point for spending was 1996, when citizens selected nearly 100 million in Brazilian reais (in 2008 currency values; at the time, one US dollar was roughly equal to 1.75 Brazilian reais). Over time, the actual amounts of resources declined. The low point for resource allocation to PB was 2005–2006, when citizens allocated just half the resources they had allocated in 1996 (see Table 4.3).

Table 4.3 Resources Allocated through Participatory Budgeting, 1994–2012

Year	Resources Allocated	In 2008 Brazilian Reais
1994	R$ 15,000,000.00	R$ 66,300,000.00
1995	R$ 18,000,000.00	R$ 79,560,000.00
1996	R$ 27,000,000.00	R$ 95,310,000.00
1997	R$ 27,000,000.00	R$ 86,508,000.00
1998	R$ 15,974,186.00	R$ 46,325,139.40
1999–2000	R$ 60,208,600.00	R$ 166,233,902.88
2001–2002	R$ 71,500,000.00	R$ 161,733,000.00
2003–2004	R$ 74,650,000.00	R$ 133,160,670.00
2005–2006	R$ 80,000,000.00	R$ 107,056,000.00
2007–2008	R$ 80,000,000.00	R$ 97,880,000.00
2009–2010	R$ 110,000,000.00	R$ 110,000,000.00
2011–2012	R$ 110,000,000.00	R$ 110,000,000.00
Total	R$ 689,332,786.00	R$ 1,260,056,712.28

Source: Prefeitura Municipal de Belo Horizonte 2013b.

Mayors Pimental and Lacerda dedicated fewer resources to PB Regional because this type of policymaking was no longer central to their political strategies. PB Regional was at the core of the policymaking process during the 1993–2002 period, but the mayors from 2002 to 2012 did not prioritize the program, as demonstrated by the declining level of funds provided by Mayors Pimental and Lacerda. The more limited allocation of funding to PB helps explain why CSO leaders and citizens became critical of the government's role in PB Regional and PB Housing: CSO leaders argued that the PB continued to play a vital part in ensuring that public resources were allocated in favelas and *vilas*, but these same citizens were also aware that the government was decreasing the relative level of spending in PB. The direct impact of citizens on the overall budget thus decreased as government officials directed resources elsewhere. By altering the level of resources dedicated to a project, government officials can change the extent to which citizens gain access to constitutionally guaranteed rights.

Redistributing Resources to Build Infrastructure in Favelas

The techniques of access, discussed in chapter 3, comprise the rules and institutions that allocate greater levels of resources to poor communities, typically favelas and *vilas*. The techniques of access allow the government to link the amorphous category of "social justice" to popular participation through the use of an innovative set of rules. Table 4.4 shows the spatial distribution of resources across the city of Belo Horizonte, thus confirming that PB's pro-poor rules allocated greater levels of resources to poor communities.

Table 4.4 Resource Allocation across Communities, 1994–2008

Social Vulnerability of Region	# of Public Works	Population	% of City Population	Resources Spent	% of Total PB Resources
High	529	761,453	34	$312 million	57
Medium	350	849,611	38	$180 million	33
Low	121	627,224	28	$55 million	10
Total	1,000			$547 million	100

Source: Veronica Sales, personal communication, November 11, 2011.

Table 4.4 demonstrates that the poorest neighborhoods with the least amount of public or private infrastructure received the greatest amount of resources in both absolute and per capita terms. This is a clear reversal of spending patterns in which upper- and middle-class neighborhoods traditionally received the lion's share of local resources (Holston 2008; Ross 2006). This data demonstrates that PB has been quite successful at achieving the stated goal of increased spending in communities with high degrees of social vulnerability. More broadly, the data demonstrates how state reform, popular participation, and an effort to bring "social rights" to life come together. The state was restructured internally in order to induce public officials to work closely with citizens. The "rules of the game," namely the Quality of Life Index, were altered to encourage increased state spending in poor favelas and *vilas*. Citizens, in turn, were induced to participate because they would be making decisions that affected their neighborhoods and because they would have formal representation in a decision-making body in which authority was jointly shared with public officials. As a result, social justice concerns are addressed because government officials are spending increased resources in poor communities.

Table 4.4 offers the best evidence demonstrating that state spending was redirected to promote the broad political project of social justice. On an absolute basis as well as a per capita basis, more spending was directed to neighborhoods that had the lowest levels of public infrastructure. However, it is impossible to know whether the government would have spent the same level of resources without the presence of a PB program. In order to address this concern, we turn to research from São Paulo that allows us to engage in comparative analysis to think about how PB is altering spending patterns.

Renata Bichir carried out a detailed study on the spending patterns on small infrastructure projects by mayoral administrations in São Paulo. From 1985 to 2000, the São Paulo municipal government allocated 36 percent of small infrastructure spending to poor neighborhoods, which had 29 percent of the population (Bichir 2005, 255, 256). It allocated 43 percent of the funds to middle-class neighborhoods, which had 53 percent of the population. Finally, the government allocated 20 percent of the funds to upper-class neighborhoods, which had 17 percent of the population. This shows that in a large city (São Paulo has a population of ten million), the municipal government was investing in poor neighborhoods at a higher rate than in middle- and upper-class neighborhoods but that the spending was still lower than the spending rate in Belo Horizonte's PB program.

However, by disaggregating the spending across mayoral administrations, we see that two populist mayors, Janio Quadros and Paulo Maluf, invested 45 percent of their resources in the poorest communities. Their political style was based on clientelism, which meant that there was high spending in key favelas, but there was no effort to incorporate citizens into an institutionalized policymaking process. The spending by mayors who didn't rely so heavily on populist-clientelistic strategies was lower. Overall, the data from São Paulo demonstrates that spending in poor communities was lower as a percentage of the overall population and that it increased under populist-clientelist mayors, thus indicating that increases in spending in poor neighborhoods was most strongly associated with clientelistic exchanges.

What is different in Belo Horizonte is that there was an increase in spending in poor communities through a new democratic institution that allows citizens to exercise voice and vote. The spending patterns in Belo Horizonte's PB Regional program are remarkable because 57 percent of the PB resources were spent in the poorest neighborhoods, which had just 34 percent of the population. The comparison to spending patterns in São Paulo demonstrates that we cannot merely measure the level of spending in poor neighborhoods; we also need to carefully analyze the policymaking process. The projects implemented in Belo Horizonte went through a multichannel process of initial proposal, technical evaluation of feasibility and cost, public vote, a second and more detailed technical plan, an approval of the plan by government officials and citizens, implementation, and, finally, citizen approval of the finished project. At the broadest level, this step-by-step process improves the legitimacy of the state and democracy because citizens are involved in the allocation of resources.

An additional issue that affects the allocation of resources is the type of public works projects being implemented. Table 4.5 shows the distribution by policy sector. The data shows that over two-thirds of the projects involve infrastructure and urbanization. These sectors incorporate a wide range of projects—from street paving to water and sewage lines to building retaining walls to widening streets to tearing down houses and building new streets. Education and health care comprise 20 percent of the projects, which involve new buildings or refurbishing existing buildings.

Table 4.5 Distribution of Participatory Budgeting Projects by Policy Sector,
1994–2010

	Number of Projects	*% of All Projects*
Infrastructure	529	41
Urbanization	347	27
Health Care	134	10
Education	130	10
Sports	49	4
Social Policies	42	3
Environment	27	2
Culture	19	1
Housing	16	1
Total	1,293	100

Source: Veronica Sales, personal communication, November 11, 2011.

Thus, nearly 90 percent of all projects are designed to create basic infrastructure. Basic infrastructure already exists in middle- and upper-class neighborhoods, which is another reason to explain the absence of the middle class from PB: the middle class already has access to the basic services provided by PB.

Thus, PB in Belo Horizonte enabled the municipal state to activate already existing public and private capacity to implement services. The state was not starting from scratch but modifying an already existing capacity (building basic infrastructure) to meet the complex political, social, and physical challenges of reforming favelas and *vilas*. This observation has long been absent from most PB analyses. PB redirects existing state capacity rather than being part of an effort to build state capacity.

The data in Tables 4.4 and 4.5 demonstrate that PB Regional allocates public resources to basic infrastructure projects in Belo Horizonte's poor neighborhoods. Citizens and CSOs mobilized because their direct engagement in a democratic policymaking venue helped to transform their communities. There was an instrumental reason for being involved—citizens selected public policies that would change their neighborhoods. They were also involved in a larger project of building a more democratic state and a more inclusive democracy. PB Regional is an excellent example of bringing to life the Greek concept of *mētis* (see discussion of Scott in chapter 1):

citizens' practical knowledge of their local communities was paired with the technical knowledge of government officials.

Community Blueprints

By 2010, nearly 70 percent of all *vilas* and favelas had community blueprints designed by urban planners, which allow for long-term planning regarding how the *vila* or favela will be redeveloped. Community blueprints include small public works but also major public works, such as new roads and apartment buildings. Many of these large-scale projects are not funded through PB Regional or PB Housing but depend on the ability of government officials to secure loans from national banks and development agencies (BNDES, Caixa Econômica). In Belo Horizonte, the government initiated a program to secure funding for communities that prioritize building new housing units in existing favelas. The name of the program, Vila Viva (Community in Motion), captures the spirit of reform.

The basis for the Vila Viva program is the construction of two-bedroom apartment complexes in the same physical location as current irregular housing. The government removes existing housing stock and builds apartment buildings, which are then inhabited by residents of the houses that were torn down. The Vila Viva program evolved through the interactions of elected officials, policy experts, CSO leaders, and citizens. Because local administrators understood the need to develop coherent urban plans, the program has its roots in PB deliberative sessions, whereby citizens and government officials exchanged ideas about what local residents needed and wanted. Emphasis on larger projects was not the original plan of the PB Regional, but the mobilization of housing movements and an economic boom led the government to seek out additional funding for housing. The Vila Viva program didn't develop as a simplification scheme generated by the state, but rather involved a public learning process for both state actors and citizens that evolved over time (Scott 1998). Vila Viva is much more akin to the local learning documented by Baiocchi, Heller, and Silva in their 2011 book, *Bootstrapping Democracy.* They find that governing coalitions that are invested in promoting direct participation are likely to adapt their institutions to meet local needs. Local government may begin with a "best practice," but these institutions quickly morph to respond to local needs. What links the different local projects together is the complementary emphasis on direct participation, an effort to implement a broad range of social rights, and using state authority in new ways.

Figure 4.2   Resource Allocation in Micro-Regions, 2002–2008

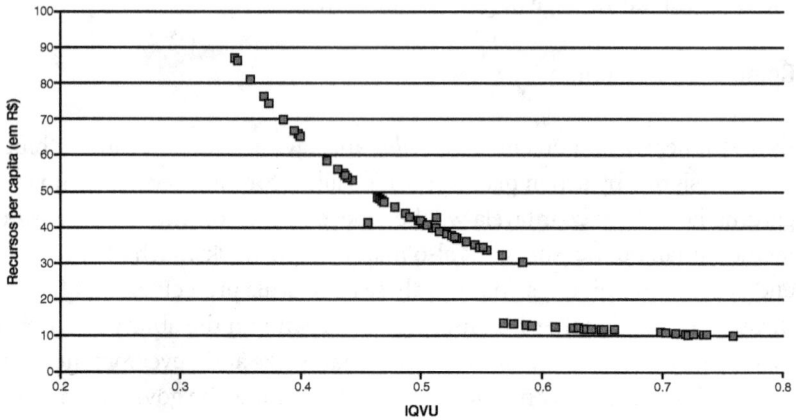

Source: Veronica Sales, personal communication, November 11, 2011.

Micro-Regions

PB Regional rules create a strong set of incentives for large, poor communities to organize themselves. One problem is that this reproduces one of the problems associated with representative democracy: those groups with an organizational advantage (e.g., education, income, dense social capital) will gain access to public goods at a higher rate than communities with limited numbers and weak social capital. As a result, small communities and poorly organized communities are the least likely to secure public goods through PB. To overcome the bias against these groups, the government created a series of micro-regions, based on the city's eighty-one planning units. Resources were allocated to specific micro-regions based on their score on the Quality of Life Index. Figure 4.2 shows that greater resources were allocated to communities with lower scores on the Quality of Life Index. Thus, small communities with greater infrastructure needs received a greater percentage of resources on a per capita basis than do communities that were better off. Very wealthy neighborhoods received very low levels of resources on a per capita basis, but the reservation of specific resources for their communities enabled them to secure a series of small public works.

The data from Figure 4.2 demonstrates that PB Regional made successful advances in three areas: promoting social justice, encouraging popular participation, and fostering the developing of interlocking institutions. Over a twenty-year period, resources were invested in poor communities, participation was promoted by government officials and CSO leaders, and the policymaking process was embedded in multiple state institutions. PB Regional in Belo Horizonte allows participants to shape their communities, the most active participants to represent their neighbors' interests, and such citizens to be represented by elected officials. PB Regional adapted over a twenty-year period, as government officials worked with citizens in favelas and *vilas* to align and realign the rules to match their mutually shared interests.

Principal Problems Associated with PB Regional

There are several clear limitations to PB Regional. First, its successful institutionalization curtails the initial political vitality associated with a new participatory venue. Participants are constrained by an intricate set of rules that govern the timing and methods of participation and deliberation as well as the types of demands that may be addressed within the program. This intricate set of rules has the benefit of streamlining the policymaking process, but there is a corresponding routinization of citizens' political activities. Citizens know that it is important to attend a specific biannual event but that it is unnecessary for them to be prepared to debate and deliberate because they defer to their community leaders, who carry out these activities. Thus, participation does not necessarily mean an engaged citizenry involved in deliberative sessions; the participation of ordinary citizens is partly political performance, as citizens and CSO leaders intuitively understand that a higher number of participants is positive.

A second drawback is that CSO leaders, who often employ the tactics of social movements—demonstrations, forging alliances with other civil society actors, discursive approaches—must now learn a technical set of skills. These skills are necessary to produce policy, but they are an additional challenge that community organizations must overcome as they try to organize their communities. There is now a "double burden" on CSO leaders: they must mobilize individuals to overcome the collective action problem, but they must also be able to engage in intricate, technical policy discussions. These are two very different types of skills, increasing the pressures on CSOs. Their leaders must gain skills comparable to professionals from NGOs, but they must also motivate individuals to turn out at multiple meetings.

In addition, CSO leaders and citizens new to PB Regional are at a tremendous information disadvantage regarding formal and informal rules.

New leaders don't necessarily fully grasp how their interests and strategies need to be adapted to correspond to the rules. Longtime CSO leaders possess an information advantage that they use in order to secure their interests, which means that government officials are concerned with the dilemma of "elite capture." Government officials worry that a small number of well-established CSOs will gain control of participatory institutions, helping these groups to secure their own interests and exclude the interests of other organizations. The institutionalization of PB programs is thus not immune from the challenge faced by any democratic institution: the control of the institution by small numbers of well-organized groups.

Municipal legislators in Belo Horizonte mobilize citizens to attend PB Regional meetings. Municipal legislators invest their time and resources into helping specific communities with the expectation that those communities will allow the municipal legislators to claim credit for public works won through PB Regional and will provide the legislators with campaign support (Mayhew 1974). Legislators from the political left (Workers' Party and the Brazilian Socialist Party) as well as those from the catch-all non-ideological parties (PMDB, PDT, PTB) are involved in PB Regional because it offers elected officials an intoxicating mix of mobilized citizens and public resources. Legislators are involved because the process has a real impact, but their participation also undermines the core tenets of the program.

A third problem associated with PB Regional is that CSO activists became a captive audience for the mayoral governing coalition (PT and PSB). There is no other political home for the CSO activists and PB participants who spent two decades building the PT. The center-right PSDB does not have a political tradition in Belo Horizonte that emphasizes direct participation. Other leftist parties such as the Communist Party of Brazil have pretensions of inverting spending priorities and investing more heavily in PB, but their small size and low likelihood of electoral victory have precluded them from gathering the support of a broader number of PB delegates. CSOs continue to participate in PB and continue to support the PT because they judge that these are the best political and policymaking options available to transform their communities.

The final problem associated with PB Regional is the gradual decline of resources over a twenty-year period, which illuminates the vital role of mayoral interest. The decrease in resources limits the impact of the program because citizens' voice directly affects a small share of the budget each year. PB Regional, as a policymaking process, had a smaller impact in

2010 than it did in 1996 or 2000 because of the smaller levels of resources. Limited social mobilization in support of PB Regional, a centralization of authority in the mayor's office, and a new federal arrangement that encourages municipal officials to seek funding from national development banks contribute to a slow decline of the program's importance.

In sum, PB Regional had a significant impact on shaping how state authority would be used to bring basic infrastructure projects to Belo Horizonte's poorest areas. It also transformed how citizens and organized groups engaged the state; instead of relying on clientelistic exchanges or contentious politics to get the attention of public officials, groups mobilized themselves to work within an incremental policymaking process. Importantly, the government's level of support for PB shifted over time, thereby weakening the relative importance of PB as a key decision-making venue. By 2010, PB Regional continued to operate as a policymaking venue, but it lacked the political vitality and the policy impact that during its first decade. This finding demonstrates the importance of elected public officials' support for the participatory citizenship regime: citizens' ability to access civil and political rights was strongly affected by the support extended by the federal government. PB Regional was initially a political venue that allowed citizens to secure access to public goods and social rights, but weakening government support limited the impact. Thus, having a government politically committed to the ideals of the 1988 constitution is a vital aspect of activating the participatory citizenship regime.

IMPACT: PB HOUSING

PB Housing was established in 1996 to address one of the thorniest policy problems from the PB Regional process: building affordable housing. The housing movement developed strong ties to public officials responsible for housing policy in Belo Horizonte. Remarkably, there was a broad consensus between 1993 and 2008 regarding policy choices and political strategies that should be used in this sector. The contentious politics of "insurgent citizenship," most often illegal land occupations, largely disappeared from the political scene as government officials and housing movement activists worked within the institutional structures (Holston 2008). PB Housing thus successfully incorporated a wide range of housing organizations and politically engaged public officials who sought to implement housing.

Table 4.6 Participatory Budgeting Housing Participants

Year	Number of Núcleos	Number of People Registered in Núcleo	Registered Participants at Biannual Policy Conference
1996	148	28,951	6,011
1997	107	26,503	3,802
1998	137	29,178	2,854
1999–2000	91	15,918	4,945
2001–2002	179	32,170	13,257
2003–2006	165	13,408	599*
2007–2008	172	13,000	5,177

*This year only included CSO leaders.
Source: Prefeitura Municipal de Belo Horizonte 2013c.

By 2010 there were 172 housing *núcleos* and roughly thirteen thousand families formally registered with the municipal government. Table 4.6 shows the number of participants in PB Housing. The evidence from the CSO leader survey administered for this project in 2009 shows that 81 percent of the housing *núcleos* met at least once a month. Frequent meetings produce bonds of solidarity among the participants but also create the links between government officials and CSO leaders (Alexander 2006). Table 4.6 also shows a drop in the number of people registered in the housing *núcleos* (from a high of 29,000 in 1998 to a low of 13,000 in 2008) is attributable to the slow progress made in building new housing units. Between 1997 and 2008, the government built 3,200 housing units that "benefited around 16,000 people," but there was a massive demand for decent housing.[9] Why hadn't the government been able to build more housing units?

The most obvious explanation is the lack of resources. The government didn't have enough locally generated resources to build housing units, which meant that it had to borrow money or receive grants from state or federal banks. During the 1990s, there was limited funding available from the state and federal governments. In President Lula's second term (2005–2008), more resources were made available for housing projects, but there was also a dramatic increase in land prices and construction cost. A second problem that complicates efforts to build new housing units is the lack of clear property titles in favelas and *vilas* (see Holston 2008 for an excellent discussion). When citizens occupy land without having official title to the property, there is a long-term struggle over land ownership. The municipal government may not build housing units in areas they don't own, which means housing units cannot be built in areas that are illegally occupied.

An additional reason PB Housing was unable to maintain high levels of participation resulted from a 2003 agreement following floods and landslides that killed dozens of people. The public defender filed a lawsuit against the municipality of Belo Horizonte ordering the government to move individuals out of areas of high risk. The municipal state lacked the resources to remove all residents from areas of risk, but it reached an agreement with the public defender in which 50 percent of all new housing units would be allocated to people living in "at risk" areas. Government officials and PB Housing representatives deliberated among themselves, and both parties agreed to this solution. This agreement dampened participation in PB Housing *núcleos* because there was an obvious decrease in the potential benefit from citizens' participation. Why participate if PB Housing is required to provide 50 percent of new housing units to people living in areas of risk? Interestingly, no one I spoke with disagreed with the decision to allocate 50 percent to people living in areas of risk, which I attribute to framing the distribution of housing units as a social justice issue. Thus the judicial order helped to advance the interests of people living in areas of risk, but it discouraged other citizens from being actively involved in PB Housing.

Problems Associated with PB Housing

PB Housing faces three significant challenges. The most difficult problem is the complexity and cost of producing housing units. Separating PB Housing from PB Regional didn't solve this problem; it just moved the problem to another decision-making venue. Tens of thousands of families continue to lack decent, affordable housing in Belo Horizonte. Although the municipal government built over three thousand housing units during the past fifteen years, the demand is much, much higher.

A second challenge for the municipal government is how to legitimize the allocation of public resources on housing units that will essentially become a private good. On a general level, there is a consensus among policymakers that governments should spend more on housing issues, but there is insufficient political pressure placed on government officials to justify the use of scarce resources for housing. Part of the reason is that housing units are an excludable policy output, different from education or health care, in which any community resident has a similar opportunity to access the public service; housing is a benefit provided directly to specific individuals.

A final, and related, problem concerns how individual apartment units should be allocated across the 172 housing *núcleos* as well as within each *núcleo*. When the government builds a housing complex with a certain number of units, a lottery is held to distribute the units to the housing *núcleos*. But the decision regarding which families are allocated specific housing units is left to the each housing *núcleo*. When PB Housing was established in 1996, the housing movements insisted that government officials should stay out of the internal politics of each organization. This ongoing situation helps to maintain CSOs' autonomy from government interference, but it also produces great conflict within CSOs because there are no strong internal mechanisms to hold CSO leaders accountable for their actions. This accountability problem also helps to explain the decline in participation: participants witnessed the allocation of specific housing units based on favoritism with the housing *núcleo*, and they chose to exit the process when they realized they would likely never receive resources. Thus, a democratic process at the municipal level may not be democratic within civil society.

In 2010, the municipal government finally turned its attention to this problem and sought to establish technical criteria that community organizations would be required to use for allocating housing units. By bringing a clear set of technical criteria into the housing debate, the government based its strategy on the well-known logic of social justice and popular participation. Families must be engaged in a community organization to be eligible. Among eligible families, those with greater levels of need are slated to receive housing.

In sum, PB Housing is an institutionalized part of the policymaking process. Government officials worked closely with CSO leaders to alter the rules in order to ensure that the program met their mutual interests. This ongoing dialogue induced cooperation, but there remained room for political contestation from the housing movement. The number of direct beneficiaries, around sixteen thousand, is substantial but represents a minority of people who need access to better housing. When the government builds the additional housing units already agreed on via PB Housing, there will be a similar number of beneficiaries. However, we must bear in mind that there are roughly thirteen thousand families registered with PB Housing who are waiting for housing units that haven't even reached the planning stage.

PB Digital

PB Digital was founded in 2006 with the purpose of expanding the number and socioeconomic characteristics of participants and to allow citizens to select larger public infrastructure projects. PB Digital has successfully met these goals. Also of note is the dramatically larger number of people who voted in PB Digital as compared to those who participated in PB Regional.

Citizens vote to select public works projects from a list developed by the government. In 2008, all projects selected were focused on improving transportation or public plazas. PB Digital thus operates like a referendum in which the government chooses a range of public works options on which people vote. Government officials risk very little because all the policy options meet their approval prior to the vote. The government also invested more resources in PB Digital because they wanted to reach out to the growing middle class and youth. PB Regional and PB Housing participants are mainly poor citizens and, importantly, are largely a captured political audience for the center-left political coalition governing the city. The government needed to reach out to the growing lower middle class and middle class to expand their base of support.

PB Digital is attracting a diverse and broad number of participants. The percentage of PB voters (see the last column in Table 4.8) is similar to the percentage of city's electorate, which means that PB Digital is attracting a representative sample of the city's population based on the Quality of Life Index. Middle- and upper-class residents are participating, thus

Table 4.7 Participation in Participatory Budgeting Digital

	2006	2008	2010
Participants	172,938	124,320	92,728
Budget	$15 million	$25 million	$35 million

Source: Prefeitura Municipal de Belo Horizonte 2013d.

Table 4.8 Distribution of Participation in Participatory Budgeting Digital by IQVU, 2006

Quality of Life Index	Number of Potential Voters	% of Citywide Voters	Number of PB Digital Voters	% of PB Digital Voters	% of Potential Voters Who Voted
Very High (0.8–1.0)	52,501	3	4,747	3	9.0
High 2 (0.7–0.8)	326,615	19	30,464	18	9
High 1 (0.6–0.7)	543,511	31	49,133	28	9
Medium 2 (0.5–0.6)	636,258	36	69,492	40	11
Medium 1 (0.4–0.5)	168,589	10	17,272	10	10
Low (0.2–0.4)	16,073	1	1,819	1	11
Total	1,743,547		172,927		10

Source: Veronica Sales, personal communication, November 11, 2011.

meeting one of PB Digital's key goals, but citizens from the poorest communities are participating at similar levels. This finding is noteworthy because much of the political science literature has found that people with higher incomes are more likely to participate and vote at high levels (Verba, Schlozman, and Brady 1995). Poorer citizens were less likely to have computers at home, and they have to rely on public computers provided at government-sponsored kiosks, which places a larger burden on them to participate. The similar participation rates are thus remarkable and are the result of a municipal participatory architecture (PB Regional, PB Housing, the public management councils) that have successfully habituated a significant subset of poor citizens to be involved in democratic politics. Although the government sought to use PB Digital as a means to incorporate the middle classes, poor groups have successfully used PB Digital at the same rates.

Limitations of PB Digital

PB Digital does not aim to produce active citizens through direct participation nor focus on social justice. Its purpose is neither to educate citizens nor to dramatically improve their knowledge of policy and government, but it is geared toward inducing greater numbers of people to vote from a menu of projects selected by the government. Larger numbers of partici-

pants in PB Digital help the government legitimize their spending decisions. But the lack of debate within these processes also means that they
are more akin to a referendum than to any sort of sustained dialogue associated with the original PB processes. In other words, the government is
trading on positive branding associated with PB to create a referendum
that legitimizes its policy preferences.

A second limitation is that PB Regional was initially designed to give
citizens decision-making authority over budget allocation, which would
help empower them while simultaneously constraining the government.
PB Digital doesn't diminish the government's decision-making authority
because the program allows the government to present to the public a list
of public works projects that it believes should be completed. Citizens select from policies that are already acceptable to the government. Accountability and oversight are not extended.

Belo Horizonte's PB programs activated and institutionalized a participatory citizenship regime. The local state has been reconfigured to allow citizens and public officials to interact with each other in a variety of new
democratic institutions. Tens of thousands of citizens participate in three
different PB programs; they make decisions that direct governmental action and outputs. The evidence presented in this chapter demonstrates
that state authority and resources are being deployed in low-income communities in ways to correspond to Scott's "state simplification" and *mētis*:
public officials working within the municipal state use technical, legal, and
financial knowledge in an effort to build infrastructure in poor favelas and
vilas, but they work with community leaders and interested citizens to implement policies. The state didn't systematically trample on the rights of
favela residents; the new incremental policymaking venues incorporated
their voices into the policymaking process. The direct incorporation of
citizens into policymaking processes does not mean that rights are always
protected or that the system only produces winners. Rather, these processes increase the likelihood that there can be a positive-sum increase in
the quality of democracy, rights protection, and state action.

Over time, the public works projects selected by citizens became more
sophisticated and more costly as a result of new rules that incorporate
technical issues directly into the decision-making process. Citizens are
making political and policy decisions that result in governmental action,
which indicates a transfer of decision-making authority to citizens. PB

programs represent the successful initiation of the participatory citizenship regime through their use of *mētis*. The exchange of information by government officials, CSO leaders, and citizens through PB broadens all of their knowledge about how the state can be more effectively deployed to achieve improvements in social well-being, deliberation, participation, and representation.

CSO leaders participating in PB are often PB's harshest critics and staunchest defenders. They are quick to identify a myriad of problems within the program. But these appear to be internal critiques, delivered to their allies and government officials. CSO leaders and citizens also staunchly defend PB as a valuable part of the political and policymaking process. Citizens and activists seem to hold contradictory positions for a couple of reasons. Perhaps most importantly, the transformation of civil society during the 1980s and 1990s was associated with the insurgent citizenship regime, the "right to have rights" and "participatory publics," which fostered the development of a critical analysis of politics and the public sphere. Thus, CSO leaders are habituated to be highly critical of how the process functions. But many of these activists also recognize that PB can transform their work, lives, and communities. CSO leaders understand that an institution providing preferential treatment for the poor gives them a greater incentive to engage in politics. They understand that PB helps to legitimize the allocation of resources to poor communities. CSO leaders are quite aware of the projects their community received through PB Regional or PB Housing. In each of the more than twenty-five in-depth interviews I conducted with CSO leaders from 2001 to 2010 in Belo Horizonte, all explained how these programs had benefited their communities. In every interview, CSO leaders argued that the program needed more resources to respond to pent-up demand.

An important part of the story in Belo Horizonte is institutional adaptation. PB is not a frozen institutional set of rules but based on the principles of popular participation, social justice, and interlocking institutions. There is no narrow set of institutions that will allow citizens and government officials to activate the participatory citizenship regime. We should expect governments and citizens to experiment with new institutions in order to produce institutional arrangements that allow citizens to access political and social rights. PB was modified to help activate the participatory citizenship regime as well as meet the political and policy needs of government officials and their key allies. Citizens initially had one format,

PB Regional, through which they were able to express voice and vote, but this expanded to three formal PB programs. There was the recognition that there was no single model for engaging citizens in the policymaking process but an effort to refine the rules to meet the needs of both citizens and government officials. The collective action problem was addressed in several different formats, as government officials and citizens sought to find the institutional incentives that would encourage mobilization and produce social change.

In sum, PB Regional and PB Housing in Belo Horizonte are state institutions that help citizens take advantage of the political and social opportunities created by the participatory citizenship regime. Both programs are based on the triple pillars of social justice, popular participation, and interlocking institutions. Citizens and government officials jointly control these bodies, thus allowing for the mutual forging of policy outcomes. The participatory citizenship regime was activated through the joint involvement of government officials and citizens.

CHAPTER FIVE

Councils and Conferences

Health Care, Housing, and Social Services

> *I am the third most important person in public health care in*
> *Belo Horizonte. . . . The council hasn't really exercised its own veto.*
> *Rather, if we disagree, then we negotiate.*
> —Willer Ferreira, president of the health care council,
> October 7, 2009

The comments of Willer Ferreira, health care council president and CSO activist, in the epigraph to this chapter illuminate competing understandings regarding the appropriate role that public policy management councils and policy conferences should play in the policymaking process. These institutions permit citizens to propose policies, gather information, engage in oversight, deliberate over policy directions, and forge new networks. This chapter analyzes three public policy arenas (health care, housing, and social services), all of which use councils and conferences. There is tremendous variation in how the participatory institutions are being employed. This chapter begins with a series of vignettes to illustrate the complexity of these new venues.

HEALTH CARE POLICY CONFERENCE

Over a thousand citizens braved a torrential downpour on a Saturday morning in December 2009 to attend the second day of a weekend-long health care policy conference. During the morning session, a public health expert, Belo Horizonte's secretary of health, and a union leader each gave twenty-minute presentations. During the presentations, there was a low buzz from the 1,500 audience members, as many listened with one ear while quietly talking to other people, thus allowing friends to renew their connections and bonds of solidarity. After an hour of presentations, things finally got interesting during the question and answer period, when a dozen participants had the opportunity to speak. The first two citizens asked pointed questions regarding overall spending and policy priorities. The next two speakers had specific questions about problems in their communities. A union leader spoke and demanded better pay and benefits for unionized workers. Finally, two longtime leaders sought to remind people about the important victories associated with the implementation of the national health care system (SUS) as they called for an increase in spending on basic health care services. Based on my experience attending participatory meetings, this range of topics was representative of the other deliberative sessions: some citizens focus on broader policies, others focus on specific problems, and others promote narrow policy changes. The most intense disputes, during the Q & A period and throughout the weekend conference, were between CSO activists advocating on behalf of public health users and union officials who focused on wages, working conditions, and specific policies.

HOUSING POLICY CONFERENCE

During the biannual housing policy conference, political alliances shifted rapidly when a long-term CSO housing leader used her opening speech to denounce fraud inflicted on her organization by a leader who disappeared with several hundred thousand Brazilian reais (roughly $150,000) from a fund allocated to improving housing in her community. This leader used her speech in an attempt to motivate the mayor, who was in attendance, and his staff to commit the resources to apprehend the fugitive and bring him to justice. Other CSO leaders, however, perceived her speech as focusing on the internal problems of her organization rather than using her prime-time speaking spot to set the agenda on broader public policies.

On the Sunday morning of the conference, political support shifted away from this longtime leader, thus allowing for the formation of a new political coalition that would win coveted seats on the housing council. During the morning meeting, there was a thoughtful and engaging discussion regarding which voting rules and procedures should be used to distribute the six seats on the housing councils among the different candidates. One group argued for the use of majoritarian voting rules because this would reflect the will of the majority of the people: the group winning the majority of the vote would have all six seats. A second group argued for a proportional voting system that would protect the rights of minorities and broaden the range of participants. As far as I could tell, everyone participating in the debate was from a housing *núcleo*, which meant that poor, traditionally excluded citizens were the key participants in a rich deliberative discussion regarding how different voting rules and procedures could support basic democratic principles.

Although the philosophical debate was of high quality, it quickly became apparent that people's arguments lined up quite closely with their perception of their likely electoral success, which meant that there was considerable political opportunism behind the lofty debate positions. The leaders were quite aware of the political effects of different electoral rules; groups who thought they would lose the election emphasized "the right of the minority voices to be heard" and "acting on behalf of those who are unable to represent themselves here today," while those leaders who were optimistic about their chances of winning emphasized "the will of the majority." The leader who aired her dirty laundry was not reelected, as political support shifted to new groups.

ACTIVATING DEMOCRACY THROUGH POLICY COUNCILS AND CONFERENCES

The most widely adopted participatory governance institutions in Brazil, as permitted under Brazil's 1988 constitution (Article 14), are public policy management councils (*conselhos*) that link citizens, interest groups, community organizations, technical staff, and government appointees (Avritzer 2009; Abers and Keck 2009). By 2009, over sixty-five thousand municipal-level councils had been adopted (Barreto 2011). Within the council system, an interlocking set of institutions produces an intricate interplay of interests, ideas, and political actors. Community organizations contribute to policy formulation and oversight; government officials depend on the formal votes exercised by council members because federal funding can be withheld if the council members don't approve the annual budget or year-end report. Government officials are directly involved in supporting the work of council members. The public policy management councils are often complemented by policy conferences (*confêrencias*), which are generally daylong or two-day-long seminars that set general policy priorities (Avritzer and Souza 2013; Pogrebinschi and Samuels 2014).

This chapter shows that Belo Horizonte institutionalized a broad number of participatory venues, far beyond participatory budgeting, that help citizens and government officials activate the participatory citizenship regime. The chapter analyzes the role of participatory institutions in three different policy arenas: health care, housing, and social services. It is the interplay of five different factors that account for the significant variation across these three policy arenas: state formation; civil society development; senior government officials' support for voice and vote; the specific rules of each participatory institution regarding representation, participation, and deliberation; and the level of resources within each public policy arena.

The public policy councils and policy conferences are integral to the interlocking institutions that activate the participatory citizenship regime. The interlocking institutions occur in three distinct fashions: vertical, horizontal, and state-society.[1] The vertical connections are twofold. First, the council system is instituted at five levels: federal, state, municipal, regional, and local councils (the last two are submunicipal). Individuals are often first elected at a lower level, after which they are eligible for election to the next level. In the health care field, for example, an individual could be first elected at the local level, then to the regional council, then to municipal council, then to state council, and, finally, to the federal level.

Second, the councils are inserted into the municipal administration, thus providing direct links between municipal councils and the top tier of municipal public officials. There are horizontal ties between councils and the bureaucratic departments and service providers responsible for implementing public policies.

Third, the councils and the policy conferences alter how citizens are positioned in relation to the state apparatus and how state officials are embedded in civil society. The councils allow government officials to build connections that permit them to develop new forms of constituency service and alter how they allocate policy provisions. The institutional design of the councils leads to the government being most willing to work with the council when the council members are in general agreement with government officials. This limits the ability of the council system to act as a counterbalance to the strong authority situated in the executive branch.

The chapter's first section details the institutional rules, with a focus on the allocation of authority and the forms of participation, representation, and deliberation processes. I explore the differences in rules for the three public policy arenas: health care, housing, and social services. The second section offers an in-depth look at the three sectors, explaining the different roles of each council in its respective policy arena.

DECISION-MAKING AUTHORITY

The authority granted to public policy management councils falls into two basic categories:

1. Co-Governance (*co-gestão*): the authority to develop and approve new policy programs.
2. Oversight (*controle social*): the authority to monitor the actions of governments and service providers.

1. *Co-gestão*: Council members influence the policymaking process based on three basic rules. Members are required to approve by simple majority (1) new policy proposals, which can be put forward by council members or government officials; (2) the department's annual budget, including budget modifications in subsequent years; and (3) a year-end accountability report that details expenditures. The council acts as a mini-legislature within the policy arena: members gather information on policy proposals, they debate these policies, and then they vote on proposed changes. A council has the potential to act as a veto point in the policymaking process because council members can refuse to approve the adoption of new policies and programs proposed by the government (Tsebelis 2002).

There are several limitations to the councils' formal legal authority. When council members approve a new program, the municipal government is under no obligation to fund it, which is similar to the constraint faced by municipal legislators (see chapter 3); policy proposals not funded and implemented can be indefinitely delayed. Municipal governments in Brazil tend to include more items in the annual budget than available resources, which means that government administrators can simply underfund the programs they are not interested in supporting. Thus, council members, just like municipal legislators, have limited authority over the way the mayoral administration allocates resources to specific programs.

Council members have the authority to reject policies proposed by government officials. There is the potential, as noted above, for councils to assume roles as vetoers. Nevertheless, many council members are involved because they want the state to do more, not less.[2] This is especially true for citizens representing potential clients (*usuários*) as well as for union members. Since the main actors in the councils tend to be CSO leaders and union officials interested in expanding the role of the state, it is rare to find anyone who opposes the adoption of a new policy programs. As health care council president Ferreira stated, "The council hasn't really exercised its own veto. Rather, if we disagree, then we negotiate" (Ferreira interview, October 7, 2009). The veto threat induces the government to negotiate with council members because a council veto could derail government activities, although this is often an empty threat because council members lack sufficient political capital to directly confront the executive.

Most council members, especially ordinary citizens and CSO leaders, are at a grave information disadvantage when they debate with government officials. CSO leaders' limited technical knowledge makes it difficult for them to hold their own in technical and policy debates or to propose alternatives to the government's proposed policies. An example from the health care field illustrates this point. On November 17, 2010, I attended a municipal health care meeting at which two public health officials gave a detailed presentation on a new policy program. The thirty-minute presentation on a specific disease as well as the strategies to combat the disease in poor communities gave the council members a lot of information to digest in a short period of time. The Q & A session following the presentation was dominated by questions about very simple issues as well as by general assertions regarding how the policy would be beneficial. It would be hard to characterize this session as informed deliberation, but the information session did expand the knowledge base of council members. Following the Q & A session, council members voted unanimously to approve the policy program.

In sum, *co-gestão* authority allows council members to engage in policymaking processes, but most council members are not on an equal footing with municipal administrators. Executive-legislative relations are the appropriate analogy here, especially in the context of a strong executive and much weaker legislative branch. In this case, it is even more extreme because public policy management councils are institutionally inserted into the executive branch, thus diminishing the legal authority held by council members. This observation confirms one of the concerns of Tanya Murray Li regarding citizen participation. Murray Li argues that "*practices of government* limit the possibilities for engaging with the targets of improving schemes as political actors, fully capable of contestation and debate. They do this by inscribing a boundary that separates those who claim to know how others should live from those whose conduct is to be conducted. Across such a divide, it is difficult to have a conversation" (Murray Li 2007, 281–82; italics in original). In Brazil's more technically oriented councils, state officials are unable to generate meaningful debates because community leaders and citizens do not have sufficient technical knowledge to engage policy experts in substantive debates. Rather, citizens and CSOs leaders are able to place both general policy concerns or very specific issues on the political agenda.

2. *Controle social*: Councils also have the authority to engage in basic oversight, which occurs on an annual basis as well as in the day-to-day monitoring of policy implementation. The ongoing process consists of council members' requests for information (such as budgetary and personnel data or outcomes indicators) to help them monitor government agencies' activities throughout the year. By having access to information, council members can engage in spirited policy discussions with each other and with government officials. This information gathering and ongoing debates over existing program implementation are part of a larger process of creating a policy network and expanding policy debates.

The monitoring of policy implementation is an oversight power provided to council members, who are recognized as official members of a state-sanctioned institution. This gives council members increased political and social standing when they contact government officials (e.g., bureaucrats, nurses, doctors) or service providers (private companies, NGOs) for information. Roberto da Matta, a Brazilian academic, highlighted the stark divide in Brazilian culture with the phrase "Do you know to whom you are speaking?" (*Você sabe com quem esta falando?*) (Matta 1979). This phrase establishes the speaker as someone of importance, which is crucial in a socially stratified county like Brazil. Since many of the CSO leaders and citizens elected to represent civil society are from poor neighborhoods, their official status as a municipal council representative increases their social and political status because they are now official state representatives. This allows them to enter government departments as someone of importance, since bureaucrats understand that council members have voice and vote. The increase in social standing partially accounts for why CSO leaders representing poor communities are willing to participate in the council despite limited authority. These CSOs leaders can no longer be ignored by state bureaucrats: they are now democratic representatives with formal budgetary and oversight authority.

Budgetary oversight is also done annually, when the council must approve the previous year's financial statements. Each council must approve the corresponding department's budget to ensure that state and federal governments can legally transfer resources to the municipality. This gives the council greater authority than is held by the municipal legislature, which focuses more on approving the entire municipal budget rather than specific departments. This budgetary oversight authority thereby induces government officials to provide necessary documentation on the previous year's spending. But the "all or nothing" vote—accept or reject the budget—induces council members to avoid rejecting the end-of-year report because they don't want to stop the flow of resources into municipality coffers. Therefore, council members legally have a greater veto power than municipal legislators but are also less likely to use their veto because of potential negative consequences. For example, the health care council could reject the annual budget accountability report, which could, in turn, mean that the federal government would stop its transfers, which totaled $1 billion in 2010. As argued before, the political risk for council members diminishes the potential power of the veto threat.

Contradictory Incentives

These two types of authority create contradictory incentives for council members and governments. The incentives associated with acting as a *cogestor* is part of a longer history in Brazil whereby groups outside of the executive branch seek to align their interests with the sitting government to secure policy goods. This induces CSO leaders to align themselves with the government in hopes they can secure constituency service, public goods, and access to state resources. These council members want to be drawn into the government's orbit, but this situation opens the possibility that such a close relationship will undercut their ability to actively carry out their second duty: *controle social*. Engaging in effective monitoring and oversight requires council members to learn how to gather information and ask critical questions that force government officials to explain their actions. Although such intense questioning can enhance accountability, it can also drive a wedge between government officials and council members. Council members generally seek to be closer to the government rather than further away. Therefore, council members are in a paradoxical situation: *co-gestão* draws them closer to government officials, whereas their oversight authority creates a wedge between them and officials. Of course, this relationship is comparable to legislative-executive relations in representative democracy, since many legislators depend on constituency service and support from the executive branch to attend to their constituents' needs. The contradictory set of incentives places greater limitations on the authority of the councils.

Policy Conferences

Thematic policy conferences, held at the municipal, state, and federal levels of governments, incorporate interested citizens and community leaders into daylong or weekend-long meetings. The frequency of the policy conferences varies greatly. The more established policy conferences (i.e., health care, housing, education) are held every two or four years, but other policy conferences can be one-time affairs. The purpose of these policy conferences is twofold.

First, they are designed to mobilize large numbers of citizens and allow them to interact with policy experts and government officials. The mobilization has the effect of linking CSO leaders to each other, which helps to produce "bonds of solidarity" (Alexander 2006). It also has the effect of demonstrating to government officials the strength of their numbers and the worthiness of their cause (McAdam, McCarthy, and Zald 1996). This serves as an institutionalized form of a mass demonstration. Instead of rallying one thousand people in front of a government office, a thousand people are organized to attend a policy summit. From a social movement perspective, this change limits citizens' ability to get the attention of their fellow citizens and media outlets; disruptive politics is often crucial in publicizing the demands of social movements and CSOs. However, directly including citizens and CSOs in the policy conferences links them to key decision makers in the government. Strong turnout can be used by government officials to pressure the mayor's office to pay more attention to the policy arena.

The second purpose of policy conferences is to make broad policy recommendations to the municipal council as well as to relevant departments (Avritzer and Souza 2013; Pogrebinschi and Samuels 2014). Given that the average number of participants in these weekend-long conferences is between eight hundred and a thousand people, participants are divided into small group sessions to deliberate over policy options and to propose new policy directions. There are different themes each year to expand the realm of deliberation. Votes exercised by citizens are symbolic, rather than binding votes that direct government policies. Participants attending the policy conference gather information as well as deliberate over and vote on general policy proposals. The conferences allow citizens to vote on general policy proposals intended to direct the actions of the relevant public policy management council and policy department. The final decisions of the conference participants are not binding but are best viewed as policy benchmarks. The policy conferences have no sources of authority that resemble a veto point, so it is better to conceptualize them as a framing and agenda-setting moment of the policy process (Tsebelis 2002).

The public policy councils and policy conferences are interconnected in two ways. First, the council representatives may be elected during the conference meetings. To be elected to a policy council, individuals must attend the relevant policy conference and organize inter-CSO alliances in order to win elections. Second, council members develop the content and the agenda for the policy conferences, thus interlocking these two forms of participatory governance. For example, it was citizens elected to the governing board of the health care council that worked with government officials to develop the agenda for the municipal-wide health care conference.

In sum, the combination of limited authority of the policy conferences and the contradictory incentives within the public policy management councils limits the overall impact of these institutions on policy outputs. In participatory budgeting programs, there is a direct connection between individuals' vote and policy decisions. The public policy management councils suffer from a similar problem experienced by the legislative branch: there are no clearly drawn lines of authority, limiting the councils' impact on specific policymaking and political outcomes. Despite this limited authority, there continues to be substantial involvement in these participatory governance institutions. Why do government officials and civil society leaders continue to work within a space that doesn't produce specific policy outcomes? Why are hundreds of thousands of Brazilians engaged in these processes? The rest of the chapter answers these questions.

BROADENING THE STATE: EXPANSION OF INSTITUTIONAL VENUES

In Belo Horizonte, as documented in chapter 3, there are 41 municipal-wide councils, nearly 30 regional-level councils, and hundreds of local participatory venues (e.g., health care clinics, schools, park commissions). Over half the members serving on these councils are representatives of CSOs, and just under half of the seats are representatives from the government. Although variation occurs among the different councils regarding the distribution of seats and the voting power of civil society members and government officials, the councils serve the important role of linking citizens to government officials. Policy experts, government officials, private sector actors, union representatives, and civil society leaders are thus in constant communication regarding problems and potential policy solutions.

Two issues are analyzed in this section: formal representation on the councils and the different deliberative formats used in each council. Overall, government officials hold the largest plurality of seats on municipal councils, followed closely by citizens and CSOs (see Table 5.1). Each department decides which of its officials will serve on the council: the head of a department, a political appointee, or an interested civil servant. This provides compelling evidence that these new venues are institutionalized points of contact between citizens and government officials, fostering the development of new networks.

Representing Civil Society on Municipal Councils

A total of 408 seats are available to CSOs, citizens, unions, and service providers at the municipal level. Citizens and CSOs, not including union representatives, hold 58 percent of civil society seats.[3] Table 5.2 shows that 37 percent of civil society seats are held by citizens, and 21 percent are held by citizens from other councils—that is, citizens and CSO leaders selected by another council, thus creating interlocking institutions. The citizens

Table 5.1 Public Policy Management Councils and Seats, 2009–2010

	Municipal	*Regional (9)*	*Local*	*Total*
Participatory Governance Venues	41	52	479	571
Seats for:				
Government officials	325	124	1,406	1,855
Citizens/CSOs	309	377	2,725	3,411
Union officials	35	132	141	308
Service providers	64	N/A	N/A	64
Total	733	633	4,272	

Source: Adapted from Martins 2007.

Table 5.2 Distribution of Seats by Civil Society Sector (Municipal Level)

Civil Society Category	*Number of Council Members*	*% of Total*
Citizens and CSO representatives	151	37
Citizens from other councils	84	21
Professional associations	41	10
Unions	35	9
Service providers	64	15
Policy experts (e.g., professors)	16	4
Others	17	4
Total	408	100

Source: Adapted from Martins 2007, 157.

and CSO leaders elected to these councils are both participants and representatives. By "participants" I mean that they are citizen-volunteers working within a democratic institution jointly controlled by government officials and private citizens. But they are also representatives of a greater body of citizens; they represent social movements, specific communities, and community-based organizations.

One-third of the seats are allocated to union representatives, professional associations, and service providers. Public employees and private companies have significant representation within these councils; in this way councils bring a broad selection of the relevant policy actors into a common venue to discuss policy outcomes. An analysis of each policy arena (housing, health care, social services) will demonstrate that there is wide variation in the number of union representatives on the council (regulated citizenship), which greatly affects how they function.

Overall, the data in Table 5.2 demonstrates a plurality of actors involved in the councils. Since people voluntarily participate in these councils (with the exception of government officials, who are generally appointed from within their departments), there is a broad range of interests, ideas, and actors involved in these processes. The broad range of actors means that council members can present their interests to different groups and, importantly, also be exposed to other groups' agendas.

Regional and Local Councils

Beyond the municipal-level council, there two other levels of institutionalized participation in Belo Horizonte: regional and local. Citizens have multiple opportunities to be elected in one of the nine regions. The positions for citizens are elected.

At the regional level, citizens hold a majority of seats, followed by union officials and government officials. Municipal-level council members in the areas of health care and social services must first be elected to a regional council to be eligible to stand for election to the municipal council. Candidates for the municipal council thus build support for their candidacy by working with fellow representatives at the regional and local levels.

Table 5.4 shows citizen involvement at the local level, where the highest number of participants engage in participatory venues. Local councils serve as an entry point for new policy ideas and citizens. New participants start at the local level and may then work at regional, municipal, or state levels, thus contributing to the interlocking institutions. Large numbers of citizens are directly engaged in their local schools, mirroring the participation of parents in other countries (Verba, Schlozman, and Brady 1995). We also see that citizens are involved in local health care clinics, which is attributable to the fact that poor Brazilians rely on the public health care system. Citizens are elected to the councils for local health centers, Vila Viva, education, and social services. There are nearly fifty civil defense teams (e.g., response to flooding and landslides) across the city, which

Table 5.3 Distribution of Regional-Level Seats

	Health Care	Social Services	Conselho Titular	BH Transports	Parks	Total
Number	9	9	9	10	15	52
Government officials	75	9	9	40	45	178
Union officials	92		0	40	0	132
Citizens	183	54	45	50	45	377

Sources: Martins 2007, 64; Magalhes and Ferreira interviews.

Table 5.4 Distribution of Local-Level Seats

	Vila Viva	Local Health Center	Education	Social Services	Civil Defense	Total
# of Venues	25	141	186	54	48	454
Citizens	276	141	1,700		400	2,517
Workers		141	186	108		435
Government officials	10	141	1,116	54	10	1,311

Sources: Martins 2007, 64; Ana Flavia Martins, personal communication, April 14, 2010; Flávia Julião, personal communication, April 19, 2010; Savio Araújo, personal communication, April 16, 2010; Marcus Annibal Rego, personal communication, April 23, 2010; Magalhes and Ferreira interviews.

don't have elections but depend on the voluntary participation of interested citizens.

The institutionalization of participatory governance has created multiple opportunities for civil society activists, social movement leaders, community leaders, and ordinary citizens to engage each other and government officials in public venues. At the municipal level, government officials hold the largest number of seats; the second largest group is comprised of representatives from civil society. This demonstrates the institutionalization of contacts between citizens and government officials. The interlocking institutional connections among municipal, regional, and local councils create information feedback loops and accountability mechanisms.

The data discussed above demonstrates how the local state has been extensively broadened in Brazil to directly incorporate citizens into state policymaking institutions. There are thousands of positions to which citizens can be elected. In each of these elected positions they exercise some type of formal vote that allows them to approve or reject policy proposals and budgets. The establishment of these venues has given citizens an unprecedented level of access to formal state institutions, which now permit them to secure basic social rights such as education, health care, and housing.

Deliberation

The councils are a space of ongoing deliberation through which policy and political problems are raised, information is shared, and technical issues addressed. It is a space in which a common language and understanding of policy problems are established so as to allow interested parties to create a community. A focus on deliberative processes shows new forms of communication being initiated among community leaders, government technocrats, appointed officials, and elected officials. The councils induce a constant flow of information among different sectors of society. The members of the council are intermediaries, representing different sectors of the policy community; their monthly meetings are complemented by participation in technical committees, by interaction with other council members outside of the council meeting, and, finally, by their dialogue with members of their own constituencies.

There are commonalities across the three councils (housing, health care, and social services) regarding the deliberation process:

1. The agenda is established by the council's governing body prior to the meeting.
2. New issues can be added to the meeting's agenda, and the agenda's order can be changed based on the approval of a simple majority of council members (show of hands).
3. Any council member has the right to speak during scheduled blocks of time, as does any citizen who signs up to speak. Speakers are generally given three to four minutes to speak. Individuals may speak again after others have had the opportunity to speak. Council members have a right to respond if other speakers' comments are directly related to the same topic.

4. Government officials have the right to respond. These responses are generally clarifications of technical, administrative, budgetary, or legislative issues. The three- to four-minute time limit on speaking does not apply to government officials.
5. An official quorum of half of council members allows the meeting to begin. Voting decisions are based on majoritarian principles—50 percent plus one wins. However, a quorum is not required when the voting takes places, which means that individuals who leave prior to the end of the meeting do not have their votes included.

This analysis highlights three important issues. First, a small minority of council members elected to a governing body establishes the agenda. From an organizational standpoint, this is a step toward improving efficiency because it ensures that issues can be addressed in a timely fashion. This is similar to the work in legislative chambers: those who are well-positioned on committees and in leadership organize the agenda. This allows the leadership to set the agenda. A government official at a municipal policy conference stated to the assembled crowd: "We are not going to prohibit new proposals from being introduced, but we don't want to undermine the previous work done in the district conferences. We want to build on what was done" (municipal health care policy conference, December 5, 2009). The core idea is that a smaller elite within these participatory institutions sets the tone of the debate.

Second, and related to the first point, policy experts and government officials are actively engaged in the deliberative process to clarify misunderstandings and provide relevant policy material. They provide information to improve the quality of the deliberations. Within the health care council, a tremendous gulf exists between the policy knowledge of citizens and government officials. This gulf is much narrower in the social service council because there are few "clients" (*usuários*) among elected council members. This illuminates the vital role played by government officials in supporting the work of the councils. If government officials only provide the legal minimum of information to council members, it is highly unlikely that the council will be able to hold vibrant policy discussions.

Third, individual citizens and council members have the right to speak during the meetings, providing council members and any interested citizens a formal, institutionalized space to present issues not included on the agenda. Thus the governing body that sets up the meeting doesn't have full control over deliberation. However, denouncing governmental actions is a tactic of last resort. It is only used when council members believe there is no other way to draw government officials' and other council members' attention to the issue. The "right to denounce" is held in reserve because council members do not want to jeopardize their relationship with government officials.

A final observation is that the deliberative processes take place formally and informally. The formal deliberative process involves the public exchange of ideas. Informal deliberative exchanges occur prior to, during, and after the council meetings. This point was particularly striking to me at several of the policy conferences I attended. The meetings started late, although all key personnel were present and sound equipment was ready. The opening of the meeting was being purposefully delayed to allow participants to socialize as well as to exchange information about policy and political topics. For many years as I conducted research on participatory venues, I found myself frequently thinking, "Just start the meeting; everyone is ready." It was only after living in Brazil for four years over a fifteen-year period that I realized starting late was important to building bonds of solidarity and policy networks because it allows CSO leaders to interact with each other as well as with government officials. This helps to build trust and connections, linking CSO activists to each other and to the broader policy apparatus.

The council system provides the opportunity for constant communication among council members and government officials. Deliberation is not limited to the formal venues, which is what sharply distinguishes deliberative processes like deliberative polling (Fishkin 1993). There is a blurring between formal and informal deliberative exchanges. A CSO leader on the social service council stated in an interview, "My job is to bring issues and problems from the community to the council. My job is to then take information back to the community. I bring and I take" (Marcelo interview). This role is crucial to council members, as it allows government officials to better understand the concerns of the most active members of civil society. It also provides a check on street-level bureaucrats and independent service providers because there is a well-known public forum that allows citizens and councils to register wrongdoings and incompetence. Finally, it allows government officials to build a constituency to support new policies and programs as well as to create or maintain an electoral base.

In sum, this section demonstrates how the councils and policy conferences fit into the broader participatory citizenship regime. Citizens now have regular access to a host of policymaking institutions that permit them to exercise voice and vote. The rest of this chapter looks at the five explanatory factors that best account for the variations across the different policy arenas: state formation, the configuration of civil society, government support for voice and vote, rules specific to each participatory institution, and level of available resources.

HEALTH CARE

In the broader health care policy community, the municipal council is at the heart of how the participatory citizenship regime is being activated. The key features that define how the participatory citizenship regime is activated in the health care field include: (1) extensive local state involvement in the provision of public services; (2) a vibrant and well-organized civil society that includes community activists, union officials, and medical personnel; (3) limited engagement of senior government officials; (4) limited technical knowledge of CSO leaders; and (5) internal rules that limit the involvement of government officials. As a result of these factors, the health care council thus plays a fundamentally different role in shaping policy outcomes and civil society mobilization than the social service and housing councils.

State Formation and Civil Society Development

The provision of health care from the 1930s to the 1988 constitution utilized three distinct tracks (Viana 1987; Draibe 1993). First, there was a private market (direct payments or private insurance) for a small minority of the population with the financial means to pay for it. Second, union members had access to medical facilities and care; this was one key benefit of the regulated citizenship regime (Santos 1979; Wolfe 1993; French 1992; Carvalho 2002). Third, the vast majority of Brazilians relied on *Santa Casas*, which were hospitals and health care clinics run by the Catholic Church and other philanthropic organizations (Viana 1992). Thus the poor majority had limited access to public health care facilities.

During the 1970s, when Brazil was under a military dictatorship, a broad health care social movement developed that linked community leaders from favelas to young medical professionals seeking to change how health care services were provided. There was a unionized workforce of health care professionals, who were employed to provide services to citizens who had access to the regulated citizenship regime. The health care movement was initially forged in São Paulo and had three guiding principles (Jacobi 1989). First, access to quality health care was conceptualized as a moral and constitutional right: health care is a right that should be provided to all Brazilians by the state. Second, it advocated for the decentralization of health services to favelas and other poor communities in the form of public facilities providing desperately needed services. The third and final claim of the health movement was that ordinary citizens should exercise voice and vote in the deliberative meetings. Citizens should make decisions regarding policies. The health care movement was extended to other urban areas such as Belo Horizonte during the 1980s (Campos et al. 1998).

The 1988 constitution grants all Brazilian citizens the right to health care services provided by the state. The health care system was decentralized, with municipalities in charge of most health care services. The universal health care system (Sistema Unica de Saúde, or SUS) is funded through federal tax receipts, which are transferred to municipal governments. Municipal governments can provide the services themselves, or they can outsource the services to private hospitals and clinics. The amount of resources allocated to Belo Horizonte's health care department was roughly $1 billion in 2010, which dwarfs municipal spending in any other policy area. Given the level of resources, the health care council can potentially have an enormous impact on social well-being outcomes; actions taken by council members can affect the allocation of substantial financial and human capital resources. The health care department is a complex bureaucracy responsible for a wide range of services, from public health campaigns to family health to heart surgery.

The development of the SUS in Belo Horizonte began in the early 1990s and accelerated under Mayor Patrus Ananias in 1993. The vice mayor, Celio de Castro, was a medical doctor, a former member of the outlawed Communist Party, and a member of the Brazilian Socialist Party (PSB). When the mayoral administrations of Ananias and Castro built the administrative structure to implement a new health care system, they did so in conjunction with the core principles of the national health care movement—decentralization of services, citizen participation in decision making, and universal access to health care. Belo Horizonte thus had three consecutive municipal governments dedicated to ensuring the consolidation of the SUS program. Over time, however, the upper echelon of the government withdrew from the health care council system, which signifies declining elite support for participatory democracy.

Who Participates?

By 2010, the main actors engaged in Belo Horizonte's health care councils were CSO leaders representing their regional districts and union representatives. The citizens representing civil society had a wide range of interests, but a common theme in almost all my conversations was that they wanted the municipal government to provide more services and to provide existing services more efficiently. A second common feature is that many of the CSO activists employed the language of SUS—decentralization, democratization, and universal access—but they didn't have the technical knowledge to contribute to policy debates. Union officials were also actively involved in the health care council. They have greater levels of knowledge about medical and administrative practices. Union representatives did not necessarily advocate for the expansion of universal access to health care but focused on increasing spending on state-run facilities (as opposed to outsourcing services) and more specialized service areas. Thus there is a clear division between union representatives, who push for specific, specialized services, and civil society representatives, who tend to advocate for the expansion of basic medical services.[4]

A council member representing the private sector was always present at the council meetings. However, I never heard him speak. He was present to monitor the actions of the council but not necessarily to actively participate. Nearly 60 percent of all resources spent on health care by the municipal government were spent through outsourcing, which means that the government was contracting with for-profit and nonprofit providers to provide basic service.

Only four government officials serve on the council (out of thirty-six members), none of whom are in the first or second tier of government appointees. The health care movement has its roots in the struggle against the 1964–1985 military dictatorship; this helps to explain why social movement activists were distrustful of government officials. One consequence of the mistrust is that the health care council typically provides a smaller venue for formal representation by government officials than other councils. Government officials find themselves in a minority position, which further reduces their role in the council because the amount of time and energy required to build solid majorities does not appear to be a good use of senior administrators' time. No first-tier government officials were involved in the council during my research in 2004 and 2009–2010. However, in 2010, the secretary of health care finally established a weekly meeting with government representatives on the health care council so that they could inform him about the main issues and concerns of council members. No one inside the health secretary's key decision-making circle participated in the council on a regular basis.

Citizen Participation in Meetings

Council meetings are held every two weeks. The meetings formally begin on a weekday at two thirty p.m., but only a handful of CSO activists are usually present. The midday meeting time makes it difficult for people employed during regular business hours to be present. People slowly arrive, and the meetings generally begin at three. The first thirty to forty-five minutes are a general information session. Speakers are almost exclusively council members. They inform their fellow council members about upcoming events (e.g., mental health workshop in Region Y, inauguration of health care clinic), denounce problems in basic service delivery, and question government officials regarding policy solutions to these problems.

Just one government representative is elected to the council governing body. The representative takes the lead in responding to questions posed by speakers because the representative typically has access to information that can correct misunderstandings and they can respond to ill-founded rumors and myths. Interestingly, when the government official responded to a person who brought a problem to the council, the official would often suggesting that the two of them discuss the problem during the coffee break or after the meeting to resolve the problem.

This information session serves multiple functions: sharing information among CSO leaders, an accountability session whereby any registered citizens can question the council members (especially the government representative), a problem-solving process whereby the speaker alerts the government representative to their concerns, and an opportunity for individual CSO activists to press their claims on public officials.

Following the general information session, the health care council addresses issues related to policymaking (*co-gestor*). Two types of activities are most common. First, subcommittees (e.g., finance, primary health) provide updates on their ongoing work. These subcommittees do the bulk of the information gathering, hold deliberations, and then present policy recommendations to the council. This is another example of interlocking institutions. Second, government officials give presentations on a specific topic (e.g., annual budget, year-end report, proposed new hospital). After the information is provided, a question and answer period occurs during which council members seek qualification of the proposed changes.

During the ten months I attended meetings and had contact with council members, the policy discussions were limited to council members' responding to the government's policy proposals. It was common for policy experts from the government to present new policy programs. They would provide information on the technical merits of the plans, the targeted audience, and the cost. The experts would address the concerns and questions of council members. Questions regarding how the policies would function were common, but it was exceedingly rare that anyone would oppose the implementation of a new program. This is because council members representing civil society firmly believe that more programs and more resources are necessary to improve the quality of health care. Union representatives also support new programs because they will likely result in expanding employment opportunities. There is no political cost to supporting new programs because the council is not being asked to make the hard decisions regarding the allocation of resources.

In the case of the health care council, it was very difficult to forge a real conversation because of stark differences in education and technical knowledge. There are continual efforts to improve the skills and knowledge of participants, but the key problem remains a major educational deficit among many council members. This is the principal tension present in the council: many of the members represent and are themselves from low-income communities, but they lack the technical skills to contribute to complex policy formulations. This education deficit is particularly apparent in the health care policy arena with its technical complexity. The informed deliberation essential to the argument of deliberative democrats is not present but resembles an initial stage of building a policy community as well as serving as a school of democracy to habituate citizens and government officials to the process of exchanging ideas and information. Although government officials seek out to gather information about the councilors' interests and local knowledge (*mētis*), this information plays a smaller role in policy areas that are more technically complicated.

During the time that I observed the activities of the health care council, there was one policy moment in which the council acted as a veto point, thereby altering how the municipal government acted. In December 2009, the government came to the council meeting with plans to build a new hospital. The government needed the council's quick approval of the plans to open the bidding process to begin construction. The council refused to approve the plan because they had virtually no information about the proposed hospital. The council members asserted that the proposed hospital first be approved by three different subcommittees before the council could legally vote on the plan.

Government representatives were thus forced to present different aspects of the hospital proposal to each of three subcommittees. Council members told me they felt the government was "disrespecting" the council. They all supported the hospital but insisted that the government must follow established rules and procedures. After receiving information from government officials, all three subcommittees voted to approve the plan. The entire council voted on the plan, and it passed with overwhelming support.

This example demonstrates that a council has the potential to slow down or block a government's plans. A government seeking to establish new policies must receive the council's approval, which means that the government must carefully attend to council members' policy and political concerns. This example also shows the limitations of the council: the council members have a strong bias toward approving projects, and they lack the technical skills to assess policy proposals.

Another problem related to policymaking is that the government provided an extremely limited and superficial year-end report, with only a general overview of spending in broad categories (e.g., personnel, medicines, public health campaigns). The cliché "the devil is in the details" was not well understood by council members; they asked very generic questions about the annual report. After the round of questions, they voted to approve the report. The council has the potential to be actively involved, but members lack the incentive and knowledge to hold government officials accountable.

Interestingly, the two most contentious debates I witnessed over the ten months I attended meetings concerned issues not directly related to public policy outcomes. One contentious debate involved the selection of two council members who would travel, at the municipality's expense, to a regional conference in Salvador, Bahia. This led to acrimonious accusations regarding the quality of different individuals' participation and work on the council. The second contentious debate was highly personal because it revolved around the theft of supplies from a storage closet used by council members. This shouting match pitted CSO representatives against government officials, with a host of accusations. These examples suggest that the councils are far from a deliberative democrat's ideal forum. Rather, these new participatory formats are functioning democratic bodies that reproduce many of the petty disputes and rivalries characteristic of other organizations.

The Participatory Citizenship Regime in the Health Care Field

Health care councils have a limited impact on the specific, technical part of the policymaking process. Policy proposals come from the government. CSOs and citizen representatives lack the technical skills and expert knowledge that would allow them to reshape policy initiatives. The union representatives focus on narrow sets of interests that are difficult to translate into general public policies. The health care council serves as the hub of an intricate web of coalition building and information sharing. There is a mixing of social movement and union activity as groups try to forge a broad coalition that will maintain pressure on government officials to increase the resources dedicated to participatory budgeting. Sharing information is crucial because it allows council members to better understand the health care system. They swap stories with other CSO leaders; they learn how services are provided in other sectors of the population. Because civil society members are first elected at the regional level, they take this information back to the regional council meetings. This information is then carried back to the local councils and, finally, into community meetings. The CSO leaders seek to activate the interlocking institutions to increase the flow of information from communities to the municipal secretary's office.

The council plays a limited role in agenda setting as council members respond to the initiatives and actions of the municipal health care department. The council does assume a key role of oversight of the public provision of health care services, but this activity is constricted by the limited knowledge and technical capacity of CSO leaders, who must monitor a complex policy environment. What is most noteworthy is that the vertically and horizontally integrated council system serves to improve the quality and distribution of information among new networks of citizens, CSOs, and public officials. In Belo Horizonte's health care councils, the technical gulf between CSO leaders and policy experts is sufficiently large that it is difficult to generate a real policy conversation.

CSO leaders actively participate in local, regional, and municipal councils. The expansion of these democratic policymaking venues links them to other CSO leaders as well as to government officials. CSO leaders also represent their followers within this vertically integrated council system. Thus council members are participants in the policymaking processes but also represent their CSO members and community members. The municipal-level council members are, in turn, represented by other council members on state and federal councils as well as by government officials in other policy spaces. The direct participation of council members links them to multiple actors, thus helping to expand their policy networks.

As a result of these connections, systemic policy problems as well as individual grievances now work their way up and across the state through the interlocking institutions. Citizens' voices are incorporated by local and regional administrators, who look for novel ways to respond to high demand and insufficient resources. Citizens and CSO activists use their political rights within the councils in order to secure social rights. These social rights are collective and individual. The collective rights involve securing public goods, such as health care clinics or additional personnel, that serve broader communities. But CSO activists also develop the connections that allow them to secure specific benefits for individuals within the state. For example, CSO activists get to know public servants (e.g., doctors, hospital administrators), allowing them to develop the necessary connections to gain specific public goods, such as admission to a hospital.

CSOs leaders are involved in establishing or strengthening various kinds of networks. First, they participate in networks within civil society, allowing them to foster bonds of solidarity with other CSOs. Second, they are becoming part of policy networks. Their access to information and decision makers allows them to fine-tune their response to policy proposals and to better monitor ongoing policy implementation. This is an important power because they can change specific provisions. Third, council members use their involvement in the council system to develop personal networks that tie them to government bureaucrats, union representatives, and political appointees. These ties are crucial if a community leader needs to request a favor or bypass bureaucratic rules to help a constituent. Finally, council members are part of a political network, whereby community leaders develop connections to government officials that are vital to both groups during the biannual campaign season.

CSO leaders are involved in health care council systems because it is part of a vertically integrated system of bringing demands to the attention of key government decision makers. Policy problems at the local level now travel through two distinct routes: one pathway is through the councils, and a parallel pathway goes through the government bureaucracies. At the local, regional, and municipal levels, there are horizontal links between the council and government officials, which produce the interlocking institutions connecting CSO leaders to government officials.

Although oversight is a central responsibility of council members, council members have limited influence for a couple of reasons. First, council members lack the technical skills to evaluate a complex health care system. As one might expect, there is no clear method as to what information should be collected or how it should be collected. The results of subcommittees were generally based on anecdotal evidence. The details and stories of problems uncovered were usually gripping and disturbing but difficult to translate into broader public policy changes. Nevertheless, the reports did allow government officials present to begin to work on the identified problem.

Council members' legal right to approve the annual budget as well as the year-end report creates two additional veto points, since the government is obligated to have council approval. There is a great deal at stake because if the council doesn't approve the budget and annual reports, the federal government can stop the transfers that sustain the health care system. Government officials must provide information to council members, which helps explain why council members would continue to participate. From the perspective of council members, it is a high-risk strategy to block the government's reports because it could stop the transfer of much-needed funds.

HOUSING

The housing council is marked by (1) extensive involvement of high-level political appointees, (2) policy support provided by state bureaucrats and policy experts, (3) CSOs' broad policy knowledge, and (4) limited state action. This council focuses on generating the necessary political capital for pressuring government officials to allocate budgetary resources to housing projects. The housing council is far more politicized than either the health care or social assistance council, since its most active participants are government officials and activists who work together to find additional funding. The municipal government in Belo Horizonte lacks the basic resources to implement the policy programs, which means that activists and government officials focus on where and how they can secure financial resources.

State Formation

For most of the nineteenth and twentieth centuries, the Brazilian state did little to provide housing for poor citizens priced out of the market (Holston 2008). Favelas emerged around the country as former slaves and new immigrants built housing on unoccupied land. The building of irregular housing on property that was either unoccupied or in legal dispute became the primary means for poor Brazilians to create new housing stock (Holston 2008). The housing units were generally informal, built with material found or purchased cheaply by the residents, and communities were organized in a somewhat haphazard fashion (Perlman 2010).

Under the logic of the regulated citizenship regime, federal and state governments began building housing units in the 1930s and 1940s for union employees and their families. The new professional and middle classes, which were growing as a result of incipient industrialization, had access to housing through the private market. Under the regulated citizenship regime, there was extensive industrialization from the 1940s through the 1980s, which was accompanied by an influx of rural migrants from the northeast to the southeastern cities of Belo Horizonte, São Paulo, and Rio de Janeiro. Many of these migrants were initially employed in the informal sector. Given that government programs provided little support to workers employed in the informal sector, this meant that migrants had to piece together housing in ever-increasing distances from jobs, schools, and hospitals (Perlman 2010).

An important difference between the fields of housing and health care is the absence of public sector union activity in housing. The construction of housing units was historically and continues to be outsourced to private (typically nonunionized) companies, which contrasts sharply with the health care sector, which developed an extensive network of public and unionized employees.

The national urban reform movement developed in the 1970s and 1980s under the military government in response to strong demands from individuals and families that lacked adequate housing and basic infrastructure (Holston 2008). Like the health care movement, the housing movement also had its roots in the São Paulo metropolitan region and drew from extensive professional and bureaucratic knowledge of the topic. The national urban reform movement counted on the support of local community organizers seeking to improve their neighborhoods through the building of infrastructure and housing units. The housing movement in the 1980s spent considerable time and energy promoting "self-help" housing, whereby individuals worked in collective organization to build simple housing stock (Erundina 1990, 1991).

The housing movement had the support of urban planners and lawyers who sought to devise broader solutions to the massive housing deficits faced by Brazilians (Holston 2008). This paralleled what occurred in the health care sector: community leaders were linked to a growing number of educated urban professionals who sought to transform Brazilian society and politics. This fusion created a social movement based on ideas associated with the concept of *mētis* (see discussion in chapter 1). That is, the social movement was founded with an effort to explicitly link local, common sense and technical forms of knowledge.

During the military dictatorship in the 1960s and 1970s, the housing movement in Belo Horizonte emerged as the city's most active and strongest social movement for several reasons. Industrial expansion from the 1950s through the 1970s provided a substantial base of wealth, attracting new residents to Belo Horizonte, most of whom came from rural areas in the state of Minas Gerais and the northeast (Eakin 2001). When these new migrants arrived, available housing was limited, so they built informal housing in new favelas and existing favelas. The 1980s were marked by a period of intense occupation of land by social movements. Holston's work on "insurgent citizenship" in the city of São Paulo during this period is illustrative of a similar process in Belo Horizonte. Social movements organized themselves under the banners of the right to the land, the return to democracy, and the establishment of public infrastructure that would benefit the poor majority. The progressive wing of the Catholic Church, which advocated liberation theology, promoted the right to land and housing and was visibly involved in Belo Horizonte's housing movement (Somarriba, Valadares, and Afonso 1984; Soares 1982). Finally, there is a topographic specificity to Belo Horizonte. The city was built in the 1890s as the new state capital. The internal core of the city is located in a fairly flat valley, but much of the rest of the city's topography is hilly. Favelas were built up the mountainsides (similar to Rio de Janeiro) because the wealthy didn't initially want to build their own housing on the hillside because of the cost. Housing and urban development in these communities are rather precarious.

Who Participates in the Council System?

Mayor Patrus Ananias (1993–1996) was a strong proponent of the housing movement. His administration voluntarily founded the housing council in 1994 as well as PB Housing in 1996. Prior to being mayor, Ananias was a leader in leftist social movements, which cemented his relationship with the housing movement. During 1988–1992 municipal legislative session, when Ananias was the Speaker of the Municipal Legislature, he spearheaded an effort to revise Belo Horizonte's master plan, based on many of the key ideas promoted by the National Urban Reform movement, including the right to housing (Gonçalves 2008). Ananais created the political expectation that the principal political actors in the housing arena should also be involved in the housing council (Medeira interview, May 19, 2010). Thus, important government officials are at the heart of the housing council rather than having been sidelined, as occurred in the health care council. The housing council is more of a political forum rather than part of an effort to create a new stage in the policymaking process.

A wide network of CSO leaders are active in the council and policy conferences. Council members are elected at the biannual housing public policy conference (interlocking institutions). Individuals voting must be registered members of a *núcleo*; this requirement induces ordinary citizens to attend housing conferences. Over thirteen thousand people were relocated to housing built with funds from the municipal government, which gave other citizens the hope that they too would be able to secure housing. Thus CSO activists leading these housing *núcleos* tend to be highly politicized because they are elected from a political body demanding the right to affordable housing. Unlike the health care sector, there is no stable source of funding transferred from the federal government, which means that CSO activists involved in the council dedicate considerable time finding the necessary political support to find funding to build housing stock.

Government officials must seek out government agencies and bank (public and private) to find the necessary financial investments. Within the housing council, there is no formal participation for union officials and a very limited participation of private contractors.

Citizen Participation in the Meeting

Housing council meetings are held once a month, beginning at six thirty in the evening. People slowly filter in, coming from work. Government officials often arrange for a van to pick up people who live in distant communities. Prior to the beginning of the meeting, light refreshments are provided, and people mingle, chatting and catching up. When quorum has been achieved, the secretary of urban affairs, who is the second or third most powerful political appointee in the city, starts the meeting. There is a general information session, but this tends to be short because only a handful of activists and CSO leaders are in the room.

Government officials lead the policy discussion. They provide updates on ongoing projects, including the status of loans, permits to build, and construction, and they also help to set the long-term agenda by introducing new programs and ideas. The government introduces its proposed plans and then provides the opportunity for council members to critique the proposals. The debate that follows is charged and quite contentious because the participants believe that the principal reason for lack of investment is due to the political interests of the mayoral administration. CSO leaders are constantly demanding that housing officials place additional pressure on the mayor and his inner circle to dedicate the necessary time and political capital to secure resources. It is a passionate debate because CSO leaders are participants in movements to secure decent housing for individuals and families who live in favelas and *vilas*.

Government officials and housing activists worked closely between 1993 and 2010 to build more housing units. The leading housing social movements have consistently partnered with the PT and PSB mayoral administrations because the CSO leaders believe that institutional processes and political coalitions in charge of the municipal government are working in the general interests of the housing movement. This doesn't mean that the housing movement accepts government proposals uncritically, but rather it means that it seeks to work with government officials.

One indication of this deep political alliance is the absence of new land occupations (or invasions) in the city of Belo Horizonte between

1996 and 2009. The housing movement leaders were persuaded that their interests would best be met by working with government officials through formal institutions. In 2009, for the first time in more than a decade, a new housing social movement organized two large land occupations, allowing hundreds of families to build housing on unoccupied land. The argument of the leaders leading the land occupation mirrored arguments of the late 1980s and early 1990s: people have a right to decent housing, the government is not providing the housing, and where there is a good housing location and idle land, people have the right to occupy the land.

Interestingly, civil society representatives on the housing council opposed this land occupation. CSO activists argued that there was an institutionalized process in place for the building and distribution of housing units. Longtime CSO activists argued that the new CSO needed to withdraw from the land it had occupied, enter into the institutionalized process, and wait its turn for access to housing. Council members wrote a letter to the leaders of the land occupation calling on them to end their land occupation. The letter was written in the offices of URBEL, the public-private company that is responsible for the urbanization of favelas (Martins interview). Thus, a CSO that was incorporated into a formal, state-sanctioned participatory process objected to another CSO using extra-institutional means to advance its agenda.

The incorporation of social movement activists into the housing system led them to align their interests with the government's. These activists continued to pressure government officials to find the resources to fund the program, but there was widespread agreement that the policies and institutional rules designed in Belo Horizonte offered the best solutions to the housing crisis. Government officials argued that because financial resources were limited, they were unable to purchase land and build housing units. Building new housing units is expensive, time-consuming, and fraught with legal problems. An opaque property rights regime makes it difficult for municipalities to purchase land, and construction costs in Brazil are high (Holston 2008).

It was hoped that the economic boom of the first decades of the twenty-first century generated resources that would finally allow the government to build new housing units. Through PB Housing (see chapter 4), the government built half the units they had promised to build. The introduction of a new housing plan, My Home, My Life (Minha Casa, Minha Vida), as well as the freeing up of credit from two federal financial institutions (Caixa Economica and BNDES, which was run by a former secretary of urban affairs of Belo Horizonte), created an atmosphere in which citizens and activists believed that their decades of work were going to result in the building of thousands of new housing units. However, skyrocketing land costs associated with a housing bubble made it difficult for the municipal government to buy land. Although it finally had resources to spend on housing, but the rising land values effectively neutralized the increase in their resources.

The Participatory Citizenship Regime and Housing

The housing social movement is well organized in Belo Horizonte, and its strong participation in the city's political life predates the 1988 constitution and the 1992 electoral realignment. Following the 1992 election of the Workers' Party, the government established the housing council, formed PB Housing, and included policy experts in the new housing venues to expand the policy debate and improve the quality of technical discussions.

CSO leaders involved in housing policy are politically active across a host of institutionalized spaces because of a widely held perception that the government has "correct" policies in place but lacks the necessary resources to implement a shared vision of change. Thus political pressure is necessary to force the government to act. The housing council and PB Housing are examples of interlocking institutions whereby citizens and government officials work together to promote their shared interests. Housing activists attended meetings held at the municipal legislature, they organized their followers to attend a federal and municipal policy conference, a small number of council members attended weekly meetings, and there was constant communication with the 172 registered housing *núcleos*. Their participation was widespread because they were attempting to pressure government officials to act—through PB housing, through the housing council, and through the new federal housing program (see chapter 6 for a fuller discussion).

The CSO activists from the housing sector were the most likely of the three policy arenas to use social justice language. Emphasis on social justice claims left a deep mark on the deliberative sessions I attended, as CSO leaders continually positioned their demands based on the moral and constitutional right to decent housing. Given that many of their followers lacked the financial capital to buy affordable housing, housing movement leaders used language related to the state's protection and promotion of social rights.

The housing council exercises very limited oversight over government policy for a couple of different reasons. First, 50 percent of the members on the council are government officials. They are obviously not going to use public forums to highlight problems in how the municipality is providing services. In addition, the state doesn't directly build housing units but outsources the work to private companies. This makes it difficult for civil society representatives on the council to exercise oversight over the work. A weakness of the housing council is that oversight of the private contractors is not a strong part of the process. Finally, the founding logic of the council was to advance a policy and political agenda to build adequate housing for low-income residents. The principle of oversight, which is foundational in the health care field, doesn't strongly resonate in the housing field.

SOCIAL SERVICES

The social service council is distinguishable from the other two policy arenas in three respects: (1) the strong presence of bureaucrats, (2) the legalistic and bureaucratic nature of the meetings, and (3) the absence of current and potential policy beneficiaries in council meetings. Although this council is formally charged with agenda setting, my interviews and participant observations over a ten-month period indicate that the primary function of this council is to ensure that service providers are technically qualified and properly registered with the council so that they can legally accept government contracts to provide social services. The council has a key role ensuring that the outsourcing of social service contracts is granted legally and to qualified service providers, which means that council oversight largely focuses on how government resources are outsourced.

State Formation

The Brazilian state long had minimal involvement in providing basic social services to the population. Under President Vargas in the 1930s, the Brazilian state's initial foray into the social service policy arena was based on outsourcing service delivery. Vargas's wife, working within the tradition of Eva Perón and the wives of other corporatist-populist leaders, led an ad hoc process of social service provision (Cunha 2009; Skidmore 1999). The state relied on religious and philanthropic organizations such as the

Catholic Church to provide social services. The lack of state activity meant that a qualified and unionized workforce did not develop, as occurred in the health sector.

In contrast to the housing and health arenas, a strong member-based social movement in the social service field did not emerge. A primary reason is the high organizational barriers faced by the poorest sectors of Brazilian society when they attempt to organize themselves (basic collective action problems). But this is accentuated in the social service field because of the type of problems: domestic violence, child abuse, alcoholism, mental illness, family members with mental or physical disabilities. Families in desperate need of social services face the greatest challenges organizing themselves.

The absence of large numbers of policy experts or qualified public servants means that the problems are treated in piecemeal form, thus discouraging collective organization. The absence of a strong national social movement made it more difficult for the incipient organizing efforts in Belo Horizonte during the 1990s and 2000s. As a result, there was very limited civil society organizing. There are many professional NGOs that seek to represent the interests of the marginalized and targeted, needy population, but few organizations are run by individuals who would be the recipients of those services (Cunha 2009).

Who Participates in the Social Service Council System?

Surrounding the social service council is a dense network of social service providers and a weak network of social movements or CSOs comprised of individuals seeking to guarantee rights for themselves that were established under the 1988 constitution. There is limited involvement of CSOs comprised of individuals who directly benefit from the services provided. CSO leaders involved in the council are comprised of professionals who provide services to targeted communities. There are few organized union members because there is limited state investment in this policy arena. Educated professionals, many of whom hold master's degrees in counseling or psychology, form the core of a network within this policy arena. They advocate on behalf of targeted populations who face great difficulties in their everyday lives. There are few recipients of the intended policies at these meetings.

Meetings of the social service council are held bimonthly in the middle of the afternoon. They, too, typically begin late, allowing participants to converse, catch up, and share information. The first part of the typical council meeting is an oral reading of the previous meeting's minutes, which takes thirty to forty-five minutes. The reading of the minutes removes any vibrancy from the meeting; it is the perfect tool to remove any energy from participants. After the minutes are read, corrections are made, and a vote is taken to approve the minutes. The minutes of the previous meeting must be read because the council's purpose is to legally register CSOs and NGOs. If the council incorrectly decertifies a CSO or NGO, the council and the municipal government could face a lawsuit.

The council's executive committee sets the agenda as directed by the council president—a position that rotates annually between a government representative and a civil society representative. The agenda is generally quite technical and bureaucratic. In every meeting I attended, organizations that had applied for registration or were up for renewal were reviewed. A subcommittee had prepared a detailed report on the CSO or NGO; an executive summary of the report was read.

A major change that promotes oversight is the legal process of formally registering CSOs wishing to receive government funds for providing services. The process limits the likelihood that public resources can be given to a "front" organization—one that receives money but doesn't provide any services. CSOs are now in charge of monitoring each other to ensure that they meet the minimal requirements. This new role greatly expanded the authority of CSOs over each other, which is also worrisome because unpopular CSOs may be punished by other CSOs. There is little oversight by CSOs of the ongoing process of service implementation, but CSOs must provide information about their activities when seeking to register.

Of the three councils discussed in this chapter, the social service council had the most restrictive deliberative sessions. Most of the public debate focused on the legalistic minutia of policy implementation. There was rarely any broader debate on policy issues, as government officials were visibly uncomfortable with allowing a contentious debate to emerge. In one meeting I attended, on April 14, 2010, a contentious debate on policy directions developed. Several community leaders were attempting to hold the government accountable for its actions. The body language of the council president (a government official) suggested that she was quite upset at how the meeting was unfolding. When it was her turn to speak, she called for a vote on the issue. Her motion was quickly seconded by a civil society representative whose CSO held a service contract with the municipal government. Debate was ended. A vote was held. Most of the government officials (they have 50 percent of the seats) and several of the civil society leaders voted to end the discussion and move on to the next item. This example illustrates the heavy-handed way that an inexperienced government official approached a contentious issue and the government's limited support for developing a critical dialogue in this area.

One of the most interesting budgetary presentations I attended concerned the reallocation of funds from a 2008 budget line to a different type of program in a 2010 budget line. The government needed to secure the approval of the social service council to spend 5 million reais (roughly $3 million) in a different manner from the way the resources had been originally budgeted. The council approved the changes in spending, but more importantly, the government did not have to seek the approval of the municipal legislative branch to make the change. Rather, the government only needed to secure the approval of the social service council. On an institutional level, this gives the council a greater potential veto over the actions of the government than the one held by the municipal legislature.

The Participatory Citizenship Regime and Social Services

The state has traditionally outsourced service provision to nonprofit and philanthropic institutions. Under President Lula (2002–2010), there was a dramatic increase in resources, but the best-known social policy program, Bolsa Família, is a conditional cash transfer program that doesn't involve the delivery of social services to individuals or families. There continues to be a very limited state apparatus to deliver basic social services to the public. The outsourcing of social service provisions continues, which means that NGOs continue to be the formal intermediary between citizens and the rights formally guaranteed under the 1988 constitution. In Belo Horizonte, the lack of social movements led by individuals and groups asserting rights-based claims for themselves as well as the lack of a large body of unionized workers has weakened the impact of the council. Participation and mobilization costs are highest among the poorest people, which explains why they are less likely to be involved. As a result of the weak client-oriented CSOs, it is now well-educated professionals that make up most of the formal representatives on the council. Their claim to be legitimate representatives is based on their policy expertise and their assertion that they are working on behalf of poor citizens who need basic social services.

There are no mechanisms to gauge the extent to which the interests of service providers and their clients coincide. Deliberation is legalistic and technical because of the rules-based nature of registering CSOs to which the state can outsource services and also because the participants are policy experts. Government officials do not promote an active debate on policy proposals. Rather, government officials seek to limit the debate along very narrow, technical and legalistic grounds. The social service councils, thus, do not expand public deliberation.

This chapter shows how the participatory citizenship regime is evolving differently across the three policy arenas. Variation in state formation; the development of civil society; government support for voice and vote; council-specific rules affecting participation, representation, and deliberation; and the level of available resources profoundly affects how citizens gain access to the participatory citizenship regime. The regime was activated differently in each policy arena, so that citizens and CSOs are able to access different types of political and social rights.

These findings reinforce the argument that the participatory citizenship regime must be activated through the political interests of government officials and their allies in civil society. This finding is generalizable to states and municipalities across Brazil. In cities such as Rio de Janeiro, Curitiba, and Recife, citizens will experience significantly different participatory citizenship regimes because of how the local state developed as well as the historical development and current configuration of civil society. As Brazilians are attempting to take advantage of the economic stability and growth of recent decades, they are working within the institutional and civil society legacies of previous periods, which can enhance (Belo Horizonte) or hamper (Rio de Janeiro) their ability to activate the participatory citizenship regime.

Figure 5.1 shows how the participatory citizenship regime shifts across six participatory institutions based on the long-term development of state and civil society. In the figure, the variable "state action" aggregates the key explanatory factors of state formation, resource availability, and government support for voice and vote. The variable "civil society activity" captures the variables of the configuration of civil society and the internal rules of participatory institutions that induce different types of engagement. The typology in the figure demonstrates how democracy is being deepened across the five policy arenas. It is the combination of state action

Figure 5.1   Activation of the Participatory Citizenship Regime:
Outcomes Across Six New Democratic Institutions

Civil Society Activity

		Robust		Limited
Action / **State**	**Strong**	**PB Regional** Inclusive, local democracy	**Health Care Council** Council-oriented, networked democracy	**PB Digital** Referendum-based democracy
	Weak	**Housing Council/ PB Housing** Politicized, mobilized democracy		**Social Service Council** Exclusionary democracy

and civil society activity that explains the extent to which the participatory citizenship regime will be activated and democracy deepened.

In sum, the evidence presented in chapters 3, 4, and 5 demonstrates how the local state has been rebuilt during the 1990s and 2000s to activate the participatory citizenship regime. To gain a better understanding of what is occurring within civil society across these different sectors, chapters 6 and 7 introduce survey data to illuminate how civil society leaders are now using the new participatory citizenship regime in pursuit of their interests.

CHAPTER SIX

Transforming the Engagement of Civil Society Organizations

Adopting New Strategies in the Participatory Citizenship Regime

My job is receive and take. I take information from the community to the council. I take information from the council to the community.
—Marcelo, community leader and social service council member, April 9, 2010

PB isn't only about public works. It is also about creating community.
—Waldir, PB government administrator and former CSO activist

The proliferation of new participatory venues has redefined how CSO activists engage government officials, other CSOs, their base of support, and state bureaucrats. CSO activists now employ a broad range of potential strategies as they seek to influence the distribution of scarce public goods. Under the new participatory citizenship regime, CSO activists must mobilize their communities while simultaneously engaging in incremental policymaking processes. This chapter demonstrates that the constant engagement among public officials, citizens, and CSO activists is now at the center of civil society activity. The institutionalization of participatory institutions embeds civil society leaders and ordinary citizens within democratic and state institutions. This blurs the line between state and society, thus altering basic state-society relationships, although not in uniform or necessarily democratic ways. The blurring of the line between the state and civil society varies from one policy arena to the next because of differences in state formation, civil society development, political support of government officials, and the specific rules that define representation and deliberation within each participatory venue.

Civil society activists and citizens embedded inside the state must navigate two contradictory roles: representing their community inside the state (thus being "civil society" inside the state) and being viewed as representatives of the government within their communities (thus being the "government" in their communities and their day-to-day lives). Given the heterogeneity of both Brazilian civil society and the Brazilian state, we now see different state-society relationships across four public policy arenas, ranging from an expansion of public deliberation to a narrow focus on securing government contracts.

The demonopolization of access to the state allows CSOs and citizens to press their claims in a wide range of institutional formats, improving policy responses to significant social problems. CSO leaders have increased access to information and public officials, thus allowing them to move beyond clientelistic relationships. The coordination of state response to pressing social and political problems is improved because state agencies have access to a broader range of information.

Nevertheless, there is a clear danger that "state in society" and "society in state" will enable government officials to extend their control over the activities and strategies of CSOs, producing "participatory clientelism" or new forms of co-optation (Navarro 2003; Wampler 2007). In my interviews and informal conversations with CSO activists and government officials, both groups consistently pointed out the dangers of a civil society that loses its independence and autonomy.

VIGNETTES

Participatory Budgeting

During a PB Regional meeting in Belo Horizonte's downtown region, the local PB administrator, a longtime civil society activist prior to accepting a paid position in the government, began the meeting by speaking for five minutes on the importance of community and about working together and supporting each other. Waldir told the audience of twenty PB delegates that he had visited one of their colleagues in her home because she was in poor health, and he urged other activists to get in touch with her. He told the assembled audience, "PB isn't only about public works. It is also about creating community" (September 1, 2009). Government officials currently working with participatory institutions often seek to help CSOs mobilize citizens and strengthen their communities. Over the ten months I followed Belo Horizonte's participatory institutions, Waldir constantly reminded participants that he was a long-term civil society activist prior to his becoming a PB administrator; he emphasized that he was the people's representative inside the municipal state.

Following Waldir's comments promoting community, a longtime activist and elected PB delegate took the microphone to demand government action: "No one [in the municipal government] is doing anything. We are being called liars in our neighborhood because the public works are not being done. Seven years after we won the project, it still hasn't been done. . . . We are being called liars." Just as Waldir was attempting to promote trust among community leaders, this activist was calling attention to the problems faced by the same leaders when the government didn't live up to its agreements. The inability of the government to fulfill its commitment created a shared burden of failure: CSO leaders reported that they were sharply criticized by their community members in the same breath as state officials. The one clear drawback to interlocking institutions is that CSO leaders are now blamed for state failures. Working closely can forge community and bonds of solidarity, but the dual role of CSO leaders as activists and elected officials means that they are often blamed for how the municipal government carries out its duties.

Housing Conference

At the biannual housing policy conference in November 2009, a CSO leader named Eduardo, who identified himself as being new to the housing field offered, a series of policy proposals he hoped would be included in the official policy recommendations. His proposals, however, failed to gain the necessary votes that would have allowed them to be included in the conference's final recommendations. Following the end of the deliberative sessions, government officials in charge of the meeting approached Eduardo to encourage him to continue participating, even though his policy ideas had limited support; the government official was trying to draw the new leader into the orbit of institutionalized, incremental, and participatory policymaking. Eduardo was at a clear informational and organizational disadvantage. He didn't know how to successfully engage in a complex policymaking process. He also lacked the ties to other CSO leaders that would be vital to securing support for his initiatives. Although he was in a politically weak position, he was of great interest to government officials because he represented a link to a new community and a new organization.

Another leader at the housing conference, Patrocina, was also new to the housing policy arena, and she also lacked basic information about how the policy process worked. Patrocina had the political support of an established CSO as well as the Workers' Party in her community (Morro de Papagaio favela, featured in chapter 7). I crossed paths with her the following week at a municipal housing council meeting. She explained to me that because she was relatively new at organizing and participating, she needed to attend multiple meetings to gain information, knowledge, and skills. Patrocina was trying to master the technical language associated with policymaking while also attempting to organize her neighbors to attend participatory meetings. When I went to her house, which was located up a narrow set of steps inside the heart of the favela, she showed me with immense pride the sewage lines that had been built as a result of the PB Regional process. During the previous year she had increased her civil society participation because she wanted to see if would be possible to tear down her favela's existing houses and build apartment buildings. The policymaking processes created by the Belo Horizonte government (see the discussion of community blueprints in chapter 4) greatly expanded the number of opportunities for her to directly interact with government officials. Nevertheless, she was at a grave information disadvantage because she didn't understand the process. To overcome this informational asymmetry, she was using the participatory institutions to establish policy and political connections among her neighbors, other CSO leaders, and government officials. Patrocina had the support of the Workers' Party, as they were attempting to increase their presence in her community. This support made it easier for her to contact allies among government officials.

Community and Party Activist in PB

Julio, an active community leader in the Alto Vera Cruz favela (see chapter 7), is deeply involved in party politics (elected to the statewide leadership committee of the Communist Party of Brazil, or PC do B), multiple participatory institutions, a community organization, electoral campaigns, and cultural events. He is a full-time community leader, receiving a small stipend from the PC do B in addition to earning money as an event organizer. When Julio was a teenager in the early 1990s, he organized community dances that were well attended by other local teenagers. Leaders from PC do B noticed his organizing skills and encouraged him to attend PB Regional meetings to secure municipal funding for his cultural events. As a result of his success in PB Regional, Julio became very involved in community organizing, serving as an important bridge between an aging activist population and a younger population. Julio's community and political organizing allows him to wear many different hats: party official, communist ideologue, cultural coordinator, aide to a municipal legislator, community leader. He is able to dedicate his time to monitoring government programs, organizing the local housing *núcleo*, and hosting cultural events, among other activities. Julio is a full-time activist able to build a dense local network and a broad network across the municipality.

Participatory Budgeting and Social Services

Augusto, a combative PB delegate of the center-south region, approached me at a downtown bus stop. After catching up on local participatory budgeting news, we discovered that we were both heading to the same meeting at the social service council, which was located on the other side of town. During the course of our conversation, I asked him why he was going to this particular meeting because I had not previously seen him at social service council meetings. Augusto explained that he had just been at the Municipal Urban Affairs Department in an effort to resolve a problem in his community. Given the fact that he was already downtown, he would attend the council meeting to make contact with government officials regarding a different problem.

Augusto didn't say a word during the social service council meeting, which was very different from the role he plays at PB Regional meetings, where he is often the first to raise contentious issues and to complain about government inaction. However, there is a different deliberative dynamic at social service council meetings: educated professionals dominate the discussions; in this participatory space, there is considerable distance between the technical language of the professionals and the knowledge base of community leaders. Augusto is representative of a growing number of community activists who work in participatory venues and government offices to secure social services and public works for their communities; these leaders must learn a broad number of different skills to secure their desired outcomes. In PB meetings, Augusto is more combative and makes appeals to the founding principles of social justice. In social service meetings, his voice is more muted as he tries to master the technical language that will enable him to negotiate with administrators. CSO leaders must develop the ability to engage in different types of political performances as they move across different institutions.

RESEARCH METHODOLOGY

This chapter maps out the different strategies employed by CSO activists as they seek to use the new participatory architecture, work within representative democracy, and engage state bureaucrats. Prior to beginning the research project for this book, I attended dozens of participatory meetings at different points from 1995 to 2000 and in 2003, 2004, and 2006. While conducting research for a previous book on participatory budgeting, I noticed that community leaders were very likely to move across multiple institutional formats, while ordinary citizens were more likely to attend a limited number of meetings. Thus the empirical observation that CSO activists were using multiple venues sparked the attempt to develop a more coherent theoretical explanation that would account for the varied political strategies employed by activists. Interestingly, the political strategies used by CSO activists were more sophisticated than our methodological strategies because they didn't respect the formal lines between democratic institutions, the state, and civil society.

The research project described in this book is the first to systematically analyze the variation in political strategies employed by civil society activists across multiple democratic institutions in a single Brazilian city. The research methodology breaks new grounds, allowing me to contribute to analytical and theoretical debates. To assess the political and policy strategies of CSO activists, my research assistants and I administered a survey to CSO leaders in 2009; the survey is the principal data source for this chapter. The survey analysis is complemented by more than fifty elite interviews in Belo Horizonte I conducted (2001, 2004, 2009, 2010), additional surveys (administered to PB delegates in 2004 and to citizens of two favelas in 2010), and participant observation at a series of participatory meetings). I also attended more than 30 participatory meetings and events in Belo Horizonte between August 2009 and May 2010, which built on more than a dozen previous meetings attended in Belo Horizonte in June 2000 and March and April 2004. The number of meetings attended as well as the decade-long casework provides a rich collection of data that permits me to analyze how CSO leaders and citizens engage in the complex participatory structure. I should note that I have been conducting research on participatory venues in Brazil since 1995, with over 150 meetings attended (in at least ten cities), thus giving me a unique perspective on changes over time and across institutional venues.

Prior to the discussion of the survey results, a few methodological issues need to be addressed. An alternative research strategy might have been to conduct a survey among ordinary citizens attending different participatory meetings, such as participatory budgeting or the policy conferences (see Baiocchi 2005; Goldfrank 2011). The benefit of this "ordinary participant" approach is that we gain important insights into citizens' actions as well as their perceptions of participatory processes. The drawback to this approach is that the public policy management councils do not incorporate ordinary citizens the same way that participatory budgeting does, which means that there is no comparable group of "ordinary participants" across the four participatory venues (participatory budgeting, health care, housing, and social services).

A second strategy that could have been deployed was the use of a "snowball" technique, whereby we would have asked each survey respondent (CSO leader) to identify other organizations they had worked with recently; the subsequent step would have been to interview a leader at the organization that had been identified. This is the strategy employed by Adrian Lavalle and his coauthors in their work on São Paulo (2005). We considered this approach but discarded it for a couple of reasons. First, a snowball technique may keep researchers within a confined policy arena or civil society field because each organization may indicate a similar type of organization. Second, many small CSOs are isolated and don't necessarily have connections to others. Thus, we considered and discarded the technique because we sought to incorporate a diverse set of CSOs. The evidence demonstrates that activists without service contracts are less likely to have contact with other CSOs, thereby suggesting that service-providing CSOs are distinct from most other CSOs.

In order to compare the activities and strategies of participants across different types of participatory venues, we narrowed the field of potential respondents to CSO leaders from four distinct policy arenas. Previous survey and political ethnographic research conducted in Brazil shows that CSO leaders carry out multiple responsibilities and duties for attending public meetings, contacting state officials, and collecting information to inform their organization's members (Alvarez 1990; Baiocchi 2005; Wampler 2007; Mische 2008; Arias 2006). Participatory democracy meetings may mobilize tens of thousands of citizens across a city over the course of a planning cycle, but CSO leaders are now the "carriers" of democracy, since these leaders do the most work to sustain their organization's participation. Drawing from different public policy arenas makes it possible to engage in comparative work within the city of Belo Horizonte. Of course, the activities of ordinary citizens are of vital importance to democracy and the participatory citizenship regime. To address this issue, in chapter 7 I present the results of a second survey administered to a randomly selected group of citizens in two favelas.

The CSO leader survey was administered to three hundred individuals. To create a list of CSO leaders, our research team obtained lists of organizations and individuals from Belo Horizonte's housing, health care, social assistance, and planning (participatory budgeting) departments. Given the varied nature of public policies in each area, we drew from these four areas as a means to capture the diversity of civil society activity. The CSO leader survey included one hundred PB delegates, one hundred social service CSO leaders, fifty leaders from housing committees (*núcleos*) registered with the housing department, and fifty leaders elected to health care councils at the municipal or regional level.[1] Because of the variation in new democratic institutions as well as the configuration of civil society across the four policy fields, we identified potential survey respondents differently:

PB Regional (100 respondents): PB delegates are elected within PB Regional to monitor the implementation of small and midsize projects that were selected within the process. Delegates are locally oriented community members who are trying to find resources to improve their *vilas* and favelas. We obtained a list of 1,200 delegates; 100 respondents were randomly selected from this list to be interviewed.

Housing sector (50 respondents): Housing *núcleo* leaders were included in the survey. A housing *núcleo* must organize one hundred families, all of whom had lived in Belo Horizonte for at least two years, and all of whom must have a monthly household income of less than $300. These *núcleos* are formally registered with the city government and are on a waiting list to secure publicly financed public housing units. When the survey was conducted in 2009, there were 172 housing *núcleos* currently registered with the government, and the 50 leaders interviewed were randomly selected from this list.

Health care (50 respondents): Municipal and regional council members were included in the survey. We drew upon available lists of council members at the municipal and regional levels (nine regions). The council members were elected members representing CSOs (not including unions) within the council. The 50 respondents were randomly selected from a list of 500 individuals.

Social services (100 respondents): Community organizations formally registered with the Municipal Council for Social Services (CMAS) were included in the survey. Registration is required for these associations to receive grants and contracts from the municipalities in order to provide programs and services such as day care centers, outreach programs for the homeless, or elderly care. A hundred associations were included in the survey, from a total of 686 associations registered with the municipal council at the time of the survey.[2]

Three types of CSOs are missing from the survey. First, we were unable to systematically include evangelical associations, which are growing in number. Our research team had numerous meetings with evangelical pastors and leaders, but they were unwilling to provide the necessary contact information. Evangelical leaders are present in the social service sector, but evangelical leaders are underrepresented in the survey because these groups are not currently as active in PB, the housing field, or health care as other associations. Second, small organizations that have limited contact with government officials are not included in the survey. These organizations often have a short shelf life and face significant difficulties maintaining participation. Of the four sectors, small organizations are the most likely to be included in participatory budgeting and are least likely to be included in the social service sector.

Finally, the sample does not include organizations not seeking involvement with the municipal state. These groups, for ideological, political, or religious reasons, may avoid formal ties to state or new democratic institutions, or they may target their organizing at national or international levels. My impression, based on conducting research for nearly two decades in Brazil, is that these groups represent a small minority of CSOs. Most CSOs seek out the state. Wendy Wolford's work on the Landless Movement demonstrates that even this radical social movement is constantly negotiating with state officials over resources and state authority (2010).

The final methodological point is that summary statistics are used in this chapter to illuminate differences across the four policy arenas. Given that this is the first survey focused on how CSO activists are engaged in multiple venues within and parallel to the new institutional architecture, it was not necessary to use regression analysis because it is possible to identify key patterns based on summary statistics. Furthermore, an earlier version of the analysis used social network analysis and sociographs to illuminate the differences. In the case of this survey, the differences between the four areas are sufficiently stark that it wasn't necessary to use sociographs to show the differences.

SURVEY RESULTS: DEMOGRAPHIC PROFILES

The majority of the survey respondents were women, a finding similar to previous surveys of Brazil's participatory institutions and social service organizations (Wampler 2007; Baiocchi 2005; Nylen 2002, 2003; Cunha 2009). Brazilian women have long been central to efforts within civil society to build communities, provide social services, and educate children (Alvarez 1990). But Brazilian men have traditionally dominated formal political institutions, so the fact that women are the majority of participants indicates that these institutions are creating opportunities for women within the formal political sphere. Thus, women are occupying a community-based role they have long held but are now also engaging in public venues whereby they interact with government officials. Poor women are able to exert their voice and vote in public venues in unprecedented ways, indicating that the participatory institutions are both achieving popular participation and setting the conditions to create social justice.

The second observation about the demographic profile is that the majority of the respondents are over age forty-five. This sharply contrasts with the youth-filled mobilizations of the *direitas já* movement in the mid-1980s, the movement to impeach President Collor de Melo in 1991, and the June 2013 protests. There are four reasonable explanations for why the survey respondents and the participatory participants are so much older. First, the current participants began their political activism during the 1970s and 1980s, when they were in their teens or twenties. They were involved in the establishment of local participatory publics, and they sought to deepen the culture of "the right to have rights." Their political trajectory was shaped by direct involvement in public demonstrations, and they were habituated to engage in public, participatory activities.

A second reason is that older citizens are more willing to work within incremental policymaking processes to change their communities. The slow, and often boring, process of attending meetings, gathering information, and holding long discussions with others may be less appealing to individuals in their teens and twenties, who are often raising young children and trying to find decent employment. This coincides with the findings of Verba, Schlozman, and Brady in their work on political participation in the United States (Verba, Schlozman, and Brady 1995).

A third explanation is that the elderly (sixty and older) ride the bus for free in Belo Horizonte, which eliminates the financial cost that individual participants must bear as they travel to meetings. I directly observed how this barrier affects participation: one community leader had to ask for bus fare from another leader in order to attend a meeting. Finally, younger people in Belo Horizonte today have a greater number of educational opportunities; many attend school full-time while working, making it difficult for them to be involved in community improvement programs. Younger and poorer Brazilians are seeking inclusion in the country's recent economic expansion.

Several key differences among the four sectors are worth highlighting. First, respondents from the social service sector have demographic profiles distinct from the other three sectors. Only 14 percent of social service respondents have less than a high school degree, whereas over half of all respondents have less than a high school education. In addition, just 5 percent of social service respondents live in households earning less than $500 per month, whereas roughly a third of all respondents had very low household income. We can infer from this evidence that the social service respondents are employed at organizations that provide services to target poor individuals and families and that between a third and a half of the

Table 6.1 Demographic Profile of Survey Respondents

	Percentage Reporting			
	PB Regional	*Housing*	*Health Care*	*Social Services*
Women	60	73	45	76
Age 45 or older	78	73	82	60
Less than high school degree	58	48	56	14
Monthly household less than $500	27	33	39	**5**
Monthly household income between $ 501 and $1,300	42	53	43	47
N	100	50	50	100

Source: Wampler 2009.

other respondents are representative of Brazil's poor. Demographically, the social service group is not representative of the poor but is comprised of individuals who are working on behalf of clients, who are often very poor citizens.

The demographic characteristics of the PB delegates are similar to what was found in previous survey work (Nylen 2002, 2003; Baiocchi 2005; Wampler 2007; Goldfrank 2011). Importantly, housing and health care respondents share similar characteristics to the PB delegates. This gives us confidence that the CSO leader survey is a representative sample of community leaders working within state-sanctioned participatory institutions in urban Brazil.

In sum, the demographic profile in Table 6.1 demonstrates that the participatory citizenship regime in Belo Horizonte is successfully incorporating individuals long marginalized from formal policymaking spaces. The new moment of state-society relations is providing opportunities for the poor and for women to assume leadership roles in state-sanctioned institutions. This is evidence that the participatory citizenship regime has been activated sufficiently in Belo Horizonte to allow for individuals representing poor communities to be at the heart of political and policy debates. There are no guarantees that social justice will be achieved, but there is a greater likelihood that social justice–related issues will be addressed in public venues. We now see the election of leaders from poor communities who deliberate in public venues over the use of state authority. These leaders no longer have to rely on clientelistic gatekeepers to access public officials and public resources, but are able to represent themselves.

ACTIVATING THE PARTICIPATORY CITIZENSHIP REGIME

CSOs have a variety of strategic choices to make as they seek to first activate and then benefit from the participatory citizenship regime. The decisions made by CSO activists and their members are wrought with difficult trade-offs; CSOs must balance the ability to maintain their independence and the need to cooperate closely with public officials. Some CSOs may choose to align themselves with public officials or political parties. Other CSOs choose to act as service providers, while yet others use contentious politics and demonstrations to advance their interests. In the following sections, I analyze the variation across eight areas: (1) internal organization, (2) role as service providers, (3) social networks in civil society, (4) involvement in participatory institutions, (5) contact with municipal legislature, (6) contact with municipal public officials, (7) campaigns and elections, and (8) use of public demonstrations.

Internal Organization

CSO leaders must work within civil society to develop and maintain a base of supporters, refine their message, and provide ongoing support to community members (McAdam, McCarthy, and Zald 1996). CSOs provide the bonds of solidarity that induce their members to volunteer their time and energy to advance common goals. The evidence shows that nearly all of the survey respondents are active members of their CSO. The first important piece of information is that nearly all respondents report attending meetings of their associations at least monthly. The housing, health care, and PB CSOs typically hold meetings with their association members to exchange information among CSO leaders and members, build morale to maintain support for incremental policymaking processes, and refine

CSOs' objectives. Importantly, this means that the CSOs are an active part of their members' lives. Social service organizations typically hold internal staff meetings on a regular basis and public meetings with their service recipients less frequently. The social service CSOs are thus a step removed from the lives of their constituents and social service recipients.

Most associations use internal elections as a means to select leaders. This confirms one of the claims of the participatory publics argument: that CSOs have incorporated democratic procedures within their internal processes (Avritzer 2002; Wampler and Avritzer 2004). We can infer from this evidence that CSO activists in Belo Horizonte are being habituated to use democratic institutions; the leaders are using these venues to represent their members' interests. In these cases, internal elections promote accountability by providing an institutional check on leaders and allow new leaders to emerge during moments of conflict, stagnation, or internal differences. However, it is also quite common that founding leaders are elected multiple times because they are the "owner" (*dono*) of the CSO. The electoral process can be pro forma, allowing entrenched leaders to maintain their control over the organization by discouraging electoral competition (Cleary 2010). In other cases, an individual is elected CSO president because there is no one else willing to volunteer to serve in an often thankless, time-consuming, tiring job.

Overall, the evidence indicates CSO activists included in the survey are regularly engaging their members and holding elections. The uniformity of the responses is striking because the formal rules associated with the participatory citizenship regime don't affect the internal organization of CSOs. These practices were initiated during the renewal of civil society during the 1980s as a result of the proliferation of participatory politics (Avritzer 2002; Wampler and Avritzer 2004). The evidence suggests that a wide selection of CSOs are now habituated to holding elections and using meetings to communicate with their members on a regular basis. The active use of civil society organizations sustains the participatory citizenship regime because CSO leaders and members have the opportunity to renew their connections, interests, and bonds of solidarity. This ongoing dialogue among CSO leaders and their organizations' members allows both parties to exchange information, which increases the likelihood that the participatory citizenship regime can be used to help citizens secure rights guaranteed by the 1988 constitution. Where civil society is weak or thin, there are few ways for citizens to hold CSO leaders or government officials

Table 6.2 Internal Activities of CSOs

	Percentage Reporting			
	PB Regional	Housing	Health Care	Social Services
Currently involved in CSO	83	92	84	99
Weekly meetings	17	12	22	31
Monthly meetings	61	84	59	57
Internal elections	73	83	73	79

Source: Wampler 2009.

accountable, thus producing a participatory citizenship regime that formally exists on paper but doesn't exist in the day-to-day political activities of civil society. Under this scenario, CSO leaders could become the new clientelistic gatekeepers, or they could be targets for co-optation. However, in the case of Belo Horizonte, the evidence in Table 6.2 points in a new direction: ordinary members of CSOs now have internal mechanisms to hold their leaders accountable.

Role as Service Providers

A significant difference among the four policy sectors is whether a CSO has a formal contract with the government to provide social services. Over three-quarters (77 percent) of the social service associations have government contracts, which starkly contrasts with the other CSOs (just over 10 percent had contracts). With regard to the CSOs from housing, health care, and PB, the evidence suggests that they are seeking to engage the state but that they don't necessarily receive government contracts to support their work. This finding contrasts sharply with the findings of Lavalle, Acharia, and Houtzager, who found that a majority of CSOs had service contracts (2005).

The social service organizations, given their formal role as service providers, are characteristic of Third Sector organizations (Pereira and Grau 1999). The "Third Sector" refers to professional, nongovernment organizations that receive government contracts to provide services to the

Table 6.3 Formal Contracts to Provide Service

	Percentage Reporting			
	PB Regional	Housing	Health Care	Social Services
Formal government contract (*convênio*)	15	12	6	**77**

Source: Wampler 2009.

population. Government officials outsource the provision of basic services to private organizations, many of which are professional CSOs. Service-providing associations are a key part of civil society today because they directly engage with government officials and their clients, but their leadership demographic characteristics and their leaders' behaviors are quite distinct from those of other CSO leaders. Social service CSOs engage the state differently because they have formal contracts with government agencies. This difference suggests that the Third Sector organizations are not representative of the majority of CSOs in Brazil.

There are two important findings. First, it is rare for most CSOs to hold social service contracts. This finding limits the claims that the new forms of state-society engagement under the participatory citizenship regime are based on the outsourcing of contracts to engaged CSOs. To be sure, 15 percent of the PB respondents worked in CSOs that had contracts, but this is a distinct minority. Second, when the municipal state in Belo Horizonte outsources services, it does so to professional, Third Sector CSOs. The demographic data presented in Table 6.1 shows that social service respondents are well educated and from middle- to upper-income households. It is technical, professional CSOs that are receiving state contracts, rather than community-based organizations.

Social Networks in Civil Society

To assess how CSOs are connected to other CSOs, our survey respondents were asked if they could identify two other associations that they had contact with in the previous two months. It was our expectation that respondents would be able to identify two other organizations, given survey and

Table 6.4 CSO Contacts with Other Associations

	Percentage Reporting			
	PB Regional	*Housing*	*Health Care*	*Social Services*
Unable to identify any CSOs	40	33	60	19
Able to identify 1 other CSO	26	23	19	31
Able to identify 2 other CSOs	34	44	21	50

Source: Wampler 2009.

ethnographic data that demonstrates extensive, constant communication among civil society activists in participatory budgeting, councils, and policy conferences (Lavalle, Acharia, and Houtzager 2005).

The evidence shows that 35 percent of all survey respondents were *unable* to identify any other associations with whom they had contact in the previous two months. Health care associations are the most isolated, since 60 percent of the respondents were unable to identify other organizations they had contacted in the previous two months. Among the PB respondents, 40 percent were unable to identify other CSOs. Health care and PB respondents are thus linked to participatory governance institutions, but they have weak ties to other CSOs. This limits their ability to form the necessary alliances (bonds of solidarity) that might allow them to pressure government officials to be more responsive to their demands.

At the other extreme, 50 percent of social service respondents were able to identify two other associations with whom they had contact in the previous two months. These CSOs are involved in much denser networks within civil society, allowing them to exchange information with others and to maintain pressure on government officials. Finally, 44 percent of the housing respondents had ties to at least two other CSOs. The housing movements in Belo Horizonte are extremely active in civil society because it is vital for them to build the necessary political support to pressure government officials to allocate funds to housing projects.

In sum, the policy arena has a large effect on the type of strategies CSOs employ to connect to other organizations. Social service and housing respondents belong to organizations that are required to formally register with the state, which suggests that the "registering" process may lead to

186 Activating Democracy in Brazil

greater ongoing contact with other CSOs. These organizations are drawn into a series of meetings led by government officials, which increases their contact with other CSOs. Conversely, the participatory budgeting and health care respondents are the most isolated, thus making it difficult for them to gather information and create new political alliances. Most of these activists are politically engaged at the local level (e.g., favela, local community association), which means that they face a more difficult time developing ties to other organizations. But one-third of PB delegates did have contact with at least two other CSOs, thus indicating that they are attempting to build networks and bonds across policy arenas. Finally, this evidence confirms the usefulness of the selection criteria and methodology used to design and administer the survey. Had we utilized a snowball technique or surveyed leaders from just one policy field, we would not have captured the heterogeneity of civil society evident in this survey.

Involvement in Participatory Institutions

There was wide variation across the four public policy sectors regarding how CSO leaders would work within the participatory democracy institutions. Survey respondents were given a selection of three types of participatory institutions and asked about their participating in each one (participatory budgeting, municipal-wide council, regional council).

Two-thirds of social service organizations indicated no involvement in participatory institutions. This is additional evidence that these are professional associations, related to service delivery, rather than CSOs seeking

Table 6.5 Engaging in Participatory Democracy Venues

	Percentage Reporting			
	PB Regional	Housing	Health Care	Social Services
No participatory spaces	10	29	8	67
1 participatory space	61	35	37	20
2 participatory spaces	29	48	43	11

Source: Wampler 2009.

to participate in the democratic process. These organizations engage the local state quite differently from other CSOs because they don't need to express voice and vote via participatory institutions. Such organizations do not need to engage in participatory governance processes because their access to government officials occurs through the formal contract process used to distribute resources (recall that 77 percent have a formal contract with the state). In addition, as was shown in chapter 4, the primary responsibility of the social service council is legalistic: council members are responsible for registering CSOs and then evaluating the work of the service providers. As a result of this legal focus, the meetings are boring, and little policy debate occurs. CSOs that don't have a contract with the municipal government have a low incentive to attend, and those who do attend are seeking to protect their status.

Second, most PB delegates are primarily engaged in PB Regional. It appears that CSO members (not necessarily leaders) are elected as PB delegates within PB Regional, whereby they engage other CSO members, CSO leaders, and government officials over the distribution of small infrastructure projects within the PB process. The evidence suggests that PB Regional is not successfully encouraging larger numbers of these ordinary CSO members to move beyond PB Regional and work in other participatory governance spaces. Thus, most PB delegates now appear to be official representatives of their community organizations in PB Regional, but they are not full-time activists.

A subset of PB delegates—29 percent of the PB respondents—were engaged in multiple venues. The most active leaders have ties to government officials, who help to link these individuals to other municipal departments. These leaders meet the profile of the full-time, fully engaged CSO activist who uses PB as one among many venues. Most PB delegates are not involved in multiple venues because government officials come to PB Regional, which means PB delegates don't have to search them out. Therefore, PB Regional funnels most leaders into one participatory venue, rather than inducing them to be politically engaged across the municipality.

The final observation is that half of housing and health care respondents are engaged in two or more participatory venues. Housing and health care activists are engaged in multiple participatory venues because of institutional design, the complexity of the public policy arena, and their history of organizing. There are participatory venues at municipal, regional, and local levels in the health care and housing sectors. There are vertical links among the participatory institutions in each sector and horizontal ties between these municipal-level participatory venues and other participatory venues. The multiple access points used by housing and health respondents result from the complexity of the policy arenas. CSO leaders need to gather information and participate in several policymaking venues. They work at local, regional, and municipal-wide levels. These activists cannot only be in one venue because authority and resources cut across multiple venues. In health care, for example, there is overlapping membership and representation with the social service council and the child and adolescent council.

A final point is that the social service council uses a set of rules similar to the one used in the health care sector to link citizens and CSOs into a vertically intertwined system. However, the social service sector is unable to generate high levels of participation because of the limited number of mass-based social movements. Professional CSOs are actively involved in participatory governance venues as a means to ensure the CSOs are properly registered. This means that CSO activists who attend these meetings focus on making sure the rules are followed rather than attempting to build new networks. In this way professional, educated sectors ensure that the participatory venues are technical and largely devoid of political content. Francesca Polletta, in an article entitled "How Participatory Democracy Became White," found a similar phenomenon in the United States (Polletta 2005). The creation of participatory venues during President Johnson's Great Society initiative encouraged the participation of well-educated whites and discouraged the participation of low-income African Americans. This comparison suggests that the Brazilian council system will not always remain in the political hands of the poor. When middle-class, business, and professional groups believe that these organizations will help them to pursue their interests, they will begin to seek election to the councils.

In sum, half of housing and health care CSO activists are engaging in more than two participatory institutions. This is clear evidence that the participatory citizenship regime is producing political strategies that induce CSO leaders from these sectors to be involved in multiple formal state venues. CSO leaders now directly engage public officials, bypassing clientelistic gatekeepers, because they are aware of different venues in which they can have their voice heard. Thus, the participatory citizenship regime helps CSOs overcome the collective action problem in health care, housing, and, to a lesser extent, PB by channeling citizen participation in formal institutional bodies.

Contact with Municipal Legislature

The survey respondents reported very different activities vis-à-vis the municipal legislature. Sixty percent of PB delegates and health care activists report having no contact with municipal legislators during the two previous months. PB Regional participants are engaged primarily with PB Regional and don't need to deal with multiple institutional formats. The health care policy arena is dominated by policy experts within the mayoral administration; there is little input from legislators. Health care activists respond by focusing their attention on the municipal executive rather than the legislative branch.

In the housing field, activists seek multiple channels of access to government officials. The municipality doesn't have a set level of resources allocated to housing projects, which means that CSOs and legislators must build the necessary political momentum to induce the mayor's office to seek funding from the federal government or national development banks. Housing members contact the legislators to build political pressure and support for increased spending.

Social services respondents also had a significant number of contacts with municipal legislators. These organizations wish to engage policymakers (city council members and policy experts) who influence broader lines of decision making. Second, many social service respondents are educated professionals who already have preexisting social and professional networks with legislators and legislative aides. But perhaps most importantly, one key informal responsibility of municipal legislators is to direct money

Table 6.6 Contact with Municipal Legislature

	Percentage Reporting			
	PB Regional	*Housing*	*Health Care*	*Social Services*
0 legislature contacts	60	39	61	38
1 legislature contact	32	35	33	38
2 legislature contacts	8	25	6	23

Source: Wampler 2009.

to specific service providers in their bailiwicks (see the section "Executive-Legislative Relations" in chapter 3). Thus, social service CSOs must maintain good relations with legislators in the hopes of securing additional contracts.

In sum, the survey confirms that civil society leaders are involved in multiple venues. With regard to the municipal legislature, CSO leaders are moving beyond participatory venues to develop ties and connections with a second branch of government. (Recall that the participatory venues are housed in the executive branch, thus weakening the potential for extending horizontal accountability.) Many CSOs recognize the importance of representing their interests in one of representative democracy's main institutional bodies. In the housing and social service fields, over half the respondents were engaged in the legislative branch and roughly 40 percent in participatory budgeting and health care. By engaging in the legislative branch, these leaders expand their access to public officials.

Contact with Municipal Public Officials

Community leaders are in constant contact with government officials as part of their strategy to secure access to different parts of the state apparatus. Survey questions tapped into CSO leaders' ties to the mayor's office, political appointees, policy experts, and street-level bureaucrats. In my previous book, I analyzed participatory budgeting programs in eight Brazilian cities, and I noted the development of ongoing connections between CSO leaders and public officials (Wampler 2007). My initial analysis of these extra-institutional interactions argued that they were subverting the rules of the democratic processes embedded in participatory budgeting by bypassing the newly established rules. For example, in a 2004 meeting I attended in Porto Alegre, I observed that prior to and after the meeting, community leaders were speaking with elected officials and bureaucrats about specific problems in their communities—public security, basic road maintenance, and so forth. My impression was that these contacts were not in the "spirit" of participatory budgeting and that they subverted the effort to create structured, institutionalized policymaking processes.

Over time I realized that I was missing something of fundamental importance: community leaders were attempting to build new networks and ties. Recall the observation that representative democracy and the modern state have a middle- and upper-class bias because of the greater difficulties

Table 6.7 Contact with Mayoral Administration Officials

	Percentage Reporting			
	PB Regional	*Housing*	*Health Care*	*Social Services*
0 direct contacts with municipal officials	26	8	16	13
1 direct contact with municipal officials	25	22	30	27
2 direct contacts with municipal officials	33	43	40	47
3–4 direct contacts with municipal officials	15	27	16	11

Source: Wampler 2009.

experienced by poor and low-income citizens trying to organize themselves and build ties to government decision makers. The new participatory governance system provides venues to build the necessary ties and networks (Schattschneider 1960). To engage in the policymaking process and to secure basic constituency service rather than rely on clientelistic exchanges, community leaders need to develop a broader base of connections to civil servants and elected officials.

Table 6.7 shows the number of contacts that the survey respondents report having in four different departments in the two months prior to the survey. There are not significant differences in the reported activities. PB respondents had the least amount of contact, suggesting that PB Regional is producing a focused, more passive participation than the housing or health care fields. Since 77 percent of the social service CSOs have formal contracts with the government, their contacts are likely related to their official duties.

The evidence demonstrates that CSO leaders are actively engaging with a wide range of policy actors within the municipal administration. The institutional architecture permits CSO activists to creatively engage public officials, thus allowing them to overcome their lack of ties to public officials.

Campaigns and Elections

Community groups and associations are essential parts of biannual campaigns and elections. In Brazil, municipal elections are held every four years (2004, 2008, 2012), and there may also be elections of federal senators in those same years. Presidential, gubernatorial, state legislature, and most federal legislature elections are held in the intervening year, such as 2002, 2006, and 2010. Given the importance of local politics to municipal, state, and national politics, we would expect community leaders to be actively involved in campaigns and elections. Barry Ames, for example, shows that federal legislators have their own "bailiwicks," whereby a majority of their vote comes from a specific area (Ames 1994, 1995a, and 1995b).

The first important finding is that 58 percent of housing respondents and 45 percent of PB respondents indicate they worked for a political party during the 2008 mayoral elections. This contrasts sharply with social services respondents (14 percent), thereby providing additional evidence that social service associations are professional, service-delivery organizations. The health care respondents are less politically involved than the PB and housing respondents, indicating that they focus on policy issues rather than attempting to directly influence electoral outcomes. Importantly, the housing and participatory budgeting respondents work in policy arenas in which the municipal government has greater autonomy regarding how they will spend their resources. Health care respondents know that municipal legislators are not involved in policymaking (see chapter 3) and that the municipal government is required by federal law to spend 25 percent of its total budget on health care. As a result, health care activists don't need to spend as much of their time influencing campaign outcomes in their arena. Their time is spent on oversight of ongoing policy activities. Conversely, participatory budgeting and housing resources are discretionary spending whereby the municipal executive is responsible for deciding the level of resources to be spent. There are much stronger incentives for these leaders to be involved in electoral processes—more to lose and more to gain.

Interestingly, PB respondents—those leaders and associations focusing on community-oriented issues—had the highest number of leaders who indicated that they held paid campaign positions. Paid positions are obviously a step up, in terms of prestige and influence, in a campaign. Politicians are aware that roughly forty thousand people participated in

Table 6.8 Campaign Activities

	Percentage Reporting			
	PB Regional	Housing	Health Care	Social Services
Work for a political party	45	58	25	14
Paid work for party/candidate	18	12	10	5
Election Day work	14	35	8	5
Attended campaign rally in 2008	29	57	33	11
Try to convince association members to support specific candidate	48	61	41	28
Try to convince neighbors to support specific candidate	55	65	51	31

Source: Wampler 2009.

PB Regional in 2007 (as well as thousands of others who attended community meetings on PB-related issues but didn't attend formal PB meetings). It is thus advantageous for candidates running for office to have contact with leaders active in PB Regional because these community leaders have active membership bases. PB delegates are involved in day-to-day organizing of community activities, giving them an ideal position to understand the demands of their neighbors.

In Table 6.8, the final two rows tap into the vital role of social networks in electoral campaigns. The work of Huckfeldt and Sprague (1995) in the United States as well as that of Baker, Ames, and Renno 2006 in Brazil demonstrate that individuals often make voting decisions based on their social networks. The data here thus supports these previous findings. Community leaders are now positioning themselves as new intermediaries between the state and society as they seek to influence their constituents and neighbors during campaigns and elections. Nearly two-thirds of housing members, half of the PB delegates, and 41 percent of health care members asserted that they attempt to influence members of their organizations to vote for a specific candidate. Building on the evidence of Baker, Ames, and Renno, this finding suggests that CSO leaders occupy a key place in poor communities. Again, the social service sector is significantly different, since only 28 percent attempt to influence members of their association. Overall this is compelling evidence that CSOs act as political intermediaries between elected officials and ordinary citizens.

The percentage of respondents who assert that they attempt to convince their neighbors to vote for a specific candidate increases slightly in each of the four policy arenas. Community leaders, beyond trying to convince their association members, are reaching out to their neighbors to inform them about which political candidates they support. Building on Huckfeldt and Sprague's seminal work on community social networks, we find that community leaders have higher levels of knowledge about and interest in politics, so they help to inform their less-informed neighbors. This finding provides additional evidence that CSO leaders play a vital role in linking low-income communities to the broader political system. Recall the demographic composition of the CSO: most of the PB Regional, housing, and health care respondents are low income and from the communities they seek to represent.

In sum, by focusing on campaign and elections, we can assert that PB Regional and housing association leaders are involved in a greater number of overtly political venues than are social service and health care leaders. A key reason is that PB and housing leaders depend on discretionary state spending; they need to be politically involved to maintain pressure on government officials. Second, PB Region and housing leaders need to be able to mobilize and connect with extensive numbers of local members. If they don't have members, then they will be unable to work within their respective participatory formats to secure resources or the attention of government officials. Third, service-oriented associations do not find it necessary to engage in campaigns and elections to be in the good graces of the local government. They don't need to be involved in campaigns and elections because their future funding depends to a greater degree on their professional qualifications and networks. Finally, leaders of PB Regional, housing, and health care associations are extensively involved in discussions through which they help to convince members of their association as well as their neighbors to vote for a specific candidate. Surprisingly, survey respondents asserted that they are more likely to campaign among neighbors rather than among their association's members. This is likely due to general agreement among members regarding voter choice; it is the community leaders' neighbors who can be influenced to vote for a candidate supported by the CSO leader.

Use of Public Demonstrations

A political tactic often used by CSOs is contentious politics, which generally involves public demonstrations to draw attention to a specific issue or demand. Politically marginalized communities have long used public demonstrations in order to advance their political claims (Tarrow 1998). "Collective action becomes contentious when it is used by people *who lack regular access to institutions,* who act in the name of new or unaccepted claims, and who behave in ways that fundamentally challenge others or authorities" (Tarrow 1998, 3; emphasis added). Although evidence shows that citizens and CSO leaders now have regular access to state institutions, some CSOs continue to use demonstrations and contentious politics on a regular basis.

The survey results also demonstrate significant variation in how CSOs use public demonstrations across the four sectors. Roughly 50 percent of the housing and health care sectors respondents participated in a public demonstration in the two months prior to the survey. These respondents were willing to move beyond formal institutional venues and use public demonstrations in an attempt to pressure government officials. Only a third of the PB Regional respondents and less than a quarter of the social services respondents used demonstrations. PB Regional respondents employ public demonstrations at a lower rate because they focus on issues

Table 6.9 Demonstrations and Contentious Politics

	Percentage Reporting			
	PB Regional	*Housing*	*Health Care*	*Social Services*
Participate in demonstrations	32	51	45	23

Source: Wampler 2009.

specific to their neighborhoods and because they depend on government officials spending discretionary funding on their projects. Given that 77 percent of the social service associations have contracts with the government, it should come as little surprise that they are less willing to use extra-institutional demonstrations to press their claims. The contracts are short-term and often rewarded based on a combination of objective and subjective criteria by government officials, creating the need for service-providing organizations to maintain positive relationships with government officials. In addition, social service respondents are generally well-educated members of the middle class who are working on behalf of others rather than working on public policies that directly affect their access to public policies.

EXPLAINING VARIATION ACROSS FOUR POLICY ARENAS

Third Sector: Social Service Delivery Organizations

The CSOs that dominate the social service policy arena are professional associations most accurately described as "Third Sector" organizations. The social service civil society field is most prominently defined by CSOs' formal government contracts to provide social services (77 percent) and their policy connections to policy experts and bureaucrats. In this policy arena, CSOs have limited engagement in participatory institutions, in electoral campaigns, and in public demonstrations, and their CSO leaders have much higher levels of education and income than CSO leaders from the other fields. The instrumental, or short-term strategic decision making of CSOs, is driven by a need to secure government contracts.

Third Sector CSOs' alliance with the state is based on mutual needs: government officials outsource service delivery to professional organizations as a means of reducing the cost of providing social services, and the CSOs rely on government funding to support their organization. The roots of this outsourcing extend back to the development of the social service policy arena that began under President Vargas in the 1930s. As a consequence, there has been limited state development, which means that it is not possible to "mobilize the state" because the state is an empty shell (Abers and Keck 2009).

In turn, this leads to a second problem: service contracts are short-term and are awarded based on a combination of professional competence and government officials' discretion. CSOs seeking state contracts must demonstrate that they are professionally competent. But these CSOs are also politically vulnerable because of the discretionary authority of the municipal government, which allocates the awards. This diminishes the likelihood that they would engage in overt political actions against the incumbent government (i.e., demonstrations). These Third Sector organizations therefore seek to meet professional qualifications and benchmarks to ensure they continue to receive government funding while simultaneously not antagonizing government officials. Relatedly, these professional CSOs cannot be strongly partisan because a change in control of the municipal government could cause their contracts to be canceled.

Participatory Citizenship Regime

In this policy arena, CSOs are led by professional, middle-class activists who attempt to secure government contracts in order to provide social services to the poor. These Third Sector activists have the lowest level of participation in the new participatory venues. When the Third Sector CSOs participate, their involvement is along technical and legalistic lines, rather than expanding public deliberation. Technical and legal issues dominate debates within the council, proving to be a major barrier for individuals who don't have technical or professional skills in the area. Third Sector CSO leaders are not actively involved in political campaigns and elections to represent the interests of their organizations' members. Rather, they rely on dense professional and policy networks that exist independently of the representative and participatory democracy. The professional CSOs have important policy, educational, and social ties that do not require them to use the new institutions to pursue their goals.

In sum, the establishment of new participatory institutions has not induced many of these types of CSOs to be actively involved in participatory governance. These Third Sector leaders have multiple contacts with other CSOs, indicating a dense network of civil society allies. They have extensive contacts with the social service department but limited contact with participatory institutions, thus indicating professional relationships. Participatory institutions are not producing bonds of solidarity among citizens but are reinforcing already dense networks based on professional ties that are independent of participatory institutions. These CSO leaders provide much needed social services; they act on behalf of their clients, but they do not actively mobilize their clients to be directly engaged in the new institutional venues. The clients themselves have little to no voice in the

policy arena, which is partly due to the technical nature of the policy deliberations but also due to limited civil society mobilization. In this case,
expert-based organizations represent the interests of the poor inside state
institutions.

Of the four public policy arenas, the participatory citizenship regime
has been most weakly activated in the social service arena. The limited
state formation resulted in few public bureaucrats or policy experts working within the state; as such there is no state to mobilize (Abers and Keck
2009). Relatedly, the lack of unions in this arena, because of limited state
formation, reduces the breadth of the interests represented within civil society. The longterm development of civil society has centered on the development of professional CSOs, and there has been limited involvement
of citizens who might also be recipients of these services. This indicates the
importance of the direct involvement of ordinary citizens in order to generate a vibrant debate on social justice and popular participation. In addition, during the ten months I attended the social service council meetings,
there was limited support from government officials for citizens' rights to
express voice and vote. Rather, the principal participatory policymaking
venue was a legalistic, technical body that limited deliberation and restricted representation to professional organizations.

In sum, the participatory citizenship regime related to social service
policy was weakly activated through the interlocking institutions in which
there was a deliberate effort to link government agencies and professional
CSOs. But popular participation is not encouraged by the rules, by the
government, or by the professional NGOs that dominate the process. Social justice and the extension of social rights are a weak part of the deliberative process because they are not rooted in the everyday, lived experiences of CSOs leaders who are involved in the participatory institutions.

Participatory Budgeting: My Neighborhood, My PB

The PB Regional process in Belo Horizonte is now a routinized part of the
policymaking process. A biannual participatory process provides government officials and citizens with different moments in which citizens engage in substantive deliberation, political theater, and policy selection. As
chapter 4 demonstrates, a complex set of rules now promotes social justice, interlocking institutions, and popular participation. The institutionalization of PB Regional channels participation and representation into a

single process. In sharp contrast to the Third Sector social service CSOs, only 15 percent of the PB delegates included in our survey work with a CSO that has an active government contract to provide social services. Thus we can infer that weekly or biweekly meetings were not focused on service delivery but helped to generate the bonds of solidarity so vital to helping CSOs maintain their collective action. Furthermore, these CSOs have strong connections to other CSOs, confirming that the PB rules are successfully inducing PB delegates to reach out to other organizations.

Of all PB respondents 61 percent attended only PB meetings, 10 percent used no participatory venues (including PB), and 29 percent used two or more. Belo Horizonte's PB Regional process is now institutionalized as part of a biannual participatory process. PB delegates do not have to seek out other participatory or political venues to press their claims because government officials organize the process. This is a form of channeled participation in which community leaders are participating in PB Regional, but there is little evidence that their participation extends beyond this venue. As a result, political and policy focus is narrow: my neighborhood, my PB. Perhaps the most significant characteristic of the PB sector is that these organizations' principal access point to the local state is through PB Regional.

These CSO leaders were involved in community organizing and electoral politics—attending campaign rallies and talking to their neighbors and their followers about specific candidates. PB delegates were actively engaged in the electoral process: 29 percent attended a campaign rally, and 48 percent spoke with their association's members regarding specific candidates, which provides crucial evidence for why government officials are willing to dedicate considerable time and energy to these processes. The data presented in chapter 4 demonstrates that Belo Horizonte's PB Regional program successfully allocated high levels of resources in low-income communities using social justice–based criteria. The survey data that shows that nearly half of the PB delegates spoke to their members illuminates why it is politically advantageous for government officials to attend to the political and policy needs of CSO leaders.

The CSO leaders involved in PB Regional are best categorized as neighborhood organizers; they are attempting to improve the day-to-day lives of their community members. These CSO leaders likely know many community members, and that is why these leaders are at the center of campaigns and elections. Politicians seek out these CSO leaders because of their understanding of their communities' needs, demands, and attitudes. Such community leaders participate locally as they seek to secure specific public policy goods for their communities. Half the PB delegates are willing to advocate on behalf of specific candidates, which is an excellent indicator regarding why government officials might find it so important to invest in participatory governance programs that allow citizens to have specific and binding decisions on policy outcomes.

Participatory Citizenship Regime

The most significant finding is that participatory budgeting is not serving as a springboard that encourages PB delegates to be involved politically in other policy and political venues. Nearly two-thirds of the survey respondents worked within PB to solve community problems. These CSO leaders worked within PB Regional to develop contacts and secure resources that are of concern to their local neighborhoods. Thus, PB Regional plays a much weaker role as a school of democracy than was expected or has been found elsewhere (Baiocchi 2005; Avritzer 2009). The finding confirms a criticism of PB programs: that they induce activists and citizens to narrow their political attention to their local community rather than inducing them to organize more broadly.

And yet a significant minority of respondents (29 percent) were moving beyond PB Regional to engage in other types of participatory venues. This allowed them to represent the interests of their CSOs and community members in multiple formats, indicating that new forms of participation and representation were being used by a third of the most active leaders; it is these leaders who used participatory budgeting as a springboard to a greater range of public engagement. These leaders used PB Regional as one political venue among many; they linked institutions by carrying information between different venues, and they were also intermediaries among different political groups.

Other data complement this point. My interviews with CSO leaders as well as participant observation in PB Regional showed that an active minority of leaders participated in multiple venues and were generally the individuals who chose to speak during public deliberations. These active leaders thus represented community members in participatory budgeting, but they were also the representatives of PB delegates in other institutional venues. Thus, many of the elected PB delegates rely on the active engagement of a smaller number of dedicated leaders to forge bonds with other

CSOs, gather information, and establish close connections with government officials.

In sum, the institutional architecture provided by the participatory citizenship regime has transformed how CSO leaders engage the state and civil society. PB Regional provides an opportunity for constant contact between PB delegates and state officials. These CSO leaders remain active in civil society, but they have formal venues that expand their ability to engage in public deliberation, participation, and representation. A mutually reinforcing set of incentives induces PB delegates to be involved in both PB Regional and civil society: CSO leaders use the specific benefits associated with PB Regional to reinforce the bonds of solidarity that are nurtured in civil society. PB Regional rules encourage low-income CSOs and citizens to participate in the state-sanctioned body because it offers a preferential bias for the poor. The most active participants now use PB Regional as one venue among many in which they seek to influence political and policy outcomes. These representatives now work within councils and policy conferences in the hopes of inducing changes in public policies to benefit their communities.

Council Democracy: Health Care

Social movements working in the health care policy arena led the struggle to establish public policy management councils (*conselhos*) and expand social rights, most notably the right to universal health care provided by the state (Jacobi 1989). Prior to the 1988 constitution, the Brazilian state provided minimal resources to meet the health care needs of the poor majority. The constitution produced two significant changes in the health care policy field. First, universal access to health care became an established social right in the constitution. Second, the government decentralized the provision of health care; municipalities are now in charge of providing health care services. Decentralization of authority and resources combined with citizens' universal right to health care means that collective and individual demands largely focus on the municipal government.

The municipal government is responsible for providing health care via SUS (Sistema Unica de Saúde), so it is no surprise that CSO leaders seek out policy and political venues whereby they can interact with government officials. The key for CSO leaders is to get to work closely with government officials on broader issues, such as expanding and improving care, while also working to secure the personal connections that would allow these activists to gain access to scarce public resources. For example, public deliberations involving council members and government officials address public health issues, but a private conservation after the meeting may involve the admission of a specific patient. Government officials involved in the delivery of the public health system thus have significant control over broader policy as well as very specific resource allocation.

Demonstrations and the use of contentious politics are at the core of the activity in this policy arena. This is due, in large part, to a unionized labor force that regularly organizes demonstrations; CSO leaders attend labor demonstrations in support of the unionized workers' demands. This is also due to the "repertoires of action" developed within the health care field (Tarrow 1998). During the 1980s and early 1990s, the health care social movement field was a core part of the "insurgent citizenship" whereby individuals engaged in direct action against the state in order to secure their rights (see chapter 2 and Holston 2008).

Federal transfers make up the bulk of the resources for health care spending. Thus CSO leaders know that holding public demonstrations to publicly pressure government officials is a politically viable option because funding will not be cut. This is in sharp contrast to PB, housing, or the social service policy arenas, where discretionary funding makes up the majority of municipal spending; in these areas, the government can simply choose not to fund programs in these areas.

Health care CSO respondents represent themselves and their communities in the political and policymaking debates as clients (*usuários*) of the public health care system (SUS). They are not professional, skill-based organizations (only three of fifty have contracts). When the municipal health department outsources, it contracts with professional organizations (such as medical clinics and hospitals), not user-based social movements. Professional organizations are not involved in the participatory venues in part because there are few formal seats allocated to service providers. In the health care council meetings I attended, one individual representing the interests of service providers always attended, but I never heard him speak during the meetings. (This was also my experience in São Paulo during the 1990s.) The consequence is that an important actor in the health care policy debates is not present. Union members and civil society activists dominate the participatory process rather than producing a broader dialogue across a diverse selection of interested groups.

The health care council system is markedly different from the social service council in its lack of professional, technically oriented CSOs. In the social service policy arena, professional CSOs participated in the social service sector to protect their short-term government contracts. This was compounded by the absence of a broad-based movement of citizens demanding social services. The health care field has a long history of mobilization by social movements and community-based organizations around health care issues. In addition, private companies that receive government contracts to provide health service do not have to work within the health council to defend their rights. The health care council systems provide much greater political representation to citizens and union officials, thus limiting the direct participation of private contractors.

Participatory Citizenship Regime

Neighborhood leaders and social movement activists are the principal activists working within the participatory institutions (councils and conferences) in the health care policy arena. As demonstrated in chapter 5, the council system produced an institutionalized participatory governance architecture (municipal, regional, and local councils, as well as councils in each of the 141 health care clinics) that allowed people to directly participate in state-sponsored participatory venues. There is now a policymaking system based on the trifecta of popular participation, interlocking institutions, and social justice.

Community activists engage with the new participatory architecture (council system) by entering at the local level and then moving to regional and municipal councils. The council election system is based on the vertical filtering of CSO leaders from the local to the municipal. The proliferation of local health care facilities and programs such as the Family Health Program (Programa Saúde Familiar) induces activists to work locally. The integrated council motivates activists to work closely with government officials in order to solve policy issues.

There are several lessons to be learned from the patterns of network activities in the health sector. First, CSO leaders participate in a broad number of venues. Participation is not tied to any single institution, but CSO leaders enter the state at multiple points, including council meetings, policy conferences, and through direct contact and conversations with public officials. These venues allow for diverse types of deliberation—from raising contentious issues to working on the intricacies of policy design. CSO leaders work closely with government officials at local, regional, and municipal levels in hopes of improving policy outputs. Thus, the institutional architecture has led to the proliferation of access points, which now induces health care activists to be involved in multiple venues.

Beyond formal participatory venues, health care CSO leaders also participate in public demonstrations and contentious deliberations. Direct contestation enables them to expand the public dialogue; CSO leaders can repeatedly force contentious issues on the agenda. Health care social movements led repeated public demonstrations during the time I was living in Belo Horizonte (2009–2010). These protests were held in front of city hall or the building that housed the municipal heath department. The presence of social movement leaders meant that political tools of public contestation were available to them. And yet this contestation is carefully managed because it is also vital for CSOs to maintain close connections with public officials. CSO leaders use their direct connection with public officials to discuss specific public goods provisions in their communities (e.g., shortage of nurses). These connections also enable CSO leaders to discuss specific, often individual-level problems (e.g., admitting a patient to the hospital, arranging for transportation of an elderly patient to the hospital).

As a result of the new institutional architecture, CSOs activists represent their followers in multiple venues, thereby expanding the frequency and location that ordinary citizens' political issues are expressed in the political system. Interested citizens—generally CSO leaders—are elected at the local level to represent the interests of their CSOs or, more broadly, of their neighbors. These activists engage in multiple formats so as to establish connections and gain information allowing them to be better representatives. The health care system thus permits citizens and CSOs to gather information to signal their preferences to government officials, but many CSOs lack the technical knowledge central to this policy arena, limiting their impact on public policy.

Housing: Full Engagement Across Multiple Arenas

Of the four policy arenas, the housing movement in Belo Horizonte is the most active within civil society and across a broad range of local state institutions. As explained in chapter 5, the housing movement was mobilized in the 1980s, prior to the formal establishment of the participatory citizenship regime. CSO activists' political activities are in alignment with

Holston's account of insurgent housing movements in São Paulo (Holston 2008). Within Belo Horizonte's housing movement are two distinct patterns of mobilization. One group of activists participates in demonstrations, attends public hearings at the municipal legislature, and works in electoral campaigns. This is the "contentious politics and elections" track. A second group of activists is involved in participatory venues, attends CSO meetings, and has frequent contact with the housing department; this is best labeled the "participatory democracy" track.

The diversity of participatory repertoires is due to a history of social mobilization, the extensive demand for housing, and a wide-open institutional decision-making apparatus. First, during the 1980s and early 1990s, social movements in the housing field were extremely active, engaging in multiple land occupations across the city. These contentious land occupations (also referred to as "illegal invasions" by property owners) forged a strong identity among activists working in the housing field. Thus social movement activity prior to the establishment of the 1988 constitution had a significant impact on the ability of CSO leaders to sustain their mobilization during the 2000s. This finding, in conjunction with the finding from the social service field, supports the broader argument that the long-term development of civil society within a policy sector has a strong effect on how new participatory institutions will be used. This confirms a long line of work on participatory institutions that identifies the configuration of civil society as being a vital component of how these new democratic institutions will function (Heller 2000; Avritzer 2002; Baiocchi 2005; Wampler 2007; Baiocchi, Heller, Silva 2011).

Second, movement leaders work within multiple municipal agencies, two different participatory spaces, and the municipal legislature to build support, and federal development agencies such as BNDES and the Caixa Economica as they pursue their policy agenda. The policy and political complexity and broad numbers of actors mean CSO leaders have to position themselves within multiple venues. The density of their political activities is a response to the configuration of the state, particularly the internal distribution of resources and authority. There are more public agencies involved in health care than in the other three areas, which leads CSOs to actively engage public officials at multiple points.

Third, internal rules used to distribute housing units built by the city government continue to encourage civil society participation. The housing *núcleos*, around which the housing movements organize, are based on rules created by the municipal government and two participatory governance institutions (housing council and PB Housing). These rules encourage maintaining bonds of solidarity among citizens. Finally, this political struggle is both collective and individual. Groups must organize collectively for years, but the public works goods are provided to specific individuals.

It is revealing that only a small minority of the CSOs surveyed held active government contracts. These CSOs do not rely on the state to support their organizations. The two public policy arenas (housing and health care) in which CSO leaders are the least likely to have social service contracts are policy arenas in which CSO leaders are the most likely to use demonstrations. We can infer from this data that the presence of active government contracts reduces the scope of activities employed by activists.

Participatory Citizenship Regime

The housing public policy arena is an appropriate bookend to the social service policy arena. Housing leaders are active participants in multiple spaces. They are the most active in exercising political rights formally established in the 1988 constitution. This robust and dynamic civil society field has closely partnered with government officials to promote policy outcomes. The demonopolization of the state and the absence of specific budgetary resources dedicated to housing induce CSOs leaders to be active across the state. Of course, this places a major burden on the housing movements because they juggle multiple new roles: as social movements, policymakers, and public interest groups. Not all groups have the skills and knowledge to carry out this complex set of tasks.

Second, CSO leaders deliberate in multiple venues—local CSO meetings, participatory venues, and public demonstrations. In the meetings and sessions I attended, there were constant references to social justice and to the right to decent housing. These broader themes were developed within the national housing reform movement of the 1980s as well as within the Workers' Party government during the 1993–2000 period. These deliberative venues were used to continually draw attention to the issues of social justice and rights. Deliberation occurs within formal venues, but it also involves ongoing conversations among housing activists and public officials.

Finally, CSO leaders involved in the housing field represented their members in multiple formats. In small planning sessions, CSO leaders responsible for the housing *núcleo* commonly asserted the number of people involved in their CSOs. In their conversations with key government decision makers, they would mention their numbers and the frequency of their meetings. This was all part of a process to show that their organizations were worthy of support (McAdam, McCarthy, and Zald 1996).

The survey data presented in this chapter illuminates the different ways CSO leaders are now working within the state and civil society to take advantage of the participatory citizenship regime. Many CSO leaders actively participate in multiple venues, which means that they engage a wide variety of public officials. The increased number of access points allows CSO leaders to gather information, expand the breadth of their interactions with state and government officials, deliberate in public and private, and maintain bonds with other CSO leaders. For CSO leaders, key moments in the biannual political cycle include elections, large participatory budgeting meetings, and policy conferences. But on a weekly and monthly basis, these leaders are active in participatory meetings, they speak with government officials, they hold meetings in their own communities, and they reach out to other CSO leaders. For CSO leaders participation is an ongoing, everyday affair. This is significant because it allows CSO leaders to expand their political choices and strategies. Under the conceded and regulated citizenship regimes, political choices were more limited.

What is most remarkable about the participatory citizenship regime is the proliferation of multiple venues, formal and informal, that CSO leaders can choose from as they seek out their interests. The data demonstrates that the majority of survey respondents are able to take advantage of the new municipal state; most of the CSO leaders engage in multiple formal venues. We can infer from this data that CSO leaders are no longer forced to choose between the blunt instruments of clientelistic exchanges or public demonstrations. Rather, they are directly participating in a wide range of venues.

Second, the new venues allow CSO leaders to represent their members in new ways. The Brazilian state has long been a complex and heterogeneous set of institutions with different departments addressing some part of the policy problem. CSOs are now able to represent the interests of their followers in engaging a wide range of arenas. Those who study electoral behavior must be able to better understand local networks, access points, and venues for direct state-society engagement. Those who study participatory institutions need to trace the activities of activists and citizens as they leave these venues.

The data also shows that a plurality of interests in civil society is matched by the diversity in strategies. The growing complexity of Brazil's economic and social structure is producing a broader range of political and social interests. The survey shows that different types of organizations are producing distinct "mini-publics" of activity within their public policy arenas (Junge 2012). The diversity of activity within the public sphere highlights the need for local or micro-level approaches to civil society. Patterns of civil society organizing shift over time, across territorial units, and among policy arenas, thus requiring that researchers drill down to better understand how citizens and CSOs are working to gain access to rights and public goods.

CHAPTER SEVEN

Transforming Favelas

*I have something to say to the leaders of Morro de Papagaio. It is
important that you mobilize as many people as possible this year.
When people say that PB never does anything, you should remind
them of BH Cidadania [social service center], of the new health post,
of the pedestrian overpasses. . . . I would strongly encourage Santa Rita,
Santa Lucia, and Esperança to enter as many demands as possible this
year because what doesn't get funded may end up in Vila Viva or another
program. Have you noticed that what gets approved and what barely
misses getting approved is often funded through other sources? . . .
Starting today, begin to mobilize to ensure a big turnout.*
    —Waldir, PB coordinator of the central-south region, April 6, 2010

*I believe in the PB, but it is not working. We approved a PB process
many years ago, but it is very different from the PB that is currently
being conducted.*
    —Paulo, community leader in Morro de Papagaio, April 20, 2010

MORRO DE PAPAGAIO

Morro de Papagaio is a sprawling favela with an estimated twenty thousand to twenty-five thousand residents. Outsiders often view it as a singular

community, but favela residents view themselves as living in a conglomeration of five communities. CSOs leaders and residents living in these five smaller communities have remarkably different relationships with the new participatory citizenship regime, based on the timing and pace of land occupation, each specific community's topography and geographical position, and the public goods built by the local state. Similar to the situation in most favelas across Brazil, residents lack legal property titles, which hampers their ability to access public goods. Two of the five communities are formally classified as "areas of risk" because of the potential for flooding and landslides; these households are therefore ineligible for public works because the state doesn't want anyone living in those places (although the state or market is unable to provide housing elsewhere). The other three communities are not classified as areas of risk, which allows different government programs to be involved in the implementation of a variety of public goods.

The diversity of the Morro de Papagaio favela is best captured by three modes of transportation I witnessed on my return visit to the community in September 2011 after a seven-year absence. I was waiting by a small road leading into the favela. A late-model BMW sedan passed by me, heading into the favela. Drug trafficker? Friend of someone in the community? Community member? Politician? I have no idea who was in the car, but it provided a stark reminder that the favela is ringed by some of the wealthiest neighborhoods in Belo Horizonte. Wealth surrounds the favela and occasionally enters it. As I continued waiting, an elderly gentleman passed by me riding a donkey. Based on his greetings to others standing around me, it was clear that he was a community resident. Did he live in the poorest part of favela, where livestock continue to be corralled? Or was he from an older section of favela that had larger plots of land and US-style backyards? Shortly after this gentleman passed by me, a mini-bus stopped in front of me. A new bus route now travels within the favela, moving people between the lower area and the upper area; the bus brings residents to three different locations where they can catch buses to various parts of the city. The public bus is able to provide transportation to residents because the roads had been paved and widened through participatory budgeting and other urbanization programs (see chapter 4). These three modes of transportation are illustrative of old and new ways residents are connected to each other within the favela as well as to outsiders.

ALTO VERA CRUZ

On a fall day in 2010, two community leaders from Alto Vera Cruz were giving me a walking tour of the favela. This community comprised of several smaller communities, but the differences are not as significant as in Morro de Papagaio. The community leaders first took me to the site of a new infrastructure project. A private company was tearing down houses to extend a road that would connect the community more effectively to a main transportation artery at the base of the community. Community members and CSO leaders worked through PB Regional to secure this project; residents whose houses were being demolished received compensation for the value of their houses but not for the land, since there was no clear legal title. As the CSO leaders related to me, with considerable pride, how their organizing efforts were leading to major improvements in the neighborhood, a man in his mid-twenties began to chat with us about the project as well as to inquire about my presence. We had an amiable conversation for about fifteen minutes. After we left, the community leaders remarked on my calmness. I naively asked, "Is there a reason that I shouldn't be calm?" I was informed that the young man was the local drug boss. He was there to check me out and to make sure that everything was okay. The two community leaders made it clear that they have a good relationship with him; government officials and private companies working in the favela often used these two community leaders as their contact point with the drug traffickers (see Arias 2006; Arias and Rodrigues 2006 for a fuller discussion).

The next stage on the walking tour led us by two new, three-story housing complexes that were being completed. The municipal government secured a federal loan to build the housing units, which were part of the community's urbanization plan (a community blueprint; see chapter 3). Residents from Alto Vera Cruz—those living in high-risk areas—would occupy the sixty-four apartments. Each owner would pay a small monthly mortgage payment (about $30 to $50) over a twenty-year period. On one side of the apartment complex was a stream being cleaned up through the use of federal funds. On the other side were hundreds of informal, small houses. Within a small section of the favela it was possible to identify a federal program and a municipal program working to improve the conditions, as well as the homes of hundreds of residents who were currently living in a risk area (because of landslides) but who might eventually be aided by the urbanization process.

A CASE STUDY OF TWO FAVELAS

This chapter turns our attention to two favelas in Belo Horizonte, each home to tens of thousands of individuals. Favelas are based on irregular housing settlements, typically occupied by individuals who lack formal property rights (Perlman 2010; Arias 2006; Holston 2008). Favelas—especially older ones—are characterized by a physical use of space that does not require wide roads to accommodate cars and trucks. Streets are narrow, allowing passage of a single car at a time. Staircases cut through neighborhoods, allowing residents to easily move from area to area but not permitting cars to pass through. Population density is typically high because there is an effort to use all available land for housing. Well-organized communities may designate land for community use, set aside for schools and health care clinics.

The Morro de Papagaio and Alto Vera Cruz communities experienced extensive infrastructure improvements during the 1990s and 2000s.[1] In the early 1980s, there were no schools, no health care clinics, few paved roads, and no sewers or other basic public infrastructure in these two communities (Gomes 2004). Today, the vast majority of residents in both communities have legal access to water, electricity, and sewage in their homes. The roads are, in most areas, paved. However, a significant minority of households continues to lack access to these public goods. In the poorer sections of both favelas there are houses not connected to the sewage system, residents use pirated electricity, and water has to be purchased separately. A marked heterogeneity within the two favelas has long been noted in Brazilian academic literature (Marques and Torres 2005; Perlman 2010). The better-off parts of both favelas have basic public services enjoyed by lower-middle-class neighborhoods, but some parts of the favelas have virtually no public services. Thus there are now greater differences within the favela than between the better-off parts of the favela and lower-middle-class neighborhoods in the city. In both favelas, there is high density and ongoing drug trafficking.

This chapter accounts for how these two favelas are being transformed by citizens, CSOs, and government officials who are working closely to activate the participatory citizenship regime to alter political activities, attitudes, infrastructure, and the overall quality of life. In both favelas, technical and participatory innovations were employed to bring *mētis* to bear on the new policymaking process (Scott 1998). The chapter first explores

Table 7.1 CSOs in Morro de Papagaio and Alto Vera Cruz

	Morro de Papagaio	*Alto Vera Cruz*
Residents	16,000–25,000	30,000–40,000
CSOs	98	66
Number of residents per CSO	173	457

Sources: Ana Flavia Martins, personal communication, April 14, 2010; Gomes 2004, 161.

how state presence changed within the favela during the 1990s. Unlike the popular image of an "absent state" or a "parallel state," we find active state presence in both communities. They both have health care clinics, schools, and an active police presence. But there is an uneven state presence inside them. The state can be overbearing (authoritarian police presence) and mediocre (poor quality of education and health care), and it operates in grey areas (police and military officers complicit in drug trafficking) (Auyero 2007; Arias 2006). The state can also have a constructive role: the municipal government actively promotes participatory programs and innovative social programs.

The second section of this chapter analyzes the principal modes of political and civil society organizing. In Alto Vera Cruz, the Communist Party of Brazil has long had a strong presence but is slowly ceding ground to the center-left Workers' Party. In Morro de Papagaio, there is no dominant political party, which limits the ability of the community to organize collectively as well as influence legislators and members of the mayoral administration. There is an active civil society life, but it is separated from party politics. Many of the organizations focus on rights, culture, and education.

STATE PRESENCE

Prior to the 1990s, there was limited ongoing state presence in either favela (Gomes 2006; Cruz interview). Schools and health care clinics were located outside community boundaries. State presence often had a negative presence in two ways. First, in Morro de Papagaio, massive power lines and a huge electrical substation are owned and operated by the state-owned electric company. The company worked to ensure that the housing settlements would not adversely affect their power lines, but the company was unwilling to allocate resources to move people away from the lines. The company was also unwilling to concede property titles to the thousands of people living on their land.

Second, military police played an active and repressive role in both communities in the 1970s and 1980s. They repressed political opposition to the military government and targeted suspected criminals for harsh treatment. One community activist stated when I asked her about the most important set of rights she was granted in the 1988 constitution: "It was the right to come and go from my house without being bothered by the police. . . . It was the right to not have a gun shoved in my face by police officers. . . . It was the right not to have police barge into my house whenever they felt like it" (Beatriz interview). Her sentiments are representative of the feelings I heard expressed by many community activists when they discussed the presence of the state during the 1970s and early 1980s. The state did not provide social services or basic public goods, and the military police acted with impunity. During my interviews with community leaders in 2009 and 2010, all requested that my audio recorder be turned off when we discussed police-related issues.

Prior to the 1992 realigning election in Belo Horizonte, government officials made little effort to build infrastructure in these two communities (Gomes 2004; Cruz 2009). The primary state presence was that of the military police, which residents and CSO leaders viewed as playing a repressive role rather than guaranteeing public security. Mayor Patrus Ananias's administration worked closely with local CSO leaders to activate the participatory citizenship regime within both favelas.

Morro de Papagaio has multiple sites for retail-level drug sales, much of it to nonresidents (although the increase in retail sales to nonresidents has led to an increase in the number of local residents and consumers). Close proximity to middle- and upper-class neighborhoods as well as the excellent quality of major transportation avenues makes it easy for drive-through illegal drug procurement. It's easy for consumers to get in and out.

Morro de Papagaio was subjected to high levels of gun violence between 2000 and 2005, indicating the inability of the state to provide basic public security. In 2004–2005, according to numerous sources, over two hundred people were murdered in Morro de Papagaio. There was general agreement among residents that the increased police presence in their community sparked the wave of violence, but there were very different stories about the specific nature of police involvement. In some stories, police officers murdered a drug trafficker who wouldn't pay them protection money. In another version, police officers sold weapons to drug traffickers. And in yet another version, the police killed a drug trafficker to protect the community and to clean up the growing problem of illegal drug sales. The drug business introduced greater numbers of guns into the community, but according to most of the people I spoke with, most of the murders related to a revenge cycle for previous murders.

The cycle of violence involving drugs, alcohol, jealousy, and retribution was broken by the introduction of a community policing program in 2005–2006; there was a reduction in violence beginning in 2005. Most of my sources cited the active presence of the new community policing program, which discouraged young men from openly carrying weapons to late-night parties and bars. Getting handguns out of the community's nightlife made it less likely that alcohol-related conflicts would turn deadly. The active presence of community policing had an enormous impact, reducing the number of murders and lowering the overall tensions within both communities. This demonstrates the vital importance that a positive police presence can have in a community.

Although my research did not focus on police officers' involvement in drug trafficking or their role in perpetrating violence against community members (see Arias 2006 for an excellent account), there is little doubt retail drug transactions took place despite police presence. The community policing program was staffed twenty-four hours a day, but there were ongoing drug sales less than a quarter mile from the police center. The role of the police was tangential to the research project I conducted, but police presence was something that most community leaders brought into our discussions. Did the police merely overlook the drug sales, or where they involved? No community leader I interviewed was willing to discuss police-related issues while the audio recorder was turned on. Once it was turned off, people gave me detailed accounts of illegal behaviors attributed to police. Since this was not a focus of my research, I was unable to verify the extent to which police officers may have been actively involved in drug trafficking or rough treatment of young men and women.

CIVIL SOCIETY

The configuration of civil society varies significantly between and within the two favelas; citizens' and CSOs' use of the new participatory institutions

during the 1990s and 2000s are therefore different. The differences between the two civil societies are best explained by looking at (a) timing
and form of occupation; (b) geography of the favela, both internally and
location within the city; and (c) role of religious institutions. Civil society
in Morro de Papagaio is plural but splintered, whereas civil society in Alto
Vera Cruz is built around a cohesive housing movement and strong party-
based organizing.

Plural but Splintered: Morro de Papagaio

In Morro de Papagaio, the occupation process began slowly at the end of
the nineteenth century and beginning of the early twentieth century. The
newly established community was on the outskirts of Belo Horizonte, the
state capital built in the 1890s. The first residents were freed slaves (slavery
was ended in 1888; see Marx 1998) in search of a new place to live and
work. Morro de Papagaio is comprised of five distinct communities, which
were occupied over a hundred-plus-year period. Individuals and families
slowly occupied the land, many moving from rural parts of the state. Thus,
people establishing homes did not result from a single event through
which community members forged a common identity but from the slow
transformation of agricultural land to housing. The first occupation took
place in the 1890s and 1900s; the most recent occupation was initiated in
the 2000s and is ongoing.

   Second, the Morro ("hillside" or "mountaintop"), as it is called, is a
sprawling area that is difficult to traverse on foot. People living on the lower
side are not likely to walk up the hill to visit the upper part and vice versa.
Two major avenues border the community, which means that as residents
leave the favela, those residents living in the lower part use one avenue, and
the residents of the upper part use the other. This limits contact between
people living in these two areas. Until the mini-bus started functioning in
the 2000s, walking was the only way to move easily throughout the favela.

   In addition, two of the five communities are officially located in "areas
of risk." A major rainstorm could produce a deadly landslide; the state has
the legal right to remove those houses at any time. Although residents in the
other three communities don't have legal property titles, they can only be
removed from their houses by the state through cumbersome and time-
consuming legal processes. The favela's geography has made it quite difficult to forge a common identity.

The third factor that creates a plural but splintered civil society is that Morro de Papagaio is surrounded by some of the richest neighborhoods in Belo Horizonte. Morro de Papagaio now occupies a spatially advantageous position: twenty minutes by bus from downtown in one direction and twenty minutes by bus to a major shopping mall in the other direction, as well as other employment opportunities available within walking distance. It is a stone's throw from the favela to the margins of the upper-class neighborhoods. Many of the community residents are employed in low-wage service jobs in the surrounding upper-class neighborhoods, which helps explain why unemployment is lower than in Alto Vera Cruz. By the 1990s and the 2000s, Morro de Papagaio resembled the famous favelas in the southern part of the city of Rio de Janeiro. This spatial location has encouraged the development of theater, human rights, and cultural and religious groups.

Citizens in Morro de Papagaio have stronger connections to wealthier parts of the city (where there are cultural and education events) and more leisure time they can dedicate to civil society (see Perlman 2010, chapter 8). This helps to account for a broader plurality of CSOs in Morro de Papagaio than in Alto Vera Cruz. Educational, cultural, and religious groups work inside the community alongside more overtly political groups that focus on rights, resources, and political mobilization. The types of cultural groups include a theater group (Grupo do Beco), a community radio station (Radio Popular), and the organization of religious festivals (Semana Santa) (Cruz 2009). This plurality and density of civil society allows for more opportunities for citizens to participate in the CSO of their choosing, but no single organization is strong enough to mobilize hundreds, let alone thousands, of residents. There is no political party with a strong following. The Catholic Church competes with evangelical groups for residents' religious commitment.

An important generational shift occurred in the late 1980s and early 1990s as a group of young women and some men (late teens and early twenties) began to organize themselves around the role of citizenship (*cidadania*) rights (Gomes 2004, 126–29; Cruz 2009). This fits within the logic of the renewal of civil society. These young citizens were educated within the traditions of liberation theology and the progressive, social justice–oriented wing of the Catholic Church. They first addressed the role of the military police within the community (Cruz 2009, 69). When the Workers' Party government created the participatory budgeting process in 1993, this group of activists sought to use the new institutions, but there was resistance among older, more deeply entrenched community leaders (see chapter 4 for more on participatory budgeting). Community organizing during the 1980s was largely based on clientelistic exchanges, which forced older leaders to develop new strategies for organizing their followers, deliberating in public, and engaging in incremental policymaking (Abers 2000; Baiocchi 2005; Cruz 2009). The newer generation of leaders had ideas that corresponded more closely to the new participatory formats and rights making, but they initially lacked a strong following in the community. Throughout the 1990s and 2000s, ongoing political struggles were along generational lines, as different CSOs sought to mobilize their supporters and actively engage in the participatory formats. This new generation of leaders organized around the concepts of "citizenship" and "social justice" in the hopes that they would be able to work with the government in a different way. As participatory budgeting consolidated into an important program that allowed for voice and vote, the old-time leaders adapted their strategies to work within PB Regional in order to secure public goods.

The geographic position of Morro de Papagaio is another reason that civil society is now increasingly plural. As of 2010, there were over 250 students studying at the university level as well as several dozen recent university graduates. The high numbers of university students can be explained by (1) privileged geographic position, which lowers the travel time to classes; (2) the existence of college-entrance exam (*vestibular*) classes, which were organized by a local priest; and (3) free tuition to the Catholic university (PUC-MINAS), as arranged by the local priest. Of the three research assistants I employed while doing research in Morro de Papagaio, one was a recent college graduate, another was in her final year, and the third was in his first year of university. A local Catholic priest placed intense pressure on the Catholic university to provide free classes for Brazil's notoriously difficult college entrance exam. The exam is "merit-based," which means that wealthy families send their children to expensive private schools to help prepare them for the test; many upper-income students spend an entire year after high school preparing to take the test. The top performers are granted admission to federal and state public universities, which are free and generally the best in Brazil. Students from Morro de Papagaio who pass the test are then provided with tuition waivers to attend the Catholic university (PUC-MINAS).

There is another geographic advantage held by Morro de Papagaio: New Year's Eve festivities. In Brazil, New Year's Eve is the source of a major celebration because it occurs in the middle of summer and because African-derived religions have renewal and cleansing ceremonies with the transition from one year to the next. The location of Morro de Papagaio places it at the center of a New Year's Eve celebration, bringing together its residents with upper-class and middle-income residents from the surrounding areas. On the western side of Morro de Papagaio, a steep hillside gives way to a small reservoir and a park with soccer fields and basketball courts. The reservoir has a one-kilometer walking trail around it. Residents from the favela and upper-class neighborhoods told me that there is an unwritten set of rules concerning the use of the walking trail. Upper-class residents use the walking trail in the mornings, prior to work, as well as in the evening until the end of dusk. The favela residents use the public facilities during the workday and at night. The residents of the favela are the exclusive users of the soccer fields. New Year's Eve is the only time that residents from both communities come together to share their use of public space in order to cohost an elaborate fireworks show.

The close proximity of the Morro de Papagaio favela to upper-class neighborhoods allows community leaders from Morro de Papagaio to create and then reaffirm their "weak ties" to residents from the upper-class neighborhoods (Granovetter 1973; Arias 2006). These ties are informal and beyond the realm of party politics. Community leaders working in Morro de Papagaio are well aware that many municipal and state government officials live in the surrounding areas. As one community leader said, "We would arrange to 'bump into' these government officials so that we could discuss our problems" (Marcos interview). This was confirmed by a government official who had occupied several key positions in municipal government: "It was always easier to know what was going in the Morro because I would run into community leaders when I walked to the bakery or when my wife and I were walking around the lake" (Lott interview).

Although there is an active civil society, the residents in Morro de Papagaio have never been able to elect a single member to the municipal legislature. Roughly five thousand votes are needed to secure a seat in the municipal legislature. The Workers' Party is the strongest party in the community, but the leaders are internally divided. The generational split among CSO leaders has made it difficult to forge enduring political alliances. The lack of political unity has diminished the community's representation in the municipal legislature, but this is tempered by the informal connections linking CSO leaders to government officials and the mayor's office. Civil society pluralism has splintered the potential impact of the community on municipal politics.

In sum, the Morro de Papagaio has an active, plural, and splintered civil society. Multiple organizations provide different groups with the opportunity to pursue their interests. However, many of the organizations have weak links to each other; the absence of a strongly organized civil society has made it more difficult for the community to organize itself to secure public resources. Thus, density itself is not sufficient to generate the collective action necessary to activate the participatory citizenship regime.

Cohesive Party Organization: Alto Vera Cruz

Alto Vera Cruz was occupied much more recently than Morro de Papagaio—during the 1960s, 1970s, and 1980s, when Brazil was under military rule. The community is located on the edge of Belo Horizonte, on a hillside above a middle-class neighborhood. Alto Vera Cruz was originally subdivided into single-family housing plots in the 1960s, and it was supposed to developed into a middle-class neighborhood. The streets are laid out in a grid, resembling a well-planned suburb. However, a series of shady land deals in the 1960s made the property rights unclear, which decreased the market value of the land and spurred the residents to develop community organizations to sort out the land titles (Gomes 2006; for an in-depth discussion of similar processes, see Holston 2008). The housing movement and the Communist Party of Brazil (PC do B) took advantage of the protracted legal battles to lead a series of land occupations, which produced informal housing in areas that were not initially developed. Members of the community refer to themselves as living in a favela, even though several parts of the broader community are more similar to lower-middle-class subdivisions (*loteamentos*).

During the land development of the 1960s and 1970s, physical space was reserved for future public facilities such as schools, a small park, and a community center. Several acres of forest and farmland, located a five-minute walk from the favela, are protected. This property now hosts an environmental learning center, which was secured through participatory budgeting; it provides garden plots for interested community residents. Thus, the initial occupation was not merely about gaining housing plots to live; the new residents were planning to build a community where they could reside for the long term.

The PC do B, working clandestinely under the military dictatorship, was a crucial organizing force behind the mobilization of the future residents. Its members forged the unity necessary to create and maintain collective action under the dictatorship as well as after the transition to democratic rule. The PC do B organized land occupations in other communities near Alto Vera Cruz during the 1980s. This ongoing mobilization created a strong sense of community, as the PC do B's action led to individuals securing land to live on. Today, more than thirty years after their initial organizing efforts, the PC do B remains the most active group in Alto Vera Cruz (Gomes 2006; interviews with Alto Vera Cruz residents).

A neighborhood association, also registered as a PB Housing *núcleo*, is the most active community group in Alto Vera Cruz. It holds biweekly meetings in which more than 150 families participate in some capacity. The purpose of this association is to secure housing units for their members as well as to work on general improvements within Alto Vera Cruz. It is led by individuals who were directly involved in the land occupation of the 1980s and are linked to the PC do B. Connected to the housing movement are two cultural groups, one of which is a choir whose membership is comprised of grandmothers and granddaughters. They travel throughout the state of Minas Gerais performing at cultural events. Another cultural group promotes more popular music concerts, whose intended audience is teenagers and twenty-somethings. The principal community leader in Alto Vera Cruz today got his start organizing cultural events. He then attended PB Regional and PB Housing meetings before becoming an active member of the PC do B.

The Catholic Church is present, but it does not have deep organizational roots in the community. There are no priests actively providing support to community organizations. When I inquired about university graduates or students attending college, there were usually long silences followed by the names of one or two community members who had attended college. A growing number of evangelical churches have active participation, but establishing the number of participants was not possible.

The community has long had a reputation for high levels of violence. When I first visited in 2004, my research assistant Lilian Gomes took me to a community meeting in the favela at night; after we left the favela, she mentioned that several people had been killed the previous weekend not far from where we were holding the meeting. The violence diminished over the decade, but the presence of drug trafficking continues to make it a somewhat dangerous community. One community leader noted: "Our community is not very violent. . . . You just have to be careful about stray bullets on Saturday nights" (Cordero interview).

In Alto Vera Cruz, the PC do B and the Workers' Party (PT) have strong bases of support. The PC do B was able to elect a city council member, Paulão, to two terms in office. He lost his seat in 2008 to a PT candidate Party. The political left is strongly organized, providing the community with formal representation in the municipal legislature, councils, and participatory budgeting. Alto Vera Cruz is much better connected to the political establishment than Morro de Papagaio, although the latter has much better informal ties.

In sum, the strong and active presence of the housing movement and the PC do B over a thirty-year period is the distinguishing characteristic of Alto Vera Cruz. Together, they organized the initial land occupation and forged a common identity among a large number of community residents. There is also a plurality of community groups, as in Morro de Papagaio, but the three best-organized CSOs have deep ties to PC do B. The Workers' Party has made more recent inroads into the political support traditionally garnered by the PC do B, but this support is based on trying to pry votes and support away from the PC do B rather than working to build an entirely new base of support.

PARTICIPATORY INSTITUTIONS AND STATE ENGAGEMENT

The 1992 mayoral victory of Patrus Ananias and the Workers' Party expanded opportunities for participatory governance across Belo Horizonte (see chapters 3, 4, and 5). In the 1990s, activists and citizens from both Morro de Papagaio and Alto Vera Cruz engaged in PB Regional, PB Housing, and the public policy management council system. The infrastructure of both communities was dramatically altered by projects built through the participatory governance system. It is impossible to know if governments uninterested in participatory governance would have built similar projects (the logic of this thesis is that the decentralization of authority and resources in the context of electoral democracy would have led vote-seeking politicians to invest in these two densely populated and active communities). Nevertheless, it is clear that specific political alliances, solidarity, and learning would not have taken place without the emergence of this new participatory architecture.

Within PB Regional, resources are distributed based on a region's Quality of Life Index (see chapter 4). A lower score means a lower quality of life. The purpose of the Quality of Life Index is to use technical information to promote social justice (see chapters 3 and 4 for a description). Regions and districts with a lower Quality of Life Index are eligible for a higher per capita spending through PB Regional. The Quality of Life Index used in 1994 shows that the majority of the Morro de Papagaio favela had a score of 0.25, which indicates high social vulnerability.[2] Alto Vera Cruz had a score of 0.23, which placed its residents in the highest category of social vulnerability in Belo Horizonte. As chapter 4 discussed, 57 percent of the resources allocated through PB Regional went to communities with high levels of social vulnerability, which means that both communities were well positioned to take advantage of the new programs.

Between 1993 and 2010, Morro de Papagaio secured thirty projects in PB Regional, with the government spending over $15 million, an allocation of $750 per resident on projects selected by citizens. Twenty-five of the thirty projects were urbanization projects; health care and social services made up the remaining five projects. Between 1993 and 2010, Alto Vera Cruz successfully secured nineteen projects in PB Regional, with the government spending over $8 million. This is a per capita allocation of $228 per resident on projects selected by citizens; fifteen of the twenty involved urbanization projects. Below I describe each community's experience with PB Regional and then discuss why Morro de Papagaio received more resources even though it had half the residents of Alto Vera Cruz.

Morro de Papagaio

The Morro de Papagaio community was well organized at the end of the military dictatorship, thus allowing it to take advantage of the PT's 1992 mayoral victory. When the government initiated PB Regional in 1993, the younger cohort of CSO leaders had the political and social organizing skills to flourish under the new rules. In the early 1990s, the politically active CSOs were divided into two broad camps: an older generation of leaders who had long been involved in clientelistic bargains and a new group of young women (and some men) inspired by issues related to social justice and liberation theology. A Catholic priest and community activist, Padre Mauro Luis da Silva, promoted the organizing activities of the younger activists as they sought to move beyond the confines of traditional clientelistic politics. Padre Mauro was a key instigator and supporter of the increased social and political mobilization. He encouraged the younger generation to develop new political strategies to contest government officials. There was no strong political party presence; the PT and the PC do B had a limited number of loyal supporters. CSOs were heterogeneous but also fragmented.

When PB Regional was established, the new cohort of leaders used their organizing skills to mobilize residents to work within the new participatory program (Cruz 2009; interviews with Morro de Papagaio residents). The community's first important project was a job-training center. Community members obtained the resources to construct a large building to prepare teenagers and twenty-year-olds for employment. Community leaders believed that the community's most significant problem was the lack of job skills among young men and women. Community groups organized and worked within PB Regional to secure funding for the project. As the building was being designed, government officials told community leaders that the government didn't have the resources to staff a job-training center. Instead, officials said they would be willing to build a community center to provide basic social services. This offer sharply divided the community because many leaders had spent years advocating for a job-training center. Government officials eventually got their way, which was a clear indication to community leaders that they needed to align their interests with those of the local government.

PB Regional thus was a political space in which community leaders could secure specific public works for their community but proposed projects would need to fit within parameters established by the government. This situation illuminates the heart of an ongoing tension in participatory politics: citizens exercise voice and vote but within parameters largely established by mayors elected via representative democracy. Citizens and CSOs struggle to find the balance between working closely with government and party officials while maintaining enough independence so that these same public officials don't take their support for granted.

The second major project was to secure a local health care clinic. This project was selected in 1996 through PB Regional; it was opened in 2000. The medical clinic was established in the lower part of the community and was viewed as being most beneficial to those residents living in the lower part of the favela. A second health care clinic was selected in via PB Regional in 2005 and officially opened in 2011. The building of the second clinic eased the client pressure on the first clinic and also made it easier for residents from the upper side to access health services within their community. In both cases, community members spent years organizing themselves to ensure that they would win the health care clinic through participatory budgeting. This process first involved working within the CSO to build support for the health clinic as the community's most important priority. (This was a time-consuming process that had to be repeated year after year.) The process also involved reaching out to other CSOs and potential supporters within the community. The organizing efforts then extended into formal participatory venues, both participatory budgeting and the municipal health council (an example of interlocking institutions). CSO leaders needed to develop support among CSOs from other communities so that the health care clinic would be included in the list of approved participatory budgeting projects. The bargaining among CSO leaders often led them to agree to forgo the inclusion of public work requests in year 1 or 2 to ensure that larger, more expensive public works would be included in a future year's budget. CSO leaders also worked closely with public officials, especially technical experts, to ensure that the project would be implemented.

Sewage and water lines were brought into the community over the course of the 1990s and 2000s through PB Regional. This is not an easy task in an urban, hilly environment. Many sewage and water lines had to be run next to or underneath the staircases that form the pedestrian arteries linking the narrow passage to the main streets. Residents also secured the refurbishing of an elementary school, street paving, and electrification. The organizing process to secure these public goods is similar to the process explained above.

Public resources to build infrastructure were secured over a twenty-year period via PB Regional based on the mobilization of ordinary individuals and the leadership of a handful of community leaders and organizations. No dominant organization or leader set the priorities for the community; community leaders constantly negotiated with each other regarding which public works should be prioritized. The mobilization strength of each community leader has varied over the years, producing a fragile mosaic of agreements that influence which projects will be selected in PB. The geographical diversity of the Morro de Papagaio complicates negotiation efforts because a public good built in one part of the community has a positive impact on nearby residents but would not really be used by other community members. For example, the community center, which was built in the upper part of the community, is used almost exclusively by residents who live nearby. As a result, it doesn't meet the needs of the poorest and most marginalized members of the community.

The selection of public works via PB Regional is biannual, and the implementation of the project often takes several additional years. When community leader A agrees to support community leader B's project in exchange for leader B supporting leader A's project in a subsequent vote, the likely implementation date of leader A's project is five to seven years. The problem for community leader A is that it becomes difficult to maintain collective action among her organization's followers and ongoing efforts are required to ensure that leader B will adhere to his end of the bargain. Incremental policymaking makes the work of civil society activists difficult because their appeals for mobilization are based on future benefits that may never materialize. CSO leaders are thus drawn into participatory incremental policymaking processes that require them to learn to create policy while also attempting to maintain collective action.

Community leaders also forge alliances with CSO leaders from outside Morro de Papagaio to generate the necessary support to have their programs selected at the regional level. Leaders from other large favelas are potential allies as well as competitors. PB Regional thus encourages solidarity and the formation of alliances, but these programs also produce competition among CSOs and activists. This produces similar negotiation strategies as in other democratic bargaining situations whereby actors forge short-term and long-term alliances. The actors involved in this democratic bargaining, however, are CSO leaders from poor communities, mostly favelas; long-standing political practices of parliamentary elites are now being used to guide interactions among Brazilian CSO leaders.

Complex projects also require the support of the corresponding municipal departments (e.g., health care, urbanization). Community leaders not only have to persuade their fellow citizens to support a public works project but have to convince policy experts of its feasibility. CSO leaders in Morro de Papagaio had multiple "mini-publics" with whom they need to align themselves to secure public goods: ordinary citizens, who would mobilize when necessary; other CSO leaders inside the community to develop consensus around support for the project; CSO leaders from other communities, whose support was needed at the regional level; and government officials (Junge 2012).

Through PB Regional, the community secured funding for its community blueprint, which led to an ambitious urbanization plan. (See chapter 4 for a discussion of community blueprints.) A public-private consortium of urban planners developed a long-term plan to restructure the broader community. In 2009–2010, when I was working in the community, the first important change was widening a road that would allow easier traffic flow across the favela. Part of this work involved paying people to move and then demolishing their houses to widen the road.

The next major undertaking in the community was being planned in 2010 and involves the creation of hundreds of new housing units. The purpose of the Vila Viva program, also coming out of the community blueprint, is to move people away from the electrical lines and into small apartment buildings. From an urban planning perspective, this plan has the merit of producing a more coherent living system: property rights will be established, there will be standardized apartment buildings, and so forth. But the program is controversial because many residents will be displaced to distant communities. Those who stay will see a dramatic decrease in the size of their apartments. Many of the residents whose families arrived prior to the 1970s had houses that were nearly 1,500 square feet; the new apartments will be roughly 600 to 700 square feet. The Vila Viva program depends on securing a loan from federal development banks (BNDES; Caixa Economica) to the tune of $90 million dollars. Given that the municipal government spent $15 million through PB Regional between 1994 and 2010, this project will dramatically increase state involvement.

Points of Conflict in Morro de Papagaio

In my 2007 book, *Participatory Budgeting in Brazil*, I told the story of a demonstration within the community. In 2004, Padre Mauro, a Catholic priest, led a procession of young people dressed as Franciscan monks and carrying a coffin labeled "Participatory Budgeting." The "monks," like the Pied Piper, developed a large following. They stopped at the end of a major avenue that runs along the favela. The priest then called a personal contact in the city government, informing him that they would shut down the avenue during rush hour unless the government agreed to build the pedestrian overpass (plus three other stalled projects) that the community had won in participatory budgeting. The government relented, and the pedestrian overpass was built. However, five years after this occupation, an important community leader, Paulo, was still upset because of the "funeral" demonstration. Paulo felt that this tactic had divided the community and provided few tangible benefits. From his perspective, direct confrontation was a tactic that should not have been employed by community members because it drove a wedge between government officials and CSO leaders. He feared that PB Regional would become the site of intense conflict rather than cooperation. My research as well as that of Lillian Gomes suggests that the process of deciding which projects to fund became increasingly acrimonious because of community division (Gomes 2009, 155). The initial bonds of solidarity gave way to increased competition among various community groups.

One of the most controversial decisions made within PB Regional was the establishment of an "ecological park" in an area where the favela directly borders an upper-class area. Environmentalists and community members from outside the favela worked within PB Regional to build support to protect a heavily forested section of the favela in order to preserve a watershed and maintain the beauty of the area. But the creation of the ecological park also involved the removal of longtime residents, many of whom were related to the favelas' original inhabitants. Relocating people to housing outside of the park meant moving them away from their extended families and social networks. In a series of formal and informal interviews with community residents and leaders, the establishment of the ecological park was often cited as a case where the interests of the upper and middle classes trumped the interests of favela residents. Nevertheless, government officials in interviews often cited the ecological park as an example of how environmental issues could be incorporated into PB Regional. This example illustrates how a successful participatory project can be used to legitimize government activities despite opposition from community residents.

For a brief period in the 2000s, community leaders were hopeful that the proposed ecological park would be declared a *quilombo*, which is physical space occupied by runaway slaves prior to 1888. Under the 1988 constitution, if *quilombo* communities could document their continued presence on the land since the end of slavery, then the community could win legal title to the land (French 2006; Gomes 2004 and 2009). Graduate students, all of whom were residents in the community, carefully documented that the first residents began living there in the 1890s, after the city of Belo Horizonte was built in the 1890s. This made the community ineligible for being officially registered as a *quilombo* because slavery officially ended in 1888.

The newest community within Morro de Papagaio, São Bento, was occupied during the 1990s and 2000s. It is located underneath a massive retaining wall built to support a major avenue that forms one of the favela's borders. São Bento is built on a sharp hill, leading to the lower part of the favela. The small roads and paths in São Bento are not paved. Residents' electricity is pirated, there are open-air sewage lines, and running water is not provided. Many of the houses are made from rough wood or very cheap cinderblocks. São Bento has been identified as an official "area of risk" by the municipal government because a massive rainstorm concentrated in that specific area could produce a landslide. Because of this designation, São Bento residents are unable to secure any public resources to improve their community because the municipal or state governments may not urbanize in at-risk areas. In 2010, for example, an urbanization plan for the entire favela prepared by the municipal government depicted São Bento as an uninhabited green space, effectively erasing the hundreds of homes and people who lived there. São Bento was thus "simplified" (James Scott's term; see chapter 1); the official map used by the government to engage in urban planning omitted its residents' homes. Residents of São Bento are thus in a terrible bind. They have no real reason to participate in participatory budgeting because their demands cannot be put into the budget, and there are no government or market-based solutions to move them to other areas. This situation is an excellent example of how a state simplification project can trample on citizens' rights. These residents had few formal means to access the state, and the participatory venues were not an option because their community was "at risk," a status that prohibits governments from investing in public goods. The participatory institutions and the 1988 constitution provide little recourse for this community to pursue their interests.

One afternoon I walked with two research assistants into São Bento to administer a survey to a random selection of residents. Both research assistants lived in the more established parts of the favela, which now have access to basic public services. Neither of my research assistants had ever visited São Bento. Both were shocked by the poor living conditions—the lack of sewage hookups, pirated electricity, no running water, and so forth. They were unaware that the living conditions were so terrible within their community. Both were very uncomfortable being there (similar to how middle-class university students feel when they visit a favela for the first time). Interestingly, when my research assistants were young children, their parents had to contend with the lack of basic infrastructure similar to these conditions, but it was no longer part of my assistants' lived experiences. When we came to a dirt plaza, where it quickly became obvious that drugs were being sold and used, both thought that it would be a good idea to leave the area.

This discussion shows that the state greatly increased its presence in Morro de Papagaio during the 1990s and 2000s. By 2009, children were attending school in the community, residents had access to two health care clinics, and the majority of homes were linked to water, sewage, and electricity lines. Community leaders are justifiably proud of their accomplishments, which they attribute to their ability to mobilize citizens and to work in participatory venues. But the plural nature of civil society fields makes it difficult to generate the strong political support vital to securing additional public resources. The lack of any single organization requires leaders to spend incredible amounts of time working to maintain political alliances. However, the community's geographical position is an asset because government officials would highly favor placing a large development project in this area with its high visibility.

Alto Vera Cruz

Alto Vera Cruz secured extensive resources through PB Regional and PB Housing. The PC do B and its affiliated community associations set the tone for negotiations within participatory budgeting. These organizations rely on a cadre of active community leaders who can mobilize hundreds of people. Several of the most active community leaders secured their housing through PB Housing, with the blessing of the PC do B, which means that public resources morphed into a private resource. These community leaders owe their allegiance to the party.

The most important victory achieved through PB Regional was the building of a community health care clinic. Prior to the building of the local health clinic, residents had to walk twenty minutes to a main avenue and then take a bus to a regional clinic or hospital. The establishment of the health care clinic greatly reduced the burden on residents for preventative and curative care. Residents were encouraged to participate in PB Regional rather than the municipal health care council because PB Regional was the government's preferred venue for promoting citizen participation in binding decision-making venues. PB Regional provided an opportunity to mobilize a wide base of supporters to pressure the government.

Through PB, Alto Vera Cruz also secured sewage and water lines and street paving. Once street paving was complete, community leaders were able to work with the municipal transportation department to establish a bus route into their community (an example of an interlocking institution). This is important because a resident can now walk out of her home, board a bus, and be in the downtown region in twenty to thirty minutes. A solid transportation infrastructure also means that delivery trucks can now easily enter the favela, allowing restaurants and stores to proliferate.

During the early stages of PB Regional community leaders secured funds to build a job-training center (similar to Morro de Papagaio). A warehouse was built, and different classrooms housed a beauty school (for women) and mechanics (for men). The program received donated equipment, much of it well used. However, by 2010 the job-training center was no longer in use because there was a disconnect between the skills that entry-level government civil servants could teach and the skills needed by young men and women as they entered the workforce. In 2010, the job-training center, built via PB, was being torn down to make way for a large social service center. This exemplifies the disjuncture between citizens' needs and what the local state could deliver. In both Alto Vera Cruz and Morro de Papagaio, community leaders initially mobilized around a job-training center. It was never built in Morro de Papagaio. While it was built in Alto Vera Cruz as a result of the strength and mobilization efforts of the PC do B and the community association, the physical infrastructure was an empty shell that provided minimal benefits. This example illustrates why government officials now place specific parameters on what citizens can choose to build via participatory budgeting. In this case, considerable time and resources were ill-spent because people's needs didn't match the government's ability to provide.

Another project secured through PB Regional was a community center. Cultural groups had sought this since the founding of the community in the 1970s. The community center was built, and local community associations donated much of the equipment from their temporary community center. The equipment was promptly stolen, thus creating a lasting division between the public officials destined to run the community center and the two most important community groups. The groups that won the community center through participatory budgeting have never used the center because of the theft of their equipment.

The development of a strong housing movement led to extensive involvement in PB Housing rather than just in PB Regional. Widespread participation in PB Housing was based on the central role of the PC do B and the housing movement during the occupation of Alto Vera Cruz during the 1970s and 1980s. The physical location of Alto Vera Cruz was another factor. The favela is situated on the eastern edge of the municipality, but there is open space between it and the municipality's border. The municipal government purchased the open space to build at least six large apartment complexes. Although the Alto Vera Cruz movement only secured a small share of the housing units—which were distributed through PB Housing—the implementation of so many units helped to maintain participation in the local housing *núcleo* as residents were able to see firsthand what could be accomplished. One reason Alto Vera Cruz secured fewer projects in PB Regional than Morro de Papagaio was that the Alto Vera Cruz leaders negotiated across PB Regional and PB Housing, whereas PB Regional was the only venue in which the Morro de Papagaio leaders were strongly involved.

In 2010, I was in Alto Vera Cruz on several occasions when community leaders were discussing which projects they should support in that year's PB Regional. They discussed options among themselves and in community meetings, although their association members raised questions or suggested different projects. When they heard about another community leader's proposed project, the leaders had to decide whether they would join forces with the smaller association or if they would have enough votes to win their projects without the other association. Thus, community leaders and their followers have to make decisions similar to legislators and party officials. They had to ask themselves questions such as the following: When do we need to cooperate? When do we have enough support to press ahead with our own agenda without the support of others? When do I need to raise a controversial issue in public, or when should I raise it in private? CSO leaders are now induced to think like community organizers as well as incremental policymakers, which places yet another burden on community organizers as they participate, represent their community, and deliberate in public venues.

Given the ability of the PC do B and neighborhood associations to mobilize hundreds of people, they are in a very advantageous position in the PB Regional process. These groups are able to negotiate with leaders from within and outside the community from a position of relative strength. Overall, PB Regional and PB Housing delivered a number of infrastructure improvements. The central organizing role of the PC do B and its three affiliated community organizations (one housing-oriented and two cultural) helped the community to secure a wide range of public goods. The leadership model employed by the PC do B concentrated leadership in a small group of people, but there was constant dialogue with community residents. The leaders and citizens I spoke with felt a sense of empowerment because they believed their mobilization efforts had delivered sewage and water lines, paving, public transportation, a health care clinic, and apartment complexes to the community. Their geographic position away from the core downtown area made them acutely aware that other sprawling favelas located nearby had not received the same benefits as they had. Their ability to mobilize hundreds of people for key participatory budgeting meetings in conjunction with their ties to municipal legislators enabled them to transform their communities.

SURVEY OF ORDINARY CITIZENS

The data presented in chapter 6 demonstrates that community leaders are now key intermediaries linking state and participatory institutions to their communities (see also Baker, Ames, and Renno 2006; Lavalle, Acharia, and Houtzager 2005; Lavalle, Houtzager, and Castello 2006). The final section of this chapter turns to the role ordinary citizens play in the participatory citizenship regime. Several methodological options are available to researchers to assess ordinary citizens' political activities: participant observation, ethnographies, in-depth interviews, focus groups, and surveys. Given our interest in understanding the attitudes and activities of a large cross-section of residents, we chose to administer a survey to a randomly selected group of residents from the two favelas featured in this chapter: Morro de Papagaio and Alto Vera Cruz. In both communities, local residents and college students carried out the survey. This gave them a familiarity with the byzantine network of streets. Our methodological strategy to select residents for participation in the twenty-minute long survey was to pick identifiable starting places (a store, a plaza) and then knock on the door of every fourth house. At each house we then asked to interview the adult with the most recent birthday. This research strategy allowed us to

Table 7.2 Demographic Profile of Citizens

	Percentage Reporting	
	Morro de Papagaio	Alto Vera Cruz
Women	63	55
Less than high school degree	65	66
Monthly household less than $600	50	80
Monthly household income between $601 and $1,400	35	14
N	138	195

Source: Wampler 2010.

interview 195 individuals in Alto Vera Cruz and 138 in Morro de Papagaio. The survey was conducted in April and May 2010.

First, women are well over half the sample in our survey pool. This is likely due to a greater number of women being underemployed or not working in the formal job market as they care for children. Second, two-thirds of the respondents in both communities ended their formal schooling prior to finishing high school, which is similar to CSO leaders from the participatory budgeting, housing, and health care sector (it is substantially different from the social service activists, many of whom are college educated). The population included in the citizen survey is representative of the overall education levels for urban, poor Brazilians.

There are significant differences in the levels of wealth in both communities. Thirty-five percent of the respondents in Morro de Papagaio live in households earning between $600 and $1,400 per month; they are members of the emerging lower middle class (*classe C*). In contrast, 80 percent of the respondents in Alto Vera Cruz lived in households where the monthly income was less than $600. Alto Vera Cruz is thus a community with much higher poverty rates. The timing of the land occupation and the geographical location of both communities are important to explaining this difference.

Economic diversity *within* both communities repeatedly struck me. In both communities, three-story and four-story houses allow multiple generations to live together; multiple adults were working, providing enough income to allow them to have a car, possess multiple expensive appliances (computers, flat-screen TVs, freezers), and take vacations to the distant beach. These households were doing well financially (easier access to credit in the 2000s also made this possible). Among our survey residents in Morro de Papagaio, 86 percent of the respondents owned their homes, which generally means no monthly payments and no property taxes because of the lack of clear property titles. This drops to 65 percent in Alto Vera Cruz, which is still quite high. Alongside the larger homes, there are also tiny, poorly maintained apartments in the backyards of other houses; no one was working, and families relied on a small monthly stipend from Bolsa Família to meet their most basic expenses. In these cases, residents earning $100 per month live next door to families with household incomes close to $1,500 to $2,000 per month.

Race is the final demographic characteristic that needs to be highlighted. Racial identification and individual self-classification is a notoriously difficult topic in Brazil. There is simultaneity fluidity and rigidity in racial identification (Hanchard 1994; Gomes 2010). Rigidness is evidenced by the fact that the poorest segments of Brazil are comprised of black (Afro-Descendent) individuals and families who typically live in the poorest neighborhoods with the most limited access to public goods (education, health care, sewage, decent housing). Fluidity can be seen as people change their racial identity depending on where they live as well as their class position. This fluidity can also be seen inside the favelas, as there is a great mixture of phenotypes and other physical characteristics used to differentiate among different racial categories (Marx 2004, Hanchard 1994).

It was thus surprising that 56 percent of the residents of Morro de Papagaio selected "Black" (só negro) as their racial identification. The percentage in Alto Vera Cruz was lower, at 34 percent. In Alto Vera Cruz, 28 percent identified as "white and black" whereas just 2 percent identified this way in Morro de Papagaio. In both favelas, the percentage identifying as white was around 30 percent. How do we account for this high degree of racial categorization as Black? Within Morro de Papagaio, there had been a cultural and political movement to recognize part of the favela as a *quilombo*, an area initially occupied by runaway slaves, and it was the home of the slaves' descendants. Although graduate student researchers found that the settlement had been more recently established than the legal rules required for federal recognition allowed, the cultural movement that works tirelessly to valorize Afro-Brazilian culture appears to have had a positive impact. In Alto Vera Cruz, the predominant organization mobilizing the community was the PC do B. Although this group has expanded its organizing efforts to focus on race, its primary focus continues to be class, which may help to explain why fewer people self-identified as Black.

Civil Society

As we would expect, citizens randomly selected to participate in the survey were less involved in civil society organizations and public life than were the CSO leaders. Just 7 percent of the survey respondents in Morro de Papagaio said they were involved in a community organization. This increased to 25 percent in Alto Vera Cruz, an increase I attribute to the continual mobilization efforts of the housing *núcleo* and the PC do B. But roughly half the respondents in both communities were aware of a local community organization. Given the history of social and political exclusion in these two favelas, the fact that 50 percent of the residents were aware of a community-based organization is positive. However, it was only a small fraction of the respondents who could successfully identify a CSO by name. Within the 50 percent of the survey population who were aware of the presence of local CSOs, most were quite positive regarding their impact on community life. This suggests that the CSOs are perceived as working to forge bonds of solidarity within their communities.

Respondents' engagement in community life went far beyond participation in a community or neighborhood association. In both favelas, a third attended Catholic services at least once a month, and another third attended evangelical services at least monthly. This involvement in religious associations suggests that research on civil society needs to be attentive to the multiple ways in which citizens choose to spend their time outside of work and family.

More overt political activities, such as attending demonstrations and signing petitions, is much higher in Alto Vera Cruz than in Morro de Papagaio. This is due to the role of the PC do B and its allied neighborhood associations (a housing *núcleo*, an intergenerational choir, and a hip-hop cultural group) as the key community organizers in Alto Vera Cruz. Several community leaders are financially supported by the PC do B, allowing them to organize petitions and mobilize citizens to attend demonstrations. There is no comparable organization in Morro de Papagaio. A Catholic

Table 7.3 Activity within Civil Society

	Percentage Reporting	
	Morro de Papagaio	*Alto Vera Cruz*
Currently involved in association	7	25
Aware of local community association	46	51
Of those who are aware of the local community association:		
Discuss community association with others	7	16
Know the name of a community association	11	27
Believe that CSO has positive impact on community	67	91
Attend Catholic Church services, at least monthly	36	28
Attend evangelical church services, at least monthly	30	36
Attend cultural event, at least monthly	11	24
Participate in demonstrations	9	31
Sign petition	14	51

Source: Wampler 2010.

priest in Morro de Papagaio previously organized demonstrations and petition drives, but he left the community to spend time in Rome to deepen his theological studies.

In sum, survey responses in the two communities complements the analysis presented above. Citizens in Alto Vera Cruz are more politically engaged, which is attributable to the organizing role played by the housing movement and the PC do B. Core community organizers present a unified analysis of the problems faced by the community and directed their efforts toward housing and cultural events. In contrast, the heterogeneous makeup of civil society in Morro de Papagaio is reflected in the low levels of citizen participation and engagement in political activities. The fragmentation of civil society in Morro de Papagaio is reflected in survey respondents' low participation in political activities.

Contact with Public Officials and Institutions

Citizens connect to local state and political institutions in a very different manner from the way CSO leaders connect to institutions. Citizens also connect to the state differently in the two communities. The most significant difference between the two communities is their level of contact with municipal legislators. Alto Vera Cruz is the site of extensive political organizing and contestation by two political parties: PC do B and PT. Alto Vera Cruz elected one municipal legislator in the past three elections. Even though there is a municipal-wide vote, many politicians draw their votes from specific regions, similar to Barry Ames's finding (Ames 1995). In contrast, citizens in Morro de Papagaio had almost no contact with municipal legislators. Thus, in Alto Vera Cruz there was an organized network of activists and party officials who sought out constituency service on behalf of community leaders. For example, a local health council member sought to transfer a local resident from one hospital to another hospital located closer to the community. The council member had to work through various channels—councils, municipal legislator, health care department—to accomplish this goal. In Morro de Papagaio, there was no unified, coherent organization that could provide constituency service of this sort.

In addition, half the respondents in Alto Vera Cruz had contact with PB Regional or PB Housing, whereas just 10 percent of Morro de Papagaio did so. In Alto Vera Cruz, the main neighborhood association was closely linked to the PC do B, which was involved in electoral politics. The local PC do B focuses attention on participatory budgeting and receives the support of municipal legislators to induce people to participate.

There is no similar coordinating force in Morro de Papagaio. However, one reason for low levels of activity surrounding PB in Morro de Papagaio in 2009 and 2010 is that the municipal government was involved in drawing up major infrastructure plans that were linked to other programs (the community blueprint and Vila Viva). Community leaders thus spent their time and energy on these issues and not as much on PB Regional. The amount of resources being discussed to fund the urbanization program in Morro de Papagaio was three times higher than the amount the municipal government allocated for all of PB Regional in a given biannual cycle for the entire city. It made political sense for the leaders to move away from participatory budgeting and into the new programs.

Table 7.4 Access to Public Institutions

	Percentage Reporting	
	Morro de Papagaio	Alto Vera Cruz
Contact with municipal legislator's office	2	42
Contact with mayor's office	0	2
Participated in local council	4	11
Contact with participatory budgeting	10	50
Contact with Catholic Church official	22	30
Contact with evangelical church official	24	47
Contact with government housing program	15	47
Contact with Bolsa Família	26	44
Contact with the Family Health Program (PSF)	14	67

Source: Wampler 2010.

In terms of government-provided social service programs, two-thirds of Alto Vera Cruz residents had contact with an official from the Family Health Program (Program de Saúde Familiar, or PSF), as compared to just 14 percent in Morro de Papagaio. The explanation for this lies in Alto Vera Cruz's higher poverty rates, which provides a technical justification for allocating more PSF resources in the community, as well as in the active engagement of a city council member. Greater numbers of residents in Alto Vera Cruz had recent contact with the Bolsa Família program because of the community's higher levels of poverty. Thus, access to state services corresponds to the demographic data, which suggests that the distribution of state programs matches community need.

Sharing Information within the Community

Residents of Alto Vera Cruz are much more likely than residents of Morro de Papagaio to discuss community problems with their friends, community leaders, and public officials. There is a clear interactive effect between community involvement and their political interests. Candidates are well

Table 7.5 Sharing Information

	Percentage Reporting at Least Monthly	
	Morro de Papagaio	*Alto Vera Cruz*
Speak with friends about community problems	16	31
Speak with community leaders about community problems	9	30
Speak with public officials about community problems	4	22

Source: Wampler 2010.

aware that residents of Alto Vera Cruz are more likely to vote in a unified manner, which then leads party leaders to invest in community leaders as intermediaries.

Morro de Papagaio has a large community center staffed by three full-time social workers with a basketball and soccer court, classrooms, and so forth. It is located on top of the hill, and almost all the registered users come from the surrounding area. The social workers—public officials—make sporadic attempts to reach out beyond the direct community, but there is little sustained effort. No single organization is organizing the community. Instead, five neighborhood organizations represent the five communities located within the sprawling favela. In São Bento, the president of the neighborhood association was unable to legally register the organization because the one-time registration fee of $110 was beyond its members' ability to pay. Overall, discussing community issues is much more difficult in Morro de Papagaio because no single organization advocates on behalf of the entire community.

Campaigns and Elections

The data in Table 7.6 shows that there is a significant difference between the two favelas regarding political campaigns. Citizens in Alto Vera Cruz were much more likely to be directly engaged in formal campaign work,

Table 7.6 Campaigns and Elections

	Percentage Reporting	
	Morro de Papagaio	*Alto Vera Cruz*
Work for a political party	18	29
Election Day work	9	27
Partisan ID	18	30
Received information about candidates from community leader	49	49
Talked with neighbors about candidates	17	47

Source: Wampler 2010.

which suggests that the two strongest parties in the favela, the PC do B and the PT, were working closely with citizens to get out the vote. In Morro de Papagaio, weaker political parties produced lower levels of electoral engagement.

In both communities, 49 percent of the residents indicated that they had received information about political candidates from community leaders. This confirms the importance of community leaders as conduits between political parties and voters (Baker, Ames, and Renno 2006). This survey result illustrates the role of community leaders as intermediaries between party officials and ordinary citizens. Ordinary citizens receive the information from community leaders and, in the case of Alto Vera Cruz, pass this information to their neighbors. My methodological approach didn't allow me to identify if citizens incorporated this information into their voting choices, but research by Huckfeldt and Sprague and by Baker, Ames, and Renno shows the importance of social networks influencing voting decisions.

What is striking is the difference in response rate regarding whether respondents speak with their neighbors about candidates. In Morro de Papagaio, only 17 percent spoke with their neighbors about candidates, whereas nearly half did so in Alto Vera Cruz. This helps to explain the high level of support in Alto Vera Cruz for a small body of leftist parties; neighbors are reinforcing political attitudes. This is also an indication of why political parties held fewer events: they already have a person-to-person network and don't need to spend limited resources to seek out new votes.

Morro de Papagaio and Alto de Vera Cruz were both transformed through the extension of the participatory citizenship regime into their communities. Community activists developed new forms of engagement that allowed them to be involved in a number of participatory venues. The municipal state used technical and participatory innovations to incorporate citizens' local knowledge—*mētis*—into new policies. The state did "simplify" both favelas, but it did so by combining legal, technical, and local forms of knowledge that allowed for an activist state to transform itself without violating the rights of citizens. For many residents, the "simplification" process expanded their access to housing, education, and health care services. However, the simplification was negative for those living in areas at risk because they were ignored by government officials.

The process of occupying land and the corresponding development of a shared identity were crucial to the development of civil society. The occupation in Alto Vera Cruz involved conflict with military police, the courts, and unscrupulous landowners. These struggles forged a common bond among residents, the housing movement, and PC do B leaders. In Morro de Papagaio, a drawn-out occupation process took place in different stages over a ninety-year period, which made it more difficult to forge a common identity. Thus, the political repertoires employed by civil society during the period leading up to the formal initiation of the participatory citizenship regime had a significant impact on how citizens and CSOs would engage the new political opportunities.

The geographic position and contours of each community have mattered greatly (see Arias 2006). The geographic contours of Morro de Papagaio, which includes a mountaintop, areas of risk, and a well-forested area that became an ecological park, produced five distinct communities. The geographic differences formed mini-publics that made it difficult to forge political and social alliances across the entire community. Each favela's spatial location within the city also strongly affected civil society organizing (Arias 2006; Perlman 2010). Community leaders were able to develop "weak" ties to government officials living in the surrounding areas; they would create links to officials and then use those connections as they sought help to solve pressing problems. A Catholic priest living in Morro de Papagaio leveraged his ties to the Catholic university to greatly expand the educational opportunities provided to the community's best students.

The Morro de Papagaio favela is surrounded by some of the city's wealthiest residents and is bordered by two major avenues, which create an obvious political benefit for government officials to improve the infrastructure. Morro de Papagaio residents received a greater per capita share of resources through PB Regional because fewer individuals competed for resources as a result of how PB regional maps were created. The middle and upper classes did not participate, which then allowed the CSOs from Morro de Papagaio to compete with just a single other large favela over resources.

The geographic position of Alto Vera Cruz did not afford it the advantage of being noticed on a daily basis by government officials or by the upper middle class. Its most important asset was vacant land on the far side of a small river to the east of the community. This land was not occupied during the military dictatorship but was obtained by the municipality during the 1990s and 2000s to build apartment complexes, which helped to maintain bonds of solidarity within the local housing movement. Community leaders from Alto Vera Cruz could not exploit informal ties to government officials the same way that leaders in Morro de Papagaio could. The leaders' "weak ties" were through political parties (PT and PC do B) and the participatory governance structure. Further, there are multiple favelas in the same region, which means that the competition for resources is much higher.

Political activities associated with more contentious forms of politics, such as demonstrations and petition drives, were more common in Alto Vera Cruz than in Morro de Papagaio. This is attributable to the PC do B's strong presence in Alto Vera Cruz as well as their common identity forged through land occupation. In Morro de Papagaio, the 2004 demonstration (the funeral procession for participatory budgeting) had a divisive effect among community leaders. The older generation of leaders opposed the effort at the time and still believed years later that it was a mistake. The younger, "right to have rights" leaders believe that it was the proper strategy because it engendered a series of reforms by government officials.

Finally, we see that citizens and CSOs now have much greater access to government officials and public goods. Citizens are able to exercise their political rights because they have multiple forums in which to participate, to represent and be represented, and to deliberate. The burden of ongoing participation is carried by a small number of CSO activists. Funding support from outside the community—the Communist Party and the Catholic Church—helped sustain participation. As community leaders participated in multiple venues, they sought to represent their members and the broader community. Why do government officials pay attention to them?

Because as half the survey respondents indicated, citizens receive information about specific candidates from community leaders. Thus, a small body of politically active leaders successfully uses the participatory governance citizenship regime.

A key dimension of the participatory citizenship regime is the protection of social rights. In both communities, there was a significant increase in the allocation of public goods. Citizens have much better access to basic services provided by the state, such as education, health care, utilities, and transportation. Unfortunately, I have no data on the quality of education or health care services. This obviously tempers any claims about the impact of reforms, but I want to emphasize that the local state is investing in projects that will help residents to take advantage of Brazil's expanding educational and economic opportunities.

This chapter demonstrates how a new governing model, based on participation, social justice, and interlocking institutions, initiated a broad number of changes. Interactions among citizens and local public officials were significantly altered. Mayor Patrus Ananias and the Workers' Party activated the participatory citizenship regime in Belo Horizonte in 1993. The emphasis on popular participation is evident in both communities, since citizens and CSOs now have multiple opportunities at local, regional, and municipal levels to advance their agendas. The emphasis on social justice can be identified through the allocation of greater public works in these two poor communities than in surrounding wealthier areas. Finally, the most complex housing and infrastructure projects that have been built as well as those being planned require the direct engagement of multiple municipal departments, as well as ties to state and federal governments, producing an interlocking series of institutions.

CHAPTER EIGHT

Activating Democracy

Belo Horizonte and Beyond

> *All power emanates from the people, who exercise it by means of elected representatives or directly, as provided by this Constitution.*
>
> —Article 1, Brazil's 1988 constitution

Brazil's 1988 constitution initiated a participatory citizenship regime that has dramatically increased the number of democratic institutions citizens access in pursuit of their political and social rights. Across Brazil, citizens, government officials, and CSOs are activating the regime to provide citizens with voice and vote, improve citizens' access to public goods, and reform a fragmented and authoritarian state. Ensuring that citizens have access to political and social rights formally guaranteed in the 1988 constitution is a contested political process. Acrimonious political disputes in Brazil now revolve around who has the right to be included in policymaking, which rights should be extended to the broader public, and what are the appropriate institutional venues for political negotiations among public officials, citizens, and CSOs (Yashar 2005).

Although the 1988 constitution formally guarantees a universal set of political, civil, and social rights, there is broad variation across Brazil in citizens' ability to secure these rights. The ability of citizens and public officials to activate the participatory citizenship regime results from the long-term development of the state and civil society as well as from more immediate factors, such as the availability of public resources, the governing coalition in charge of local municipalities, and specific institutional rules that regulate participation, representation, and deliberation. The importance of this finding is that citizens' ability to access rights, public goods, and democratic institutions varies as a result of the combination of long-term macro-structural factors (state formation, civil society development) and more recent, micro-level factors (resources, governing coalition, rules).

At the core of the new participatory citizenship regime is the institutionalization of a broad participatory system; CSO activists and citizens have multiple access points through which they can engage public officials. Control over policymaking processes has been demonopolized as new democratic institutions have proliferated. Citizens and public officials can now use participatory venues to develop policy proposals, deliberate over policy directions, raise contentious issues, and engage in oversight. The new participatory architecture draws citizens and CSOs into an interlocking set of institutions that improves policy coordination but also blurs the line between state and society. The blurring of this line places a new set of burdens on both CSO activists and public officials. CSO leaders are expected to work closely with government officials to develop new projects and policies, but they are also expected to raise contentious issues and engage in oversight. Public officials are expected to work closely with citizens and CSO activists within participatory venues but are also supposed to administer public policy programs for the wider public, which is not participating in the new intermediary institutions.

This book is the first longitudinal and cross-sectoral analysis that closely examines the process of building multiple democratic institutions in a single Brazilian city. In the 1990s and 2000s, Brazilian government officials and citizens greatly expanded the number and contours of democratic institutions in order to respond to a host of social, policy, and political problems (Abers 2000; Avritzer 2002, 2009; Baiocchi 2005; Baiocchi, Heller and Silva 2011; Santos 2005; Wampler 2007, 2008). Belo Horizonte is an exemplary case of reform, given the widespread adoption of new participatory venues that encourage popular participation, promote social justice, and link citizens and government officials in a complex set of overlapping institutions (Sandbrook, Edelman, Heller, and Teichman 2007). Five successive mayoral administrations built and now maintain a complex, participatory structure that includes nearly six hundred councils (municipal, regional, and local) and five thousand elected positions in which citizens exercise some degree of authority and oversight (see chapter 3). In addition, government officials promote rules that allocate greater resources to poor communities, thus increasing the likelihood that poor citizens have access to public goods and basic social rights (see chapter 4). Belo Horizonte is leading municipal-level reform in Brazil, as citizens and government officials are struggling to expand citizens' ability to exercise social and political rights formally guaranteed by the 1988 constitution.

This book's analysis of Belo Horizonte demonstrates that there is considerable variation across policy sectors regarding how the participatory citizenship regime has been activated. A close examination of six participatory institutions, the executive and legislative branches, four public policy arenas, and two favelas provides a rich empirical basis to explain variation regarding how the participatory citizenship regime is being activated in Belo Horizonte. The focus on a single city proved to be extremely fruitful: this methodological approach provided the opportunity to hold multiple factors consistent, thus permitting me to more clearly identify the key factors that explain variation across different institutions, policy arenas, and communities. The principal benefit of narrowing the empirical focus to a single city is that it allowed me to create an analytical framework that can now be used to explain variation across Brazil.

This concluding chapter has four sections. The first demonstrates how the initiation of Brazil's participatory citizenship regime created opportunities for government officials to produce innovative solutions to enduring social and political problems that have long plagued Brazil. The second section describes the five key factors that best account for the variation in the impact of the participatory citizenship regime in four of Belo Horizonte's policy sectors as well as in six distinct democratic institutions. The third section links the argument of this book to a wider canvas—namely, Brazil's federal participatory structure. The final section illuminates the key lessons from Belo Horizonte and Brazil for conceptualizing the political, institutional, and social processes associated with efforts to improve the quality of democracy.

INNOVATIVE FEATURES OF BRAZIL'S PARTICIPATORY CITIZENSHIP REGIME

Brazilians are designing innovative institutions to better address vexing policy and political problems that have long bedeviled scholars, democratic theorists, activists, and policymakers (Pateman 1970, 2012; Barber 1984; Madison 1787a, 1787b). As argued in the first chapter (see subsection "Challenges Facing New Democratic Regimes"), reformers in new democracies must contend with three interrelated problems: sustaining participation in a posttransition environment in which routine politics replaces rapid change, the bias of representative democracy in favor of upper- and middle-income citizens, and the need for governments to quickly act to produce public goods for poor citizens without violating their rights. For more than two decades, Brazilian reformers have devised new institutions to address these vexing problems.

Although institutional innovations across three areas—popular participation, social justice, and interlocking institutions—can be implemented without corresponding support from the other two areas, these new institutions have the greatest impact when they are implemented in close concert. To promote participation, government officials incorporate "pro-poor" incentives into the new institutions, thus encouraging participation by a broader number of citizens than traditionally participate in formal policymaking venues. Increased participation helps to mitigate some of the bias in favor of middle and upper classes because it produces a new political coalition capable of winning elections and maintaining pressure on government officials to allocate resources to public goods favored by low-income citizens. The direct participation of poor citizens in public, democratic policymaking venues decreases the likelihood that the state will trample on their rights because these citizens are directly involved in decision-making venues and are also trained to monitor the implementation of public works projects.

Therefore, the greatest political opportunity for political and social change occurs when popular participation, social justice, and interlocking institutions are addressed simultaneously. When participation among low-income citizens is promoted by creating specific rules that ensure public goods to poor communities, when these policymaking processes incorporate local knowledge (*mētis*), and when the policy demands are linked to different state agencies, positive change is more likely to result. These innovative features establish the basis for a virtuous cycle of change, whereby complementary actions from public officials and citizens contribute to improvements in social well-being, the quality of democracy, and state performance. The groundbreaking institutional redesign in Belo Horizonte, initiated by Mayor Ananias and the Workers' Party, is based on an institutional redesign that address all three problems.

The participatory citizenship regime alters the structure of the state and complements representative democracy by opening policymaking processes to ordinary citizens and CSOs. In Belo Horizonte, in Brazil, and across much of Latin America, elected officials and party bosses have long controlled access to policymaking venues and public resources. Brazil's participatory citizenship regime is thus altering the foundational structures through which political power is exercised in Brazil because access to the state has been demonopolized. The participatory citizenship regime permits citizens, CSOs, and public officials to move beyond the constraints of the conceded and regulated citizenship regime (see chapter 2 for an extended discussion). The conceded citizenship regime was based on the "donation" of rights to citizens by government officials, thus effectively curtailing citizens' agency and ability to promote their interests in the public sphere (Sales 1994). The regulated citizenship regime extended rights to individuals linked to the formal labor market, which was a minority of Brazilian citizens (Santos 1979). The participatory citizenship regime moves beyond the conceded and regulated citizenship regimes because citizens have a broader range of incentives that encourages them to exercise political rights in order to claim a broad host of social rights.

Changing the incentives for citizen participation is at the heart of the participatory citizenship regime. Citizens now have specific, instrumental incentives to be involved, such as the ability to vote on specific public works (Olson 1965; Ostrom 1990). Citizens and CSO leaders participate because their involvement directly influences how state authority and resources are used; by participating they help to secure public works and social services that they believe will reshape their lives. Thus citizens are more likely to participate because they know that their participation will result in changes in how the municipal state allocates resources.

The institutional rules also induce citizens and CSO leaders to form alliances with other citizens; these bonds help to establish the bonds of solidarity and collective unity so vital to social movement organizing (Alexander 2006; McAdam, McCarthy, and Zald 1996). Citizens are induced to form groups and become part of broader political networks that allow them to more actively work together in pursuit of common interests. The new alliances inside of participatory venues are then designed to produce a larger political coalition that can win elections as well as pressure government officials to allocate scarce resources to their communities.

Researchers and institution-builders need to be attentive to multiple incentives that motivate citizens and CSOs to be directly involved in policy-making venues. Citizen participation positively affects policy, elections, state-society relations, and civil society when institutions are designed to promote dual incentives that motivate individuals to participate. The establishment of tens of thousands of new democratic institutions across Brazil enables citizens to overcome some of the basic difficulties associated with collective action (Ostrom 1990; Olson 1965; Heller and Evans 2010). Popular participation is thus an integral part of the effort to activate the participatory citizenship regime.

A second innovative feature of the participatory citizenship regime is that citizens and government officials jointly control a new series of interlocking institutions. The participatory citizenship regime thus moves us beyond the dichotomy between representative democracy and direct democracy because citizens are directly involved in policymaking venues that are administered by government officials. The joint control over these new democratic institutions helps to improve policymaking coordination within the state, since public officials are now formally linked to each other across what were previously discrete policy arenas.

These new institutions also improve the exchange of information and signals sent between citizens and public officials. By using multiple participatory venues, citizens and government officials can develop an ongoing formal and informal conversation regarding the key social, policy, and political problems citizens face. From public officials' perspective, the participatory citizenship regime broadens the number of signals received from social groups. Public officials now have ongoing dialogues with different sectors, which allow them to better understand the range and intensity of citizens' and CSOs' demands. From the perspective of citizens and CSOs, the participatory citizenship regime allows them to use formal deliberative venues to hold government officials accountable while also using informal conversations in newly established policy networks to find solutions to more immediate and specific problems.

Joint control of the new participatory and interlocking institutions incorporates *mētis*, which James Scott describes as local knowledge (1998;

see chapter 2 for an extended discussion), because citizens are expected to bring their knowledge to the policymaking process in order to improve demand making, deliberation, and project monitoring. The expanded surface area of the state creates multiple venues through which *mētis* can be linked with technical and legal forms of knowledge. Participatory institutions depend on both types of knowledge in order to produce social change. Without technical and legal knowledge, it is very difficult for public officials to transform favelas and *vilas*. Without *mētis*, it becomes more likely that state officials will ignore or trample on the constitutionally protected rights of citizens. Interlocking institutions, a key pillar of the participatory citizenship regime, represent a modern addendum to James Madison's systems of checks and balances. By incorporating *mētis* into the policymaking process, the state is more likely to be able to provide public goods without violating the rights of poor and politically marginalized communities. Many poor communities need the state to provide public goods; the combination of popular participation and interlocking institutions permits states to act quickly without violating citizens' rights.

This participatory system based on interlocking institutions is located within an already strong executive branch in Brazil (and elsewhere in Latin America). Rather than the Madisonian construct "ambition must be made to counteract ambition" operating across different branches of government, political negotiation takes place within the executive branch. There are significant accountability problems with this model: the passions of the majority could use their control of the executive branch to violate the interests of minority groups. This new institutional arrangement developed in response to an institutional and political culture environment that has long supported a strong executive. Rather than placing new veto points that might limit the executive's ability to act, this institutional environment expands the number and type of citizens and organized groups that directly negotiate with the executive branch. This helps to get things done but runs the real risk of further concentrating authority in the executive branch.

A third innovative feature is that many of these institutions focus on social justice and the social rights formally guaranteed by the 1988 constitution. The participatory citizenship regime is designed to deliver public goods to poor citizens and communities, thus helping Brazilian governments move beyond the constraints associated with representative democracy. Representative democracy has a bias toward middle- and upper-income groups, which are more easily able to overcome the collective action problem (Schattschneider 1960; Schlozman, Verba, and Brady 2012).

The 1988 constitution formally established a broad range of social rights (e.g., right to health care, retirement, housing, education) and the institutional and political context that allowed citizens and governments to create policy agendas allocating increases in public spending on issues of high relevance to poor citizens and communities. By focusing on issues that are of fundamental importance to the poor, government programs both address the bias associated with representative democracy and provide additional incentives to overcome the collective action problem (Ostrom 1990). Broadening the state, in conjunction with addressing basic collective action issues, allows the participatory citizenship regime to establish a new democratic context that helps citizens and government officials to begin to minimize the bias in favor of the middle and upper classes.

ACCOUNTING FOR VARIATION ACROSS THE PARTICIPATORY CITIZENSHIP REGIME

This book demonstrates considerable variation regarding how the participatory citizenship is being activated across different policy arenas in Belo Horizonte. The variation across the four policy arenas, six participatory institutions, and the executive and legislative branches is due to the interplay of five factors: (1) state formation, (2) the development of civil society, (3) government support for voice and vote, (4) the source and level of public resources, and (5) specific participatory rules that regulate citizen participation, representation, and deliberation. It is thus a combination of macro-structural factors (numbers 1 and 2) as well as more immediate factors (numbers 3, 4, and 5) that differentiate how the regime is activated across different policy arenas. The evidence shows that the 1988 constitution and the participatory citizenship regime is more likely to be activated when there is a reasonably capable state governed by a reformist, democratic political coalition that can deploy a combination of local, state, and federal resources. Therefore, access to rights is no longer solely based on socioeconomic status (conceded citizenship) or employment status (regulated citizenship). Citizens' access to political and social rights now significantly depends on how these five factors interact at the level of the policy arena. The research focus on the city of Belo Horizonte created the opportunity to systematically assess the factors that best account for variation in the participatory citizenship being activated.

State Formation

The vital importance of state formation to participatory politics moves the debate on participatory institutions in a new direction because there has been a limited focus on the vital role of the state and participatory politics (Kohli 2004; Migdal 2001; Abers and Keck 2009, 2013). This book's focus on multiple policy arenas (housing, health care, social services, and small infrastructure) allowed me to demonstrate how differences in state formation are highly correlated with the type of political and social rights accessed by citizens. Within the broader concept of state formation, there are several key subfactors that enable a tighter analytical explanation of change.

First, building the bureaucratic and legal structures of the state over the course of the twentieth century created a more capable state that in the twenty-first century could deliver public goods and extend social rights to poor communities. The initial establishment of state agencies in the 1930s and 1940s in specific policy arenas had long-term effects that affected local-level politics in the 1990s and 2000s. When there is basic state capacity, citizens and government officials are able to use participatory institutions to redirect that capacity to new areas (e.g., building infrastructure in favelas). In contrast, where there was limited state-building and limited state capacity, it was difficult for policymaking via participatory institutions to have a significant impact on policymaking. Participatory institutions are better equipped to redirect state capacity rather than generate new state capacity. Existing state capacity makes it easier for citizens to use political rights to gain access to social rights. A key lesson for democratic reformers and development experts is that we should expect to see more robust results when decisions made in participatory institutions can leverage existing state capacity; when state capacity is limited, citizen participation doesn't appear to contribute to its strengthening.

Across the four policy arenas analyzed, there was significant variation in state development and current state capacity. For example, Belo Horizonte's PB Regional program was based on using existing state authority to implement public goods in communities that had been traditionally underserviced by the state. The Brazilian state has long provided basic infrastructure to advance the industrialization process, which means that there is a local state capable of providing the necessary goods and services associated with urban infrastructure development. Thus one of the reasons that PB has a significant impact on the policymaking process is that citizens are redirecting existing state capacity. In contrast, the lack of a state apparatus in the social service policy arena meant there was no existing state capacity to use to implement services; it is difficult to make effective use of the participatory systems because citizens and CSOs do not have a state partner with which they can work.

The second subfactor relevant to state formation is how it generates a broader range of political and policy actors. When the Brazilian state developed its own capacity to provide specific goods (housing, health care) to workers included in the regulated citizenship regime (1930s–1970s), there was an associated expansion in the number and range of policy actors. Most importantly, the expansion of regulated citizenship created unions, which have an active presence in the new participatory citizenship regime in distinct two ways. Some union officials participate in participatory institutions seeking to represent the public employees who work in the areas. For example, in the health care council and conference, union officials were present to advocate on behalf of their members. Union officials working for public agencies can be released from their official duties (while also receiving full pay), which allows them to work with CSOs.

In sum, a key theoretical and methodological insight that applies to Belo Horizonte, to Brazil, and beyond Brazil is that our studies of citizen participation must closely analyze the long-term development of the state as well as current degrees of state capacity. Many of the most successful cases of participatory governance in Brazil involve redirecting state authority rather than generating state capacity; the single-case approach didn't allow researchers to see the fundamental importance of the state (Abers 2000; Avritzer 2002; Baiocchi 2005). This theoretical insight suggests that we (citizens, researchers, policymakers) may need to lower our expectations for the potential impact of participatory institutions where state capacity is lacking. Thus the development of participatory institutions in rural areas of Mozambique, Indonesia, and the Philippines will likely produce weaker results than in urban Brazil because of very low state capacity.

Civil Society

The development of civil society at the level of policy arena is the second key factor that explains how the participatory citizenship regime will be activated. The important subfactors include the depth of the renewal of civil society, the number of CSOs that are now service providers, the density of CSOs, and the extent to which ordinary citizens (actual or potential beneficiaries of public goods provision) are involved in CSOs.

First, when CSOs associated with the broader citizenship movement ("the right to have rights," "insurgent citizenship," and "participatory publics") are present, citizens are much more likely to pressure public officials to use participatory institutions to enable citizens to gain access to social rights. Thus the extent to which there was a renewal of civil society at the level of policy arena is important. The participatory citizenship regime is much more likely to be more fully extended if citizens are actively involved in making claims. The renewal of civil society greatly expanded the political repertories of engagement that CSOs would use (Tarrow 1998). These political repertories were then refined as citizens and CSOs responded to the specific opportunities created by the new participatory architecture. This finding is in line with a broader swath of studies that have been conducted in Brazil and the developing world (Avritzer 2002, 2009; Baiocchi 2005; Baiocchi, Heller, and Silva 2011; McNulty 2011; Van Cott 2008).

A second important subfactor is the extent to which CSOs are involved in delivering state services. The evidence shows that holding a contract (*convênio*) to provide social services (outsourcing of service delivery) is strongly associated with different types of social and political strategies. CSOs holding social service contracts are less likely to engage in demonstrations, less likely to use participatory institutions, and more likely to have direct contact with public officials. Therefore, researchers must be attentive to the types of organizations that engage in ongoing service delivery contracts. When CSOs hold service contracts, they are more likely to be professional organizations with limited direct engagement in participatory institutions, demonstrations, and campaigns and elections. This produces a Third Sector policy arena in which these organizations seek to represent others.

The third subfactor that explains variation is the density of civil society (Putnam, Leonardi, and Nenetti 1994; Avritzer 2002). The number of participants in meetings matters in terms of legitimatizing shifts in how governments allocate scarce resources. Too few participants delegitimizes the process because political opponents can point to how participants are not representative of the larger polity. Citizens and CSOs need to have allies with whom they can connect and forge bonds of solidarity. Density matters as a means to generate a larger political coalition to maintain pressure on public officials. The policy conference system now complements the council system as a means to show the density of civil society activity in an arena (see chapter 5 for a broader discussion).

The final important subfactor is the extent to which poor citizens, who are the majority of Brazil's population, are actively involved in the CSOs that are, in turn, actively involved in new participatory policymaking processes. Greater numbers of poor citizens in both the CSOs and the new participatory institutions generate the necessary pressure to force government officials to allocate public goods to their communities. But when there are limited numbers of poor citizens participating, the political and policy debates shift from an inclusionary politics to a politics of advocating on behalf of others.

This book demonstrates that the variation in the configuration of civil society strongly affects how the participatory citizenship regime operates across policy areas. The variation across civil society sectors is due, in part, to the long-term development of the state, as there is a clear interplay between state and civil society (Migdal 2001). The importance of this finding is that efforts to expand the participatory citizenship regime into new policy arenas or into different cities or countries must be attentive to CSOs' capacity and breadth of activities to contribute to these processes. In areas of low trust, high violence, and weak social bonds, the potential impact of CSOs on policy processes is likely to be quite limited. In these cases, promoting bonds of solidarity among citizens might be all we can expect.

Government Support for Voice and Vote

The political coalition that forms the government and thus jointly controls participatory institutions is the third factor affecting the activation of the participatory citizens' regime. Citizens and government officials jointly control the participatory institutions directly involved in setting policy agendas that enable individuals to access their constitutional rights (see chapters 2 and 3). At the municipal level, researchers often use the party of the mayor as a proxy to gauge government support for participatory programs (Abers 2000; Avritzer 2002; Wampler 2007). In Belo Horizonte, for example, it was a twenty-year left and center-left political coalition of the Workers' Party and the Brazilian Socialist Party that actively implemented the participatory citizenship regime. And yet we see considerable variation over time and across policy arenas even within the city of Belo Horizonte.

Mayoral administrations' political support for participatory governance waxed and waned as a result of shifting political coalitions and bases of support.

In previous work, I argued that the government support for participatory institutions stems from a combination of four factors, including the government rewarding its political supporters, reaching out to politically unaffiliated citizens, party branding (participatory, inclusive, transparent), and the mayor's party affiliation (Wampler 2008). The evidence provided in this book supports the previous argument, but with a couple of key caveats. It is not just elected officials who matter but it is also mid-tier public officials (both political appointees and bureaucrats) who strongly affect how the local state will engage participatory institutions. Thus our research need to be attentive to strategies through which government officials at different levels are willing to support or hinder participatory politics. How senior-level political appointees are involved significantly affects how the participatory citizenship regime will be activated. When more senior-level political appointees are involved, there is a greater likelihood that the decisions of the participatory institutions will have a larger impact on public policy. But their involvement also tends to make the institution more political and less technical.

Conversely, when more bureaucrats are managing the participatory institution, there is a greater emphasis on technical issues. The ongoing, day-to-day support of mid-tier bureaucrats for voice and vote is crucial to allow the participatory institutions to function well. In particular, street-level bureaucrats managing the participatory institutions need to encourage a deliberative environment that expands participants' voices (Abers and Keck 2009; Lipsky 1980). When there is little government support for the power of the vote and when the vote doesn't result in state action, there is a greater likelihood that the participatory citizenship regime will not be activated. In addition to the support of senior-level political officials, the support of mid-tier bureaucrats for voice and vote is crucial to allow the participatory institutions to function well. Mid-tier political appointees and civil servants carry out the day-to-day administration of participatory institutions, which means that their involvement will have a great effect on the extent to which participants receive timely information and are able to jointly control decision-making processes.

There is no simple solution or magic formula concerning the appropriate balance between more politicized or more technical involvement of government officials. Researchers, policymakers, and activists need to be aware of the trade-offs between establishing more political and more technical participatory venues. More politicized venues create opportunities to forge and maintain political coalitions capable of pressing government officials to allocate resources to poor communities. The obvious downside is that these politicized processes are more susceptible to "participatory clientelism" and co-optation (Navarro 2003). Conversely, policymaking processes that are extensively technical create the opportunity to develop more coherent policies, which produce extensive benefits for targeted communities. A clear downside is that ordinary citizens lack the skills to actively and constructively contribute to these technical debates. The problem is that the influence of citizens will likely diminish overtime as technical criteria dominates policymaking debates; citizens from poorer communities will lack the mobilized organizations to pressure government officials to allocate resources to low-income neighborhoods. This book highlights the importance of public bureaucrats working inside the state, but researchers continue to lack a solid understanding of the mechanisms that link citizen participation and the internal decision-making processes that result in policy implementation.

Public Resources

The source and level of resources available has a tremendous impact on the contours of political contestation and debate within each policy arena. A stable source of funding enables citizens and CSOs to narrow their policy focus to a single institutional body, thereby enabling them to develop the skills to work inside policy arenas. When there are multiple sources of funding (e.g., the federal government, public banks, and development agencies), citizens and CSOs have a strong incentive to be involved in multiple venues. For example, in the housing arena, there are no automatic federal or state transfers. The uncertainty over resource allocation encourages housing activists to be politically active in order to maintain pressure on government officials to secure resources. Officials spend their precious time and political capital securing loans and transfers from the federal government and national development banks. In the health care policy arena, resources are largely based on federal transfers, which means that attention is focused on how the money is allocated rather than on securing the flow of resources.

The level of resources available also affects the incentive structures that motivate citizens to participate. Citizens, especially those who are not CSO leaders, are more likely to be engaged when their decisions make an impact on government spending. In Belo Horizonte's participatory budgeting, the slow decline in the absolute and relative level of resources dedicated to citizen decision making was a signal from the mayor's office that it was withdrawing support for participatory budgeting. The decrease in resources weakened one of the key incentives for citizens to be involved in this type of policymaking body. More broadly, the mayor was signaling a decrease in the authority that citizens could exercise during the policymaking process. Encouraging popular participation is based on dual incentives (specific and broad), which means that having a clear, stable set of resources helps to induce citizens to participate.

Rules Regulating Participation, Representation, and Deliberation

The internal rules of participatory institutions also explain the variation in how the participatory citizenship regime is being activated across the different policy arenas. More specifically, rules regarding who can participate, who has formal representation, and who can deliberate directly affected the activation of the new participatory citizenship regime. An important insight from this book's close analysis of multiple democratic institutions is that the distribution of seats to different groups (e.g., civil society, unions, government officials) establishes the political and policy contours of how these individuals and groups will affect the policymaking process. Who had a seat at the table varied across the six participatory institutions, which meant, in turn, that who could directly participate and who could deliberate shifted significantly. The specific rules of participation, therefore, had a large affect on the content and tenor of the deliberations. As representative democracy demonstrates, there are no easy solutions to the thorny political problem of which voices should be amplified inside of institutionalized venues. A methodological lesson based on these findings is that researchers studying participatory institutions need to develop methodological approaches that are much more attentive to how specific rules affect policy and political negotiations within new democratic institutions.

In Belo Horizonte and across Brazil, there are now two basic models that used to incorporate ordinary citizens into participatory institutions. The first model directly incorporates ordinary citizens first into local meetings and then, in a second stage, into large, municipal-wide meetings. Participatory budgeting and the public policy conferences are the best examples of this participatory model. Participation at the local level is designed to focus on policy oversight and the policy proposals. Ordinary citizens participate in large, municipal-wide meetings, where they are largely spectators. Their presence is necessary to show support for the community's policy interests as well as to help the government legitimize policy changes. Under this model, CSO leaders are responsive to their members, because they are elected directly by citizens.

The second model is a multitiered system whereby ordinary citizens are primarily engaged at the local level. Citizens participate at the local level and elect individuals to represent them at regional levels. Regional representatives then vote for municipal-level representatives (see chapter 5). This model is most commonly used in the public policy management councils. Under this model, municipal-level council members are most responsive to submunicipal council members (regional and local) because these individuals are their formal constituents and voters.

With regard to representation, the processes through which individuals are elected to participatory institutions produce different patterns of engagement. There are four commonly used rules that condition how different types of leaders will represent their organizations and their constituents. The first is a "filtering" mechanism, whereby leaders must first be elected at the local level, then the regional level, and, finally, the municipal level. This encourages participants to carry information from higher-up entities to lower-level entities; individuals elected to the municipal level need to stay in touch with lower-level elected officials to increase the likelihood of future elections. The council system is the best example of this structure.

The second electoral model is mass-based, whereby ordinary citizens vote in larger meetings for their representatives. In Belo Horizonte, this occurs in the case of participatory budgeting and PB Housing. In both cases, ordinary citizens vote for their leaders. These rules thus induce leaders to directly engage citizens in order to secure their vote. It also induces them to work with other candidates running for municipal-level offices. Participatory budgeting and the public policy conferences are examples.

The third type of representation encourages interlocking institutions to link citizens across multiple policy venues. Citizens elected to one council thus have the opportunity to be elected to a second council.

The fourth type of representation involves seats guaranteed to specific CSOs (e.g., CSOs representing elderly people or people with disabilities). The obstacle is that these rules are frozen in place, which makes it hard for new organizations to gain a place at the table.

The final set of rules that significantly affect how the participatory citizenship regime is activated determines the role of deliberation. A key distinction across the four policy arenas studied in this book is the extent to which the participatory institution encourages technical forms of deliberation or if the institution seeks to incorporate local knowledge (*mētis*). When technical deliberation is emphasized, it weakens the influence of leaders from poor communities because they don't have the skills to successfully debate with policy experts. When *mētis* is incorporated into the policy debate, there is a much greater emphasis on incorporating citizens and CSOs leaders from poor communities.

It is crucial to recognize the importance of both formal and informal deliberations. Formal deliberation allows citizens and CSO leaders to raise contentious issues in public venues, to signal their support for other CSOs, and to pressure government officials. Allowing citizens from a wide range of backgrounds to exercise voice expands the public policy debate. Beyond formal deliberations, informal conversations among citizens, CSO activists, and government officials are vital to the new political moment. Citizens and CSOs are able to forge new political networks, which ease the process of exchanging information. Deliberation is not constricted to a single venue but operates on a day-to-day basis. The informal deliberations generate policy networks, but they also generate personal networks. Thus the deliberative processes permit citizens and CSOs to gain access to new democratic policymaking venues while also allowing them to forge the personal connections that remain vital to Brazil's political culture.

In sum, it is the interplay of these five factors that will allow citizens to access political and social rights. By analyzing the variation in a single city (Belo Horizonte) that has led the way on reform, we now have a better set of analytical tools to understand reform in other cities and states, as well as the federal government. This book demonstrates that it is vital for researchers to more carefully analyze the construction of democracy at the level of direct public participation. Citizens participate in a variety of formal democratic venues, but their ability to jointly control these venues varies significantly over time and across specific policy sectors.

ACTIVATING DEMOCRACY BEYOND BELO HORIZONTE

There is now an extensive effort being made across Brazil by a wide number of governments and CSOs to activate the participatory citizenship regime to allow citizens access to a wider range of political and social rights. Political reformers are using the opportunities created by the 1988 constitution to incorporate new actors into policymaking venues to increase the likelihood that they can secure social rights. This section demonstrates how the participatory citizenship regime is being activated across Brazil.

Participatory Budgeting

Table 8.1 shows the spread of participatory budgeting across Brazil. This table demonstrates that there has been widespread adaptation across Brazil. Participatory budgeting is the most well-known example of municipal governments attempting to activate the participatory citizenship regime, which is based on the three pillars: popular participation, interlocking institutions, and social justice.

Workers' Party governments now administer half of PB cases, which highlights the centrality of the PT to the adoption of the process as well as the willingness of other political parties to adopt it. Evidence we collected from a survey applied in 2012 to ninety municipalities with participatory budgeting demonstrates that 50 percent of these programs were administered with political parties other than the PT (Spada and Wampler n.d.).

To assess the impact of participatory budgeting programs on governments and citizens, Mike Touchton and I analyzed its potential impact on social well-being (Touchton and Wampler 2014). We used a database from 1989 to 2008, which gave us twenty years of observations.

Table 8.1 Participatory Budgeting, 1989–2012
(Municipalities with at Least 50,000 Residents)

Mayoral period	Total PB cases	Total Municipalities	% Adopting
1989–1992	11	448	2
1993–1996	30	484	6
1997–2000	63	495	13
2001–2004	136	545	25
2005–2008	126	575	22
2009–2012	112	604	19

Sources: Spada, Wampler, and Coelho 2013; Avritzer and Wampler 2009; Wampler and Avritzer 2005.

Our article has four key findings. First, when municipal governments adopt PB, there is an associated increase in spending by the municipal government on health care and sanitation, two public goods desperately needed by poor Brazilians. Second, adopting PB is associated with an increase in the number of civil society organizations (CSOs). . . . Third, we find a reduction in infant mortality in municipalities that adopt PB. Again, this is a public health problem that more dramatically affects the poor than middle- and upper-income groups. This finding is linked to the first because increases in spending on health programs and sanitation are associated with decreases in infant mortality, thus improving well-being. Finally, an increase in the number of years that PB operates and the political party in charge of the municipal government produce more robust results. This implies that PB is associated with a broader, structural set of changes; new patterns of governance, state-society relations, and empowerment are initiated, thus producing more durable change. (Touchton and Wampler 2014, 1444)

These effects grew stronger over time, indicating that the changes were the result of the institutionalization of new ways of governance. Sonia Gonçalves used a similar data set, but one that covers only a few years, to identify similar changes (Gonçalves 2014; see also Boulding and Wampler 2010; Donaghy 2011, 2012). This book focused on a political and policy change in a single city, Belo Horizonte, but many of the cities adopting PB are also led by political coalitions attempting to activate the participatory citizenship regime. The evidence suggests that governing coalitions seeking to activate the participatory citizenship regime produce more positive effects than governments that are not strongly incorporating participatory institutions into their governing strategies.

Public Policy Management Councils

The second institutional expansion in Brazil is the more extensive use of public policy management councils (*conselhos*—see chapter 5 for an analysis of the councils in Belo Horizonte). By 2009, there were 65,224 councils. Eight councils are required by the federal government (education, health care, FUNDEB/FUNDEF, local school, school nutrition, social services, children and adolescents, child protection services) as a condition for financial transfers. There are over 40,000 councils in these eight areas.

Table 8.2 Public Policy Management Councils in Brazil

	1999	2006	2009	2011	Required
Education	5,010	3,760	4,403	4,718	Yes
Health Care	5,425	5,541 (2005)	5,417	5,553	Yes
Kids	3,948	4,622	5,084	5,446	Yes
Child Protection Services	3,011	5,167	5,472	5,521	Yes
Social Assistance	5,036	5,497 (2005)	5,527	5,527 (2009)	Yes
Fundef/FUNDEB		5,372	5,267	5,462	Yes
Local Schools	5,425	5,541 (2005)	5,417	4,243	Yes
School Nutrition		5,375	5,466	5,303	Yes
School Transportation		2,165	2,201	1,367	No
Bolsa Família			3,761		
Environment	1,176	2,039 (2004)	3,124		No
Watershed		2,829 (2004)	1,428		No
Housing	439	979 (2005)	2,373	2,360	No
All Others	2,943	9,141	10,284	5,057	No
Total	32,413	58,028	65,224	50,557	

Source: Adapted from Barreto 2011, 225.

The most important point about the councils is that they (1) provide for inclusion of citizens in a complex policymaking process, (2) establish oversight mechanisms, and (3) allow for federal and state administrators to provide information and monitor local governments (see chapter 5).

Table 8.2 demonstrates the explosion of councils over a period of twenty years in Brazil. The number of councils doubled between 1999 and 2009. This increase was partially induced by the federal government, as the fiscal transfers often require that municipalities have public policy management councils, which is an example of the federal government's role in using its authority to activate the participatory citizenship regime.

But the increase in the number of councils is also due to the voluntary adoption of councils by individual municipalities. Across Brazil, 55 percent of all municipalities voluntarily adopt at least one council that is not required by the federal government.

Table 8.3 shows that 45 percent of municipalities in all regions are not voluntarily adopting additional councils. These municipalities are adopt-

Table 8.3 Municipalities Voluntarily Adopting Councils

	None	One	Two or More	Total Municipalities
South	519 (49%)	442 (42%)	96 (9%)	1,057
Southeast	707 (42%)	553 (33%)	408 (25%)	1,668
North	193 (43%)	156 (35%)	100 (22%)	449
Northeast	832 (46%)	629 (35%)	332 (19%)	1,793
Center-West	197 (42%)	170 (37%)	99 (21%)	466
Total	2,448 (45%)	1,950 (36%)	1,035 (19%)	5,433

Source: Adapted from Barreto 2011, 225.

ing councils when required to do so by the federal government. My original hypothesis was that municipalities in the south and southeast would have a much greater percentage of municipalities that voluntarily adopted councils. Table 8.3 shows that this hypothesis is incorrect. The size of the municipal population is a much better explanation. The implication of this finding is that larger and midsize cities are much more likely to adopt the institutions strongly associated with local efforts to activate the participatory citizen regime.

The data in Table 8.4 clearly demonstrates that the voluntary adoption of councils is taking place in larger municipalities. Interestingly, there is a steady and consistent increase in the percentage of municipalities adopting one or more councils as the municipality grows in size. The evidence in these two tables indicates that medium and large municipalities across the country are voluntarily adopting participatory institutions.

In sum, this evidence demonstrates that midsize to large municipalities are adopting a broad number of participatory venues. Adopting and building new democratic institutions is thus more related to the size of the

Table 8.4 Voluntarily Adopting Councils (by Municipality Size)

	None	One	Two or More	Total Municipalities
Less than 5,000	791	429	83	1,303
	(61%)	(33%)	(6%)	
5001–10,000	641	470	101	
	(53%)	(39%)	(8%)	1,212
10,001–20,000	627	557	215	1,399
	(45%)	(40%)	(15%)	
20,001–50,000	333	383	327	1,043
	(32%)	(37%)	(31%)	
50,001–100,000	50	84	190	
	(15%)	(26%)	(59%)	324
100,001–500,000	5	26	214	245
	(2%)	(11%)	(87%)	
More than 500,000	1	1	36	38
	(2%)	(2%)	(96%)	

Source: Adapted from Barreto 2011, 225.

municipality than its region. The implication of this finding is that democratic institutions are being built in those environments where most Brazilians live.

Public Policy Conferences

During the 2003 and 2010 period, between five and eight million people participated in seventy-four national policy conferences (Avritzer 2012, 12). Most of the participation occurred at the municipal level, but participants' policy preferences were incorporated into state and federal policies. Millions of Brazilian citizens now participating in a policymaking process that links federal, state, and municipality governments, indicating that the concept of interlocking institutions can be successfully applied to a host of institutions not explicitly analyzed in this book (see also Pires and Vaz 2012). The policy conference system is an excellent example of "scaling up," whereby the federal government is attempting to find the institutions that allow it to active the participatory citizenship regime and engage in ongoing efforts to govern for a wider public. The Workers' Party led efforts to promote local-level participation during the 1990s, when the party was most successful at winning elections in large cities. When the party won Brazil's presidency in 2002, they shifted from a strategy of municipal-level, local democracy to a focus on national-level conferences. The "scaling up" offers potential to activate the participatory citizenship regime, but the government faces significant challenges.

The system of national conferences fits within the concept of interlocking institutions. We must be cognizant that these institutions do not provide participants with binding votes, but are designed to help policymakers set general policy directions. Pogrebinschi and Samuels (2014, 325) argue that

> a quantitative assessment confirms our key point: deliberations in and recommendations from Brazil' s National Public Policy Conferences can and do provide the source of important new national-level policies. Quantitatively at least, input from NPPCs is responsible for a substantial proportion of all new statutes in two of the three policy themes we considered. This analysis also confirms that NPPCs contributed to policy production under both Cardoso and Lula; thus, their impact does not depend on the PT holding power.

This is compelling evidence to suggest that the executive branch is drawing from the conferences as it sets policies. The mass-based participation is producing social and political change.

In sum, there are extensive political and policy reform efforts underway across Brazil to activate the participatory citizenship regime. The demonopolization of the state through the creation of a vast participatory architecture is one key step forward in permitting citizens to access political and social rights. But ongoing efforts to activate the participatory citizenship regime will depend on the ability of political reformers to simultaneously incorporate policies that promote popular participation, social justice, and interlocking institutions.

KEY LESSONS

The participatory citizenship regime establishes a series of institutions that expand the surface area of the state and induce citizens to participate through complementary incentives (Heller and Evans 2011). The public policy management councils, participatory budgeting, and the policy conferences create specific incentives for citizens to work within state-sanctioned venues. The participatory citizenship regime is activated when the new institutions use dual incentives (narrow and broad) to encourage citizen participation. Individuals and groups successfully pursue narrow self-interest, thereby allowing them to secure specific benefits that reward their participatory efforts (Ostrom 1990). But these institutions also create incentives for citizens to forge bonds with other citizens (Alexander 2006; Pateman 1970, 2012; Barber 1984). Citizens are rewarded for forming alliances with CSOs, thus forging collaborative relationships within the participatory venues as well as outside them. But these relationships are not easy—citizens' needs for basic and scarce public goods leads them into conflicts with CSOs because they are operating in a context of high demand and limited state resources. (See chapter 7 for a description of the acrimonious disputes in Morro de Papagaio.) Citizens and CSOs are involved in intense political competition over these scarce resources. The activation of the participatory citizenship regime takes place within an institutional environment that simultaneously promotes collaboration, contentious political debate, and political competition.

When citizens' incentives to participate are narrowly defined (only a focus on public goods allocation), it becomes more likely that a form of participatory clientelism will emerge. In this scenario, public officials will use the new institutional venues to offer a small number of material benefits to citizens and CSO activists. The latter will have little option but to accept the limited resources offered by government officials because they will have few other alternatives. Conversely, if citizens are principally involved in participatory institutions for ideological or moral reasons ("it is the right thing to do"; "we are building a new democracy"), robust participation will be less likely to be sustained because participants are more likely to be aligned with the incumbent government. This book demonstrates that the dual focus on narrower and broader interests is vital to establishing vibrant participatory institutions through which citizens can use political rights to gain access to social rights.

A second key lesson is that the new participatory institutions allow for the incorporation of *mētis* (local knowledge) into the policymaking process, which is changing how public officials take action in poor communities. The intensity with which Brazil's participatory institutions incorporate *mētis* falls along a wide continuum. The most limited incorporation of *mētis* helps citizens and governments to better target resource allocation and produce efficiencies during the implementation phase. As a result, citizens' local knowledge improves the quality of state services, which improve the quality of governance. From a democratic and rights perspective, the more expansive incorporation of local knowledge decreases the likelihood that public officials will trample on citizens' rights. Public officials are more likely to act with restraint because they are working closely with local citizens and CSOs to design projects that will transform their neighborhoods. Public officials can use these participatory venues to enhance the legitimacy of the local government and state as well as to build support for the political coalition that sustains them in power. Citizens and CSO leaders use these policymaking venues to establish informal ties to public officials, whom they can contact when problems develop within their communities.

A third important theoretical lesson is that the new participatory architecture creates specific incentives that induce poor Brazilians, who have long been the majority of the population, to participate in policy decision-making venues. The preferential bias for poor Brazilians is created both through specific rules (e.g., Quality of Life Index, techniques of access) and through a focus on policy areas that are of great interest to poor citizens (e.g., health care and education). For example, PB Regional and PB Housing have specific rules that allocate greater per capita funding to poorer communities and individuals. The public policy management councils focus on policies that are vital to the social well-being of Brazil's majority—health care, housing, education. As a result, participatory institutions alter the rules of the game and help to overcome long-term biases in favor of middle and upper classes that have long been associated with representative democracy. The participatory citizenship regime provides a means to overcome the class bias long associated with representative democracy. Across Belo Horizonte and Brazil, the distribution of wealth, access to information, and connections to public officials continue to favor Brazil's upper and middle classes, but the participatory institutions are one step, among several, that are transforming the deep inequality and exclusion that have long marked the country.

A fourth lesson is that the participatory citizenship regime firmly establishes CSO leaders as intermediaries between state and society (Baker, Ames, and Renno 2006). CSO leaders link government officials and ordinary citizens. The evidence presented throughout the book demonstrates that CSO leaders (with the exception of social service leaders) participate in civil society and participatory institutions, and they have contact with government officials (see chapter 6). Their engagement in civil society means that they have up-to-date information regarding their members' and neighbors' needs. Thus new networks are being created that allow citizens to broaden and diversify their political and policy connections. This builds on Granovetter's key insight, "strength of weak ties," which suggests that ties outside of one's primary group affiliation are a powerful means to gain new information and access to different opportunities (1973). CSO leaders representing poor citizens in Brazil have long been constrained by having a limited number of "weak ties." The activation of the participatory citizenship regime increases the number of weak ties that CSO leaders now have to use as they pursue their interests. The demonopolization of public officials' contact with CSO leaders is reducing the conditions through which clientelism flourishes because CSO leaders now have a much broader range of potential allies. At the broadest level, this book demonstrates how participatory institutions can regenerate the state and alter basic state-society relations. The direct engagement of citizens in participatory processes opens up how the state functions. Government officials must now provide greater levels of information to citizens, they must receive the approval of council members, and they subject themselves to public scrutiny. The institutions being crafted are moving political contestations beyond the traditional confines of representative democracy. Citizens and CSOs are now inserted into multiple participatory venues.

Finally, the participatory citizenship regime has greatly expanded the number of access points into the state. It expands the surface area of the state, breaking up the clientelistic monopolies of power holders (Heller and Evans 2010). Citizens and CSO leaders now have a far greater diversity of venues and contact points through which they can reach out to public officials. This is complemented by campaigns and elections, thereby increasing the opportunities for broad participation. Participatory democracy complements representative democracy, providing the institutional means to deepen the quality of democracy.

Activating the participatory citizenship regime, and by extension the 1988 constitution, is now at the core of political competition and conflict in Brazil. CSOs and citizens long excluded from formal public institutions now have direct access to key decision-making venues. As these groups seek to use their newly won political rights to secure social rights, there is strong political resistance from their political rivals. Altering the terrain of representative democracy by creating institutions with incentives that promote the ongoing participation of poor citizens places these citizens in direct conflict with Brazil's conservative middle classes and traditional political elite. The establishment of the 1988 constitution represents the first step in a larger and longer process through which some citizens and public officials are attempting to expand political, civil, and social rights protections.

Activating the participatory citizenship regime requires the intense, ongoing involvement of citizens, CSOs, and public officials as they seek to use new democratic institutions to expand access to the political and social rights guaranteed by the constitution. We should expect that the institutional venues that promote participation, social justice, and interlocking institutions will be adapted over time, allowing new generations of citizens and activists to mold the institutional venues used to respond to pressing problems. The ongoing activation of the participatory citizenship regime and the complementary adaptation of institutions promote the deepening of democracy: citizens and CSOs are using a broader participatory architecture to gain access to political and social rights formally guaranteed by the 1988 constitution.

Notes

One. Activating Democracy in Brazil

1. Between 1995 and 2014, I have occasionally had contact with participatory institutions in which citizens and CSOs specifically sought to prohibit local officials from providing support. But even within these institutions there was an effort to reconnect the local-level participatory program to higher levels of government.

2. See Yashar 2005 for an in-depth analysis of postliberal politics in Latin America.

Two. Establishing the Participatory Citizenship Regime

1. This phrase, "Brazil doesn't have citizens," was coined in 1881 by Louis Couty, a French biologist living in Rio de Janeiro (Carvalho 2001, 64). It referred to the fact that a small minority benefited from the social order, but the vast majority of the population were systematically excluded from access to the market, to land, to housing, and to public goods.

2. The military also didn't allow for the popular vote in all state capitals as well as in cities that were of "strategic importance."

Three. Rebuilding the Local State

1. In 1988, mayoral elections were a "first past the post," thus allowing mayors with a plurality of the vote to assume office.

2. This was confirmed in a 2010 interview with Sara, a legislative aide in the city council. Given the budgeting rules, each municipal legislator is allowed to

reallocate 150,000 reais from the "rainy day" fund, which then formally drops from 10 million reais to 5.5 million reais.

3. Patrus Ananias is a deeply religious man, so the phrase "division of the waters" is embedded with profound religious symbolism.

4. There was a minimum of nine thousand participants, but probably many more because we were only able to gather participation data on nine of the nineteen conferences.

5. In order to integrate food security into civil society as well as into the popular participation project, the government created Conselho Municipal de Abastecimento e Segurança (Lei Municipal 6.739 de October 17, 1994) in 1994. It was later replaced by COMSUAN-Conselho Municipal de Segurança Alimentar (Martins 2007, 181, 188).

6. These were interviews with community leaders involved in the housing, health care, and social services movements as well as in the favela Morro de Papagaio conducted between August 2009 and May 2010.

Four. Innovation and Renewal of Participatory Budgeting

1. The US $500 million was calculated by adding up the cost of the final project as listed in official government year-end reports. It does not include the cost of administering the program (e.g., personnel, transportation).

2. There is a robust academic and policy literature on participatory budgeting. It is beyond the scope of this chapter to cover the different debates but a sampling of the literature includes single case studies on Brazil in Abers 2002 and Baiocchi 2005 and individual chapters in Avritzer and Navarro 2003, as well as multicase studies in Wampler 2007, 2008, and Goldfrank 2007, 2011. On Europe see Sintomer et al. 2012; for international studies see Guanza and Baiocchi 2012.

3. Porto Alegre, the capital of the southern state of Rio Grande do Sul, is often recognized as having the first well-established case of PB. There were precursors to Porto Alegre's PB program, most commonly recognized as being in Lages, Santa Catarina, and Recife, Pernambuco.

4. This was adapted from Wampler and McNulty 2011.

5. In 2004, I interviewed Raul Ponte, a former PT mayor of Porto Alegre. He was unwilling to admit to the possibility that PB might discriminate against small groups or against the very poor. I left the interview uncertain if he was unwilling to admit a weakness in PB's basic institutional design or if he simply couldn't conceive that PB reproduces some of the same problems associated with representative democracy.

6. In Brazil, income is typically described based on monthly earnings (as opposed to hourly or yearly). The government sets the minimum amount that an

individual can be paid. It is typical to describe someone's income based on the number of monthly incomes that they earn.

7. This was adapted from Wampler et al. 2011.

8. In Brazil, voting is compulsory. Each citizen between the ages of eighteen and seventy must vote or justify his or her absence. In PB Digital, the government has no way to ensure that an individual's voting registration number is only used by that individual, which means that there is the potential for fraud. I would argue that the likelihood of extensive fraud is low because the stakes are low. Given that only a minimum level of resources is decided through the program, the risk of engaging in fraudulent behavior doesn't outweigh the limited benefits.

9. This data and direct quotation were gathered from the municipal government's website: www.pbh.gov.br (accessed March 5, 2010).

Five. Councils and Conferences

1. This mirrors the vertical, horizontal, and societal accountability debates. See Wampler 2007.

2. The changing composition of council members over time will likely change how they use these rules. In fifteen years of research on these councils, it has been my experience that most participants want to mobilize the state—to have the state do more. One could imagine that if libertarian or antistate activists gain control of a council, they could shut down the new governance system.

3. I follow the Brazilian political and academic tradition of distinguishing between civil society (*sociedade civil*) and unions (*sindicatos*). See chapter 1 for a more complete discussion.

4. Thanks to Chris Gibson, who made this argument to me, thus allowing me to better understand the differing political coalitions that were working with the council.

Six. Transforming the Engagement of Civil Society Organizations

1. The survey was carried out between November 25, 2009, and December 5, 2009. It was administered by the polling firm CP2 in Belo Horizonte based on lists of potential respondents provided by our research team. The survey was conducted via telephone.

2. Professor Mario Fuks of the Federal University of Minas Gerais originally obtained this list from the Department of Social Services for a different research project. Fuks graciously agreed to share the list with me, with the approval of the Department of Social Services. I thank Mario Fuks for his support.

Seven. Transforming Favelas

1. You can explore both favelas by using an online mapping service such as Google; search for "Morro de Papagaio, Belo Horizonte, Minas Gerais, Brazil" and "Alto Vera Cruz, Belo Horizonte, Minas Gerais, Brazil."

2. A small number of the favela's residents were included in a different planning district, which had a score of 0.52. The higher score is largely based on residents living in the middle- and upper-class neighborhoods next to the favela. The favela residents living close to the middle-class neighborhoods had much easier access to goods and services because businesses were more likely to establish themselves outside of the favela, where the property rights regime was clearer.

References

PRIMARY AND SECONDARY SOURCES

Abers, Rebecca. 2000. *Inventing Local Democracy: Grassroots Politics in Brazil.* Boulder: Lynne Rienner.

Abers, Rebecca, and Margaret E. Keck. 2009. "Mobilizing the State: The Erratic Partner in Brazil's Participatory Water." *Politics & Society* 37 (June): 289–314.

———. 2013. *Practical Authority: Agency and Institutional Change in Brazilian Water Politics.* New York: Oxford University Press.

Abrúcio, Fernando Luiz. 1998. *Os Barões da Federação: Os Governadores ea Redemocratização Brasileira.* São Paulo: Editora Hucitec.

Abrúcio, Fernando Luiz, and Cláudio Gonçlaves Couto. 1996. "A Redefinição do Papel do Estado no Âmbito Local." *São Paulo em Perspectiva* 10:40–47.

Acharya, Arnab, Adrián Gurza Lavalle, and Peter P. Houtzager. 2004. "Civil Society Representation in the Participatory Budget and Deliberative Councils of São Paulo, Brazil." *IDS Bulletin* 35 (2): 40–48.

Alexander, Jeffrey C. 2006. *The Civil Sphere.* Oxford: Oxford University Press.

Alvarez, Sonia E. 1990. *Engendering Democracy in Brazil: Women's Movements in Transition Politics.* Princeton, NJ: Princeton University Press.

———. 1993. "'Deepening' Democracy: Popular Movement Networks, Constitutional Reform, and Radical Urban Regimes in Contemporary Brazil." In *Mobilizing the Community*, edited by Robert Fisher and Joseph Kling. Newbury Park, CA: Sage.

Alvarez, Sonia E., Evelina Dagnino, and Arturo Escobar, eds. 1998a. *Cultures of Politics/Politics of Cultures: Re-Visioning Latin American Social Movements.* Boulder: Westview.

———. 1998b. "Introduction: The Cultural and the Political in Latin American Social Movements." In Alvarez, Dagnino, and Escobar 1998a.

Alves, Maria Helena Moreira. 2014. *State and Opposition in Military Brazil.* Austin: University of Texas Press.

Ames, Barry. 1994. "The Reverse Coattails Effect: Local Party Organization in the 1989 Brazilian Presidential Election." *American Political Science Review* 88:95–111.

———. 1995a. "Electoral Rules, Constituency Pressures, and Pork Barrel: Bases of Voting in the Brazilian Congress." *Journal of Politics* 57:324–43.

———. 1995b. "Electoral Strategy Under Open-List Proportional Representation." *American Journal of Political Science* 39:406–33.

———. 2001. *The Deadlock of Democracy in Brazil.* Ann Arbor: University of Michigan Press.

———. 2002. *The Deadlock of Democracy in Brazil: Interests, Identities, and Institutions in Comparative Politics.* Ann Arbor: University of Michigan Press.

Ansell, Chris. 2007. "Collaborative Governance in Theory and Practice." *Journal of Public Administration Research and Theory* 18 (4): 543.

Arendt, Hannah. 1958. *The Human Condition.* Chicago: University of Chicago Press.

Arias, Desmond. 2006. *Drugs and Democracy in Rio de Janeiro: Trafficking, Social Networks, and Public Security.* Chapel Hill: University of North Carolina Press.

Arias, Enrique Desmond, and Corinne Davis Rodrigues. 2006. "The Myth of Personal Security: Criminal Gangs, Dispute Resolution, and Identity in Rio de Janeiro's Favelas." *Latin American Politics and Society* 48 (4): 53–81.

Auyero, Javier. 2007. *Routine Politics and Violence in Argentina: The Gray Zone of State Power.* Cambridge and New York: Cambridge University Press.

Avritzer, Leonardo. 2002. *Democracy and the Public Space in Latin America.* Princeton, NJ: Princeton University Press.

———. 2003. "O Orçamento Participativo e a Teoria Dmocrática: Um Balanço Crítico." In *A Inovação Democratica no Brasil,* edited by L. Avritzer and Z. Navarro. São Paulo: Cortez.

———. 2004. *A Participação em São Paulo.* São Paulo: Editora UNESP.

———. 2009. *Participatory Institutions in Democratic Brazil.* Baltimore: Johns Hopkins University Press.

———. 2012. *Conferências nacionais: Ampliando e redefinindo os padrões de participação social no Brasil.* Brasilia: v.

Avritzer, Leonardo, and Clóvis Henrique Leite de Souza. 2013. *Conferências Nacionais: Atores, dinâmicas participativas e efetividade.* Brasilia: Instituto de Pesquisa Econômica Aplicada.

Avritzer, Leonardo, and Zander Navarro, eds. 2003. *A Inovação Democratica no Brasil.* São Paulo: Cortez.

Avritzer, Leonardo, and Brian Wampler. 2009. "The Expansion of Participatory Budgeting in Brazil." World Bank Institute.

Azevedo, Neimar Duarte. 2003. "Orçamento Participativo de Belo Horizonte: Elementos Para Uma Leitura Institucional." Master's thesis. Universidade Federal de Minas Gerais, Belo Horizonte, Brazil.

Azevedo, Sergio de, and Rodrigo Barroso Fernandes. 2005. *Orçamento Participativo: Construindo a Democracia*. Rio de Janeiro: Renevan.

Azevedo, Sergio de, and Ana Luiza Nabuco. 2008. *Democracia Participativa: A Experiência de Belo Horizonte*. Belo Horizonte: Editora Leitura.

Baierle, Sergio. 1998. "The Explosion of Citizenship: The Emergence of a New Ethical-Political Principal in Popular Movements in Porto Alegre, Brazil." In Alvarez, Dagnino, and Escobar 1998a.

Baiocchi, Gianpaolo. 2005. *Militants and Citizens: The Politics of Participatory Democracy in Porto Alegre*. Stanford, CA: Stanford University Press.

Baiocchi, Gianpaolo, Patrick Heller, and Marcelo Silva. 2011. *Bootstrapping Democracy: Transforming Local Governance and Civil Society in Brazil*. Stanford, CA: Stanford University Press.

Baker, Andy, Barry Ames, and Lucio Renno. 2006. "Social Context and Campaign Volatility in New Democracies: Networks and Neighborhoods in Brazil's 2002 Elections." *American Journal of Political Science* 50 (2): 382–99.

Barber, Benjamin. 1984. *Strong Democracy: Participatory Politics for a New Age*. Berkeley: University of California Press.

Baretto, Daniela Santos. 2011. "Pequisa de Informações Básicas Municipais (MUNIC): Instrumento para Avaliação de Instituições Particpativas Locais." In *A Efetividade das Instituições Participativas no Brasil: Perspectivas, abordagens e estratégias de avaliação*, edited by Roberto Pires. Brasilia: IPEA.

Baumgartner, Frank, and Bryan Jones. 1993. *Agendas and Instability in American Politics*. Chicago: University of Chicago Press.

Bedê, Mônica Maria Cadaval. 2005. "Trajetória da Formulação e Implantação da Política Habitacional de Belo Horizonte na Gestão da Frente BH Popular 1993/1996." Master's thesis. Federal University of Mina Gerais.

Bernam, Sheri. 1997. "Civil Society and the Collapse of the Weimar Republic." *World Politics* 49 (3): 401–29.

Bichir, Renata. 2005. "Investimos viários de pequeno porte no município de São Paulo, 1975–2000." In *São Paulo, 2000: Segregação, pobreza urbana e desigualdades sociais*. Edited by Eduardo Marques and Haroldo Torres. São Paulo: Senac.

Bobbio, Norberto. 1993. *Thomas Hobbes and the Natural Law Tradition*. Chicago: University of Chicago Press.

Boulding, Carew, and Brian Wampler. 2010. "Voice, Votes, and Resources: Evaluating the Effect of Participatory Democracy on Well-Being." *World Development*. 38 (1): 125–35.

Bryan, Frank M. 2004. *Real Democracy: The New England Town Meeting and How It Works*. Chicago: University of Chicago Press.

Burdick, John. 1993. *Looking for God in Brazil: The Progressive Catholic Church in Brazil's Religious Arena*. Berkeley: University of California Press.

Burnham, Walter Dean. 1970. *Elections and the Mainsprings of American Democracy*. New York: W. W. Norton.

Câmara Municipal de Vereadores de Belo Horizonte. 2004. Budget Committee Data.
———. 2010. "Sistema de Controle de Emendas e Projetos de Lei do Orçamento Annual." http://www.cmbh.mg.gov.br. Accessed April 19, 2010.
Campos, Cezar Rodrigues, Deborah Carvalho Malta, Afonso Teixeira Dos Reis, Alaneir de Fatina Dos Santos, and Emerson Elias Merhy. 1998. *Sistema Único de Saúde Em Belo Horizonte.* São Paulo: Xamã Editora.
Carey, John, and Matthew Shugart. 1995. "Incentives to Cultivate a Personal Vote: A Rank Ordering of Electoral Formulas." *Electoral Studies* 14:417–40.
Carvalho, José Murilo de. 1987. *Os Bestializados: O Rio de Janeiro e a República que não foi.* São Paulo: Companhia das Letras.
———. 2002. *Cidadania no Brasil. O longo Caminho.* Rio de Janeiro: Civilização Brasileira.
Casteñeda, Jorge. 1993. *Utopia Unarmed: The Latin American Left and the Cold War.* New York: Vintage Books.
Chaui, Marilena. 1989. *Cultura e Democracia: O Discurso Competente e Outras Falas.* São Paulo: Editora Cortez.
Cleary, Matthew. 2010. *The Sources of Democratic Responsiveness in Mexico.* Notre Dame, IN: University of Notre Dame Press.
Cohen, Jean, and Andrew Arato. 1992. *Civil Society and Political Theory.* Cambridge, MA: MIT Press.
Collier, Ruth Berins, and David Collier. 1991. *Shaping the Political Arena: Critical Junctures, the Labor Movement, and Regime Dynamics in Latin America.* Princeton, NJ: Princeton University Press.
Cornwall, Andrea, and Vera Schattan Coelho. 2007. *Spaces for Change? The Politics of Citizen Participation in New Democratic Arenas.* London: Zed Books.
Couto, Cláudio Gonçlaves. 1995. *O Desafio de ser Governo: O PT na Prefeitura de São Paulo (1988–1992).* Rio de Janeiro: Paz e Terra.
Couto, Cláudio Gonçalves, and Fernando Luiz Abrucio. 1995. "Governando a Cidade? A Força e a Fraqueza da Câmara Municipal." *São Paulo em Perspectiva.* 9:57–65.
Couto, Clàudio Gonçalves, and Rogério Arantes. 2006. "Constituição, Governo e Democracia no Brasil." *Revista Brasileira de Ciências Sociais* 21 (61): 41–62.
Cunha, Eleonora Schettni Martins. 2004. "Aprofundado a Democracia: O Potencial dos Conselhos de Polítícas a Orçamentos Participativos." Master's thesis. Universidade Federal de Minas Gerais, Belo Horizonte, Brazil.
———. 2009. "Efetividade deliberativa: Estudo comparado de Conselhos Municipais de Assistência Social (1997/2006)." Doctoral dissertation. Federal University of Minas Gerais.
Cunha, Olivia Maria Gomes. 1998. "Black Movements and the 'Politics of Identity in Brazil.'" In Alvarez, Dagnino, and Escobar 1998a.
Dagnino, Evelina. 1994. "Os Movimentos Sociais e a Emergência de Uma Nova Noção de Cidadania." In *Anos 90: Política e Sociedade no Brasil,* edited by Evelina Dagnino. São Paulo: Brasiliense.

———. 1998. "The Cultural Politics of Citizenship, Democracy and the State." In Alvarez, Dagnino, and Escobar 1998a.

———. 2007. "Citizenship: A Perverse Confluence." *Development in Practice.* 17 (4–5): 549–56.

Dagnino, Evelina, and Luciana Tatagiba. 2007. "Democracia, Sociedade Civil e Participação." *Argos.* 421–52.

Dahl, Robert A. 1961. *Who Governs? Democracy and Power in an American City.* New Haven, CT: Yale University Press.

———. 1971. *Polyarchy: Participation and Opposition.* New Haven, CT: Yale University Press.

de Jong, Jorrit, and Gowher Rizvi, eds. 2008. *The State of Access: Success and Failure of Democracies to Create Equal Opportunities.* Cambridge, MA: Ash Institute for Democratic Governance and Innovation, Harvard University; Washington, DC: Brookings Institution Press.

Diamond, Larry. 1999. *Developing Democracy: Towards Consolidation.* Baltimore: Johns Hopkins University Press.

Diamond, Larry, Juan Linz, and Seymour Martin Lipset. 1988. *Democracy in Developing Countries.* Boulder: Lynne Rienner.

Diamond, Larry, and Leonardo Morlino. 2004. "The Quality of Democracy: An Overview." *Journal of Democracy* 15 (4): 20–31.

Diani, Mario. 1992. "The Concept of Social Movements." *The Sociological Review* 40 (1): 1–25.

Donaghy, Maureen. 2011. "Do Participatory Governance Institutions Matter? Municipal Councils and Social Housing Programs in Brazil." *Journal of Comparative Politics* 44 (1): 83–102.

———. 2012. *Civil Society and Participatory Governance: Municipal Councils and Social Housing Programs in Brazil.* New York: Routledge.

Draibe, Sonia M. 1993. "Qualidade de vida e reformas de programas sociais: O Brasil no cenário latino-americano." *Lua Nova* 31:5–46.

Dryzek, John S. 2000. *Deliberative Democracy and Beyond: Liberals, Critics, Contestations.* Oxford: Oxford University Press.

Eakin, Marshall C. 2001. *Tropical Capitalism: The Industrialization of Belo Horizonte, Brazil.* New York: Palgrave.

Encarnación, Omar. 2003. *The Myth of Civil Society: Social Capital and Democratic Consolidation in Spain and Brazil.* New York: Palgrave Macmillan.

Erundina, Luiza. 1990. "Sem Medo de Ser Governo." *Teoria e Debate* 11:13–15.

———. 1991. *Excercicio de Paixão Politica.* São Paulo: Cortez Editora.

Escobar, Arturo, and Sonia E. Alvarez. 1992. *The Making of Social Movements in Latin America.* Boulder: Westview.

Evans, Peter. 1979. *Dependent Development: The Alliance of Multinational, State, and Local Capital in Brazil.* Princeton, NJ: Princeton University Press.

———. 1995. *Embedded Autonomy: States and Industrial Transformation.* Princeton, NJ: Princeton University Press.

Evans, Peter B., Dietrich Rueschemeyer, and Theda Skocpol, eds. 1985. *Bringing the State Back In.* New York: Cambridge University Press.

Fausto, Boris. 1999. *A Concise History of Brazil.* Cambridge: Cambridge University Press.

Fedozzi, Luciano. 1998. *Orçamento Participativo: Reflexões Sobre a Experiência de Porto Alegre.* Porto Alegre: Tomo Editorial.

———. 2000. *O Poder da Aldeia: Gênese e História do Orçamento Participativo de Porto Alegre.* Porto Alegre: Tomo Editorial.

Fishkin, James. 1993. *Democracy and Deliberation: New Directions for Democratic Reform.* New Haven, CT: Yale University Press.

French, Jan. 2006. "Buried Alive: Imaging Africa in the Brazilian Northeast." *American Ethnologist* 33 (3): 340–60.

French, John D. 1992. *The Brazilian Workers' ABC: Class Conflict and Alliances in Modern São Paulo.* Chapel Hill: University of North Carolina Press.

Fung, Archon. 2003. "Survey Article: Recipes for Public Spheres: Eight Institutional Design Choices and Consequences." *Journal of Political Philosophy* 11 (3): 338–67.

———. 2006. "Varieties of Participation in Complex Governance." *Public Administration Review* 66 (1): 66–75.

Fung, Archon, and Erik Olin Wright. 2001. "Deepening Democracy: Innovations in Empowered Participatory Governance." *Politics & Society* 29:5–41.

———. 2003. *Deepening Democracy: Institutional Innovations in Empowered Participatory Governance.* London: Verso Books.

Garreton, Manuel. 1994. *The Chilean Political Process.* Boston: Unwin Hyman.

Gay, Robert. 1994. *Popular Organization and Democracy in Rio de Janeiro: A Tale of Two Favelas.* Philadelphia: Temple University Press.

Goldfrank, Benjamin. 2007. "The Politics of Deepening Local Democracy: Decentralization, Party Institutionalization, and Participation." *Comparative Politics* 39 (2): 147–68.

———. 2011. *Deepening Local Democracy in Latin America: Participation, Decentralization and the Left.* University Park: Pennsylvania State University Press.

Gomes, Lilian. 2004. *Entre o Legal e o Ilegal: Associativismo e participação em três vilas e favelas em Belo Horizonte—estudo de caso comparativo.* Master's thesis. Federal University of Minas Gerais.

———. 2009. *Justiça seja feita: Direito quilombola ao território.* Doctoral dissertation. Federal University of Minas Gerais.

Gonçalves, Patrícia Garcia. 2008. "Limites e Possibilidades da Democracia Representativa Na Produção Do Espaço Urbano: Uma análise a partir da atuação da Câmara Municipal de Belo Horizonte." Master's thesis. Federal University of Minas Gerais.

Gonçalves, Sónia. 2014. "The Effects of Participatory Budgeting on Municipal Expenditures and Infant Mortality in Brazil." *World Development* 53:94–110.

Granovetter, Mark. 1973. "The Strength of Weak Ties." *American Journal of Sociology* 78 (6): 1.

Grindle, Marilee. 2000. *Audacious Reforms: Institutional Invention and Democracy in Latin America.* Baltimore: Johns Hopkins University Press.

———. 2007. *Going Local: Decentralization, Democratization, and the Promise of Good Governance.* Princeton, NJ: Princeton University Press.

Gunaza, Ernesto, and Gianpaolo Baiocchi. 2012. "The Power of Ambiguity: What Travels as Participatory Budgeting." *Journal of Public Deliberation* 8 (2).

Habermas, Jürgen. 1989. *The Structural Transformation of the Public Sphere: An Inquiry into a Category of Bourgeois Society.* Cambridge, MA: MIT Press.

Hagopian, Frances. 1996. *Traditional Politics and Regime Change in Brazil.* New York: Cambridge University Press.

Hanchard, Michael. 1994. *Orpheus and Power: The Movimento Negro of Rio de Janeiro and São Paulo, Brazil, 1945–1988.* Princeton, NJ: Princeton University Press.

Heller, Patrick. 2000. "Degrees of Democracy: Some Comparative Lessons from India." *World Politics* 52 (4): 484–519.

———. 2001. "Moving the State: The Politics of Democratic Decentralization in Kerala, South Africa, and Porto Alegre." *Politics and Society* 29 (1): 131–63.

Heller, Patrick, and Peter Evans. 2010. "Taking Tilly South: Durable Inequalities, Democratic Contestation, and Citizenship in the Southern Metropolis." *Theory and Society* 39 (3–4): 433–50.

Hirschman, Albert O. 1970. *Exit, Voice, and Loyalty: Responses to Decline in Firms, Organizations, and States.* Cambridge, MA: Harvard University Press.

Hochstetler, Kathryn, and Margaret E. Keck. 2007. *Greening Brazil: Environmental Activism in State and Society.* Durham, NC: Duke University Press.

Holston, James. 2008. *Insurgent Citizenship: Disjunctions of Democracy and Modernity in Brazil.* Princeton, NJ: Princeton University Press.

———. 2009. "Insurgent Citizenship in an Era of Global Urban Peripheries." *City & Society* 21 (2): 245–67.

Huckfeldt, R. R., and J. Sprague. 1995. *Citizens, Politics, and Social Communication: Information and Influence in an Election Campaign.* Cambridge: Cambridge University Press.

Hunter, Wendy. 2010. *The Transformation of the Workers' Party in Brazil, 1989–2009.* New York: Cambridge University Press.

Huntington, Samuel. 1993. *The Third Wave: Democratization in the Late Twentieth Century.* Norman: University of Oklahoma Press.

Instituto Brasileiro de Geografia e Estatística. 2014. MUNIC Database. http://www.ibge.gov.br/home/estatistica/economia/perfilmunic/default.shtm. Accessed April 20, 2014.

Jacobi, Pedro. 1989. *Movimentos Sociais e Políticas Públicas: Demandas por Saneamento búsico e sa'de, São Paulo 1974–84.* São Paulo: Cortez Editora.

Junge, Benjamin. 2012. "NGOs as Shadow Pseudopublics: Grassroots Community Leaders' Perceptions of Change and Continuity in Porto Alegre, Brazil."
American Ethnologist 39 (2): 407–24.

Karl, Terry, and Phillippe Schmitter. 1991. "What Democracy Is . . . and Is Not."
Journal of Democracy 2 (3): 75–88.

Keck, Margaret E. 1992. *The Workers' Party and Democratization in Brazil.* New
Haven, CT: Yale University Press.

Key, V. O. 1964. *Politics, Parties and Pressure Groups.* New York: Thomas Y.
Cromwell.

Kingstone, Peter R., and Timothy J. Power, eds. 2000. *Democratic Brazil: Actors,
Institutions, and Processes.* Pittsburgh: University of Pittsburgh Press.

———, eds. 2008. *Democratic Brazil Revisited.* Pittsburgh: University of Pittsburgh Press.

Knoke, David. 1990a. "Networks of Political Action: Toward Theory Construction." *Social Forces* 68 (4): 1041–63.

———. 1990b. *Political Networks: The Structural Perspective.* New York: Cambridge University Press.

Kohli, Atul. 2004. *State-Directed Development: Political Power and Industrialization in the Global Periphery.* Cambridge: Cambridge University Press.

Lavalle, Adrián Guraz. 2003. "Sem pena nem glória: O debate sobre a sociedade
civil nos anos 1990." *Novos Estudos Cebrap* 66:91–110.

Lavalle, Adrián Gurza, Arnab Acharia, and Peter Houtzager. 2005. "Beyond Comparative Anecdotalism: Lessons on Civil Society and Participation from São
Paulo, Brazil." *World Development* 33 (6): 951–64.

Lavalle, Adrián Gurza, Peter P. Houtzager, and Graziela Castello. 2006. "Democracia, pluralização da representação e sociedade civil." *Lua Nova* 67:49–103.

Lavalle, Adrián Gurza, and Ernesto Isunza Vera. 2011. "A Trama da Critica
Democrática: da Participação á Representação e á Accountability." *Lua Nova*
84:95–139.

Leal, Victor Nunes. 1997. *Coronelismo, Enxada e Voto: O Município e o Regime
Representativo no Brasil.* São Paulo: Editora Nova Fronteira.

Lipsky, Michael. 1980. *Street-Level Bureaucracy: Dilemmas of the Individual in Public Services.* New York: Russell Sage Foundation.

Machado, Moisés, Telma Gonçalves Menicucci, and Zoraya Bernadedete de Souza.
2009. "A Experiência da Política de Segurança Alimentar e Nutricional de
Belo Horizonte: Parcerias, Participação e Controle Social." *Revista do Obser-
vatatório do Melênio de Belo Horizonte* 2 (1): 83–99.

Madison, James. 1787a. "Federalist 10." *The Federalist Papers.*

———. 1787b. "Federalist 51." *The Federalist Papers.*

Mainwaring, Scott. 1986. *The Catholic Church and Politics in Brazil, 1916–1985.*
Stanford, CA: Stanford University Press.

———. 1999. *Rethinking Party Systems in the Third Wave of Democratization: The
Case of Brazil.* Stanford, CA: Stanford University Press.

Mainwaring, Scott, and Timothy R. Scully, eds. 1995. *Building Democratic Institutions: Party Systems in Latin America.* Stanford, CA: Stanford University Press.

Manin, Bernard. 1997. *The Principles of Representative Government.* New York: Cambridge University Press.

Mansbridge, Jane. 2012. "On the Importance of Getting Things Done." *PS: Political Science & Politics* 45 (1): 1–8.

Mansuri, Ghazala, and Vijayendra Rao. 2004. "Community-Based and -Driven Development: A Critical Review." *World Bank Research Observer* 19 (1): 1–39.

———. 2012. *Localizing Development: Does Participation Work?* Washington, DC: World Bank Publications.

Marques, Eduardo, and Haroldo Torres. 2005. *São Paulo, 2000: Segregação, pobreza urbana e desigualdades sociais.* São Paulo: Senac.

Marquetti, Adelmir. 2003. "Democracia, Equidade e Effciencia, o Caso do Orcçamento Participativo em Porto Alegre." In *Inovaç o Democrática no Brasil: O Orçamento Participativo,* edited by L. Avritzer and Z. Navarro. São Paulo: Cortez Editores.

Marquetti, Adalmir, Geraldo Adriano de Campos, Roberto Pires, and Aldecy José Garcia de Moraes. 2008. *Democracia participative e redistribição: Análise de experiências de orçamento participativo.* São Paulo: Xamã.

Marshall, Thomas Humphrey. 1950. *Citizenship and Social Class: And Other Essays.* Garden City, NY: Doubleday.

Martins, Ana Flavia. 2007. "Belo Horizonte 'Democrâtica-Popular': Uma anâlise descritiva das instituições de participaç o popular em Belo Horizonte." Master's thesis. Federal University of Minas Gerais.

Martins, Paulo Emilio Matos, and Otavio Penna Pieranti. 2006. *Estado o Gestão Pública: Visões do Brasil Contemporâneo.* Rio de Janeiro: FGV.

Marx, Anthony. 1998. *Making Race and Nation: A Comparison of South Africa, the United States, and Brazil.* New York: Cambridge University Press.

Matta, Roberto da. 1979. *Carnavais, Malandros e Herois: Para Uma Sociologia de Dilema Brasileiro.* Rio de Janeiro: Zahar Editores.

Mayhew, David. 1974. *Congress: The Electoral Connection.* New Haven, CT: Yale University Press.

McAdam, Doug, John D. McCarthy, and Mayer N. Zald. 1996. *Comparative Perspectives on Social Movements: Political Opportunities, Mobilizing Structures, and Cultural Framings.* New York: Cambridge University Press.

McAdam, Doug, Sidney Tarrow, and Charles Tilly. 2001. *Dynamics of Contention.* New York: Cambridge University Press.

McAllister, Leslie. 2008. *Making Law Matter: Environmental Protection and Legal Institutions in Brazil.* Stanford, CA: Stanford University Press.

McClurg, Scott, and Joseph Young. 2011. "Political Networks." *PS: Political Science & Politics* 44 (1): 39–43.

McNulty, Stephanie. 2011. *Voice and Vote: Decentralization and Participation in Post-Fujimori Peru.* Stanford, CA: Stanford University Press.

Migdal, Joel. 2001. *State in Society: Studying How States and Societies Transform and Constitute One Another.* New York: Cambridge University Press.

Mische, Anne. 2008. *Partisan Publics: Communication and Contention across Brazilian Youth Activist Networks.* Princeton, NJ: Princeton University Press.

Montero, Alfred. 2014. *Brazil: Reversal of Fortune.* Cambridge: Polity.

Montero, Alfred, and David Samuels. 2004. *Decentralization and Democracy in Latin America.* Notre Dame, IN: University of Notre Dame.

Murray Li, Tanya. 2007. *The Will to Improve: Governmentality, Development and the Practice of Politics.* Durham, NC: Duke University Press.

Nahas, Maria Inês Pedrosa, Vera Lúcia Alves Batista Martins, Leonardo Pontes Guerra, Rodrigo Ferreira Simões, and Otávio de Avelar Esteves. n.d. *Metodologia de Construção de Índices e Indicadores Sociais, como Instrumentos Balizadores da Gestão Municipal da Qualidade de Vida Urbana: Uma síntese da experiência de Belo Horizonte.* Unpublished manuscript consulted in 2009.

Nahas, Maria Inês Pedrosa, Carla Andréa Ribeiro, Otávio de Avelar Esteves, Samy Kopit Moscovitch, and Vera Lúcia Alves Batista Martins. 2000. "O Mapa da Exclusao Social de Belo Horizonte." *Caderno Cienca Sociais* 7 (10): 75–88.

Navarro, Renato. n.d. "Democratização na gestão da política de moradia popular em Belo Horizonte, anos 1990: uma experiência possível de ser disseminada." In *Habitação Social nas Metrópoles Brasileiras: Uma avaliação das políticas habitacionais em Belém, Belo Horizonte, Porto Alegre, Recife, Rio de Janeiro e São Paulo no final do século XX.* Unpublished manuscript.

Navarro, Zander. 2003. "O 'Orçamento Participativo' de Porto Alegre (1989–2002): Um conciso comentário crítico." In *A Inovação Democratica no Brasil,* edited by Leonardo Avritzer and Zander Navarro. São Paulo: Cortez.

North, Douglas. 1990. *Institutions, Institutional Challenges and Economic Performance.* Cambridge: Cambridge University Press.

Nylen, William R. 2002. "Testing the Empowerment Thesis: The Participatory Budget in Belo Horizonte and Betim, Brazil." *Comparative Politics* 34:127–45.

———. 2003. *Participatory Democracy Versus Elitist Democracy: Lessons from Brazil.* New York: Palgrave Macmillan.

O'Donnell, Guillermo. 1994. "The State, Democratization and Some Conceptual Problems: A Latin American View with Glances at Some Post-Communist Countries." In *Democracy, Markets, and Structural Reform in Latin America,* edited by W. C. Smith, C. H. Acuma, and E. A. Gamarra. New Brunswick, CT: Transaction.

———. 1998. "Horizontal Accountability in New Democracies." *Journal of Democracy* 9:112–26.

O'Donnell, Guillermo, and Philippe Schmitter. 1986. *Transitions from Authoritarian Rule: Tentative Conclusions about Uncertain Democracies.* Baltimore: Johns Hopkins University Press.

Olson, Mancur. 1965. *The Logic of Collective Interests.* Cambridge, MA: Harvard University Press.

Ostrom, Elinor. 1990. *Governing the Commons: The Evolution of Institutions for Collective Action.* Cambridge: Cambridge University Press.

Pateman, Carole. 1970. *Participation and Democratic Theory.* Cambridge: Cambridge University Press.

———. 2012. "Participatory Democracy Revisited." *Perspectives on Politics* 10 (1): 7.

Pereira, Luiz Carols Bresser, and Nuria Cunill Grau. 1999. *O Público Não-Estatal na Reforma do Estado.* Rio de Janeiro: Fundação GetúlioVargas/CLAD.

Perlman, Janice E. 2010. *Favela: Four Decades of Living on the Edge in Rio de Janeiro.* New York: Oxford University Press.

Pires, Roberto, and Alexander Vaz. 2012. *Participação social como método de governo? Um mapeamento das" interfaces socioestatais" nos programas federais.* Texto para Discussão #1707. Instituto de Pesquisa Econômica Aplicada.

Pitkin, Hanna Fenichel. 1967. *The Concept of Representation.* Berkeley: University of California Press.

Plotke, David. 1997. "Representation Is Democracy." *Constellations* 4 (1): 18–34.

Pogrebinschi, Thamy, and David Samuels. 2014. "The Impact of Participatory Democracy: Evidence from Brazil's National Public Policy Conferences." *Comparative Politics* 46 (3): 313–32.

Polletta, Francesca. 2005. "How Participatory Democracy Became White: Culture and Organizational Choice." *Mobilization* 10 (2): 271.

Prefeitura Municipal de Belo Horizonte. 2013a. "Participação Popular no Orçamento Participativo." Gerência do Orçamento Participativo.

———. 2013b. "Valor aprovado atualizado por OP." Gerência do Orçamento Participativo.

———. 2013c. "Participação no OP Habitação." Gerência do Orçamento Participativo.

———. 2013d. "Participação no OP Digital." Gerência do Orçamento Participativo.

Przeworski, Adam, Susan C. Stokes, and Bernard Manin, eds. 1999. *Democracy, Accountability, and Representation.* New York: Cambridge University Press.

Putnam, Robert, Robert Leonardi, and Raffaela Nanetti. 1994. *Making Democracy Work: Civic Traditions in Modern Italy.* Princeton, NJ: Princeton University Press.

Roberts, Kenneth. 1998. *Deepening Democracy? The Modern Left and Social Movements in Chile and Peru.* Stanford, CA: Stanford University Press.

Roniger, Luis. 1994. *Democracy, Clientelism and Civil Society.* Boulder: Lynne Rienner.

Ross, Michael. 2006. "Is Democracy Good for the Poor?" *American Journal of Political Science* 50 (4): 860–74.

Sales, Teresa. 1994. "Raízes da Desigualdade Docial na Cultura Política Brasileira." *Revista Brasileira de Ciências Sociais* 25:26–37.

Samuels, David. 2003. "Fiscal Straitjacket: The Politics of Macroeconomic Reform in Brazil 1995–2002." *Journal of Latin American Studies* 35 (3): 545–69.

———. 2004. "From Socialism to Social Democracy: Party Organization and the Transformation of the Workers' Party in Brazil." *Comparative Political Studies* 37 (9): 999–1024.

———. 2007. "Brazilian Democracy Under Lula and the PT." In *Constructing Democratic Governance in Latin America*, edited by J. Dominguez and M. Shifter. Baltimore: Johns Hopkins University Press.

Sandbrook, Richard, Marc Edelman, Patrick Heller, and Judith Teichman. 2007. *Social Democracy in the Global Periphery: Origins, Challenges, Prospects.* Cambridge: Cambridge University Press.

Santos, Boaventura de Sousa. 2005. *Democratizing Democracy: Beyond the Liberal Democratic Canon.* London: Verso Books.

Santos, Wanderly Guilherme. 1979. *Cidadania e Justiça: A Política Social na Ordem Brasileira.* Rio de Janeiro: Editora Campus.

Saward, Michael. 2010. *The Representative Claim.* New York: Oxford University.

Schattschneider, E. E. 1960. *The Semisovereign People: A Realist's View of Democracy in America.* New York: Holt, Rinehart and Winston.

Schlozman, Kay Lehman, Sidney Verba, and Henry E. Brady. 2012. *The Unheavenly Chorus: Unequal Political Voice and the Broken Promise of American Democracy.* Princeton, NJ: Princeton University Press.

Schmitter, Philippe. 1974. "Still the Century of Corporatism?" *Review of Politics* 36 (1): 85–131.

———. 2004. "The Ambiguous Virtues of Accountability." *Journal of Democracy* 15 (4): 47–60.

Schumpeter, Joseph. 1942. *Capitalism, Socialism, and Democracy.* New York: Harper & Bros.

Scott, James C. 1998. *Seeing Like a State: How Certain Schemes to Improve the Human Condition Have Failed.* New Haven, CT: Yale University Press.

Sen, Amartya. 1999. *Development as Freedom.* Oxford: Oxford University Press.

Sintomer, Ives, Carsten Herzberg, Anja Röcke, and Giovanni Allegretti. 2012. "Transnational Models of Citizen Participation: The Case of Participatory Budgeting." *Journal of Public Deliberation* 8 (2).

Skidmore, Thomas. 1999. *Brazil: Five Centuries of Change.* New York: Oxford University Press.

Snyder, Richard. 2001. "Scaling Down: The Subnational Comparative Method." *Studies in Comparative International Development* 26 (1): 93–110.

Soares, Jose Arlindo. 1982. *A Frente do Recife e o Governo do Arraes: Nacionalismo em Crise—1955/1964.* Rio de Janeiro: Paz e Terra.

Somarriba, Maria das Mercês, Gezica Valadares, and Mariza Rezende Afonso. 1984. *Lutas Urbanas em Belo Horizonte.* Petrópolis: Vozes.

Somers, Margaret R. 1993. "Citizenship and the Place of the Public Sphere: Law, Community, and Political Culture in the Transition to Democracy." *American Sociological Review* 58 (5): 587–620.

Spada, Paolo, Brian Wampler, and Denilson Coelho. 2013. Research project funded by the Ash Center for Democracy at Harvard University and Boise State University. November 2012–February 2013.

Stiglitz, Joseph. 2007. *Making Globalization Work.* New York: Norton.

Tarrow, Sidney. 1998. *Power in Movement: Social Movements and Contentious Politics.* 2nd ed. New York: Cambridge University Press.

Tatagiba, Luciana. 2002. "Os Conselhos Gestores ea Democratização Das Políticas Públicas no Brasil." In *Sociedade Civil e Espaços Públicos no Brasil,* edited by E. Dagnino. São Paulo: Paz e Terra.

Thompson, E. P. 1996. *The Making of the English Working Class.* New York: Vintage.

Tocqueville, Alexis de. 1969. *Democracy in America.* New York: Harper Perennial.

Touchton, Michael, and Brian Wampler. 2014. "Improving Social Well-Being through New Democratic Institutions." *Comparative Political Studies* 47 (10): 1442–69.

Tribunal Superior Eleitoral. 2013. http://www.tse.jus.br/eleicoes/eleicoes-anteriores /eleicoes-anteriores. Accessed December 15, 2013.

Tsebelis, George. 2002. *Veto Players: How Political Institutions Work.* Princeton, NJ: Princeton University Press.

Urbinati, Nadia. 2000. "Representation as Advocacy: A Study of Democratic Deliberation." *Political Theory* 28 (6): 758–86.

Van Cott, Donna Lee. 2008. *Radical Democracy in the Andes.* New York: Cambridge University Press.

Verba, Sidney, Kay Lehman Schlozman, and Henry E. Brady. 1995. *Voice and Equality.* Cambridge: Cambridge University Press.

Viana, Oliveira. 1987. *Instituições Políticas Brasileiras.* Vol. 2. Belo Horizonte: Editora Itatiaia.

Vianna, Solon Magalhäes. 1992. "A descentralização tutelada." *Saúde debate* 35:35–38.

Villas-Boas, Renta. 1994. *Participação Popular nos Governos Locais.* São Paulo: Instituto Pólis.

Villas-Boas, Renta, and Vera Telles. 1995. *Poder Local, Participação Popular, Construção da Cidadania.* São Paulo: Instituto Pólis.

Wampler, Brian. 2007. *Participatory Budgeting in Brazil: Contestation, Cooperation, and Accountability.* University Park: Pennsylvania State University Press.

———. 2008. "When Does Participatory Democracy Actually Deepen Democracy? Lessons from Brazil." *Comparative Politics* 41 (1): 61–81.

———. 2009. CSO Leadership Survey.

———. 2010. "Morro de Papagaio and Alto Vera Cruz: Survey of Residents."

———. 2012. "Participation, Representation, and Social Justice: Using Participatory Governance to Transform Representative Democracy." *Polity* 44 (4): 666–82.

Wampler, Brian, and Leonardo Avritzer. 2004. "Participatory Publics: Civil Society and New Institutions in Democratic Brazil." *Comparative Politics* 36 (3): 291–312.

———. 2005. "The Spread of Participatory Democracy in Brazil: From Radical Democracy to Good Government." *Journal of Latin American Urban Studies* 7:37–52.

Wampler, Brian, and Stephanie McNulty. 2011. *Does Participatory Governance Matter? Exploring the Nature and Impact of Participatory Reforms.* Washington, DC: Woodrow Wilson International Center for Scholars.

Weffort, Francisco. 1984. *Porque Democracia?* São Paulo: Editora Brasiliense.

Weyland, Kurt. 1996. *Democracy Without Equity: Failures of Reform in Brazil.* Pittsburgh: University of Pittsburgh Press.

Wolfe, Joel. 1993. *Working Women, Working Men: São Paulo and the Rise of Brazil's Industrial Working Class 1900–1955.* Durham, NC: Duke University Press.

Wolford, Wendy. 2010. *The land Is Ours Now: Social Mobilization and the Meanings of Land in Brazil.* Durham, NC: Duke University Press.

Yashar, Deborah J. 2005. *Contesting Citizenship in Latin America: The Rise of Indigenous Movements and the Post Liberal Challenge.* Cambridge: Cambridge University Press.

INTERVIEWS

All interviews and meetings conducted in Belo Horizonte unless noted.

Ananias, Patrus. Former mayor of Belo Horizonte. November 14, 2011.

Arthuzzi, Marina. Program director of Cultural Center, Alto Vera Cruz. April 30, 2010.

Beatriz. Community organizer. Morro de Papagaio. September 19, 2009.

Bernedete. Community organizer, Morro de Papagaio. April 20, 2010.

Campos, Veronica. Director of Participatory Budgeting. October 7, 2009.

Cordero, Valdete da Silva. Community organizer, Alto Vera Cruz. May 3, 2010.

Corrêa, Sabrina Oliveira. Community organizer, Alto Vera Cruz. May 4, 2010.

Crispim, Marcos Antonio. Community organizer, Alto Vera Cruz. May 4, 2010.

Cruz, Marcia. Community organizer. November 18, 2009.

Davila. Community organizer, Morro de Papagaio. October 10, 2009.

Dutra, Ivan Matos. Community organizer, Alto Vera Cruz. May 3, 2010.

Enrique, Romeo, Municipal employee, BH Cidadania in Santa Lúcia. April 6, 2010.

Ferreira, Willer Marcos. President of municipal health care council and community organizer. October 7 and November 17, 2009.

Gonçalves, Patricia Garcia. Legislative aide at city council. April 19, 2010.

Guimarães, Ramon Izadora. *Conselho tutular*, East Region. May 3, 2010.

Humberto. Public employee, URBEL. April 8, 2010.

Indío. Community organizer. March 2, 2010.

Jacinto, Claudenia. PB administrator. September 30, 2009.

Julio. Community organizer, Alto Vera Cruz. Multiple informal conversations.

Junia. Community organizer. October 9, 2009.

Lacomini, João Carlos. Director, Centro de Apoio Comunitario, Alto Vera Cruz. May 3, 2010.

Lott, Paulo. Former secretary of government. November 17, 2009.

Macedo, Lindala de Jesus. Coordinator of Cultural Center, Alto Vera Cruz. April 30, 2010.

Martins, Ana Flavia. Chief of staff for director of URBEL. October 21, 2009.

Magalhes, Cristina. Director of planning, URBEL. October 9, 2009.

Marcelo. Municipal social services council member and community organizer. April 9, 2010.

Marcos. Community organizer, Alto Vera Cruz. November 28, 2009.

Matos, Gabriel de. *Conselheiro tutular.* May 18, 2010.

Medeira, Carlos. Secretary of housing. March 16 and May 19, 2010.

Montero, Paulo. Community organizer. March 20, 2010.

Motorista, Paulo. City council member. October 2, 2009.

Nabuco, Ana Luiz. Assistant secretary of planning. October 7, 2009; February 25, 2010.

Natalico. PT party activist and community organizer. September 9, 2009.

Padua, Antonia de. Community organizer. October 6, 2009.

Patrocina. Community organizer, Santa Lúcia. October 31, 2009.

Rezende, Silivinho. City council member. November 10, 2009.

Ricci, Ruda. Professor, Catholic University of Minas Gerais. September 8, 2009.

Santana, Elisangela Lopes. Social worker. May 4, 2010.

Sapão. Community organizer and political appointee. March 10, 2010.

Sara. Legislative aide in the city council. April 19, 2010.

Savio. Executive secretary, social service council. September 2, 2009; April 7, 2010.

Soares, William. Community organizer, Santa Lucia. Multiple conversations in 2009 and 2010.

Sousa, Biatriz Immaculada de Paz. Community organizer, Morro de Papagaio. September 19, 2009.

Sousa Júnior, Antonio David de. Former secretary of education and chief of staff for urban politics. November 27, 2009.

Souza, Alcides Pereira de. Community organizer, Alto Vera Cruz. May 4, 2010.

Vasconcelos, Lede. Chief of staff for planning secretary. March 4, 2010.

Ventura, Adriano. City council member. October 2, 2009.

Verde, Geraldo Arco. Former PB administrator. September 15, 2009.

Waldir. Regional director of PB Regional Center-South. December 8, 2009.

Wilson. Community organizer, Santa Lúcia. October 10, 2009.

MEETINGS

Health care council: October 10, 2009; November 17, 2009; February 24, 2010;
    March 4, 2010; April 15, 2010.
Housing council: November 17 and 26, 2009; December 2, 2009; April 8, 2010.
Local health care commission, Alto Vera Cruz: April 29, 2010.
Municipal health care policy conference: December 4–6, 2009.
Municipal housing conference: November 13–15, 2009.
Participatory budgeting, region-wide meeting: May 5 and 6, 2010.
Participatory budgeting workshop: March 15, 2010.
PB Regional Center-South: September 1, 2009; October 7, 2009; November 4,
    2009; December 1, 2009; February, 2, 2010; March 2, 2010; April 5, 2010;
    May 4, 2010.
Social assistance council: September 9, 2009; October 14, 2009; April 14, 28, and
    30, 2010.
Social service executive committee: April 30, 2010.

Index

Abers, Rebecca, 6
Alexander, Jeffrey, 4, 13. *See also* bonds
    of solidarity
Avritzer, Leonardo, 48–50. *See also*
    participatory publics

Baiocchi, Gianpaolo, 23, 117
bonds of solidarity
    civil society organizations, 155, 171,
        181, 182–83, 199, 236, 255–56
    conferences, 132, 139
    definition, 4, 13–14
    deliberation, 58–59, 104, 132, 147,
        228
    participatory budgeting, 96, 98–99,
        104, 106, 122
    participatory institutions, 9, 23,
        58–59, 185, 197, 201, 206
    See also Alexander, Jeffrey

campaigns
    civil society, 15, 57
    civil society organizations, 255
    definition, 192
    elections, 16, 90, 156, 192–200, 241
    First Republic, 41, 42
    participatory regime, 173, 181, 270

Cardoso, Fernando Henrique, 87, 267
Carvalho, José Murilo de, 39, 41
citizenship regime
    activation, 2, 11, 28, 76, 85, 92, 107,
        121, 127, 148, 181–88, 244–45,
        271 (*see also* mayors of Belo
        Horizonte: Ananias, Patrus)
    Alto Vera Cruz, 221–22, 230–33
    Belo Horizonte, 24, 65–67, 71–72,
        85, 97, 127, 129, 179–81
    civil society organizations, 16
    conceded, 34, 37–42, 47–50
    definition, 2, 5, 11, 16, 33
    insurgent, 67, 128 (*see also* Holston,
        James)
    Morro de Papagaio, 216–20,
        223–30
    participatory, 2, 4, 11–12, 16, 35,
        47–61, 76, 92, 105, 129, 134,
        154–56, 162–63, 166–68, 176,
        197–98, 200–201, 203–4, 206–8,
        246, 248–71
    regulated, 6, 34, 42–48, 149
    state, 17, 253
citizenship rights (*cidadania*)
    activation, 2, 60, 72, 217, 252
    civil, 20, 34, 38, 39, 43–46

citizenship rights (*cidadania*) (*cont.*)
  definition, 35, 48
  England, 36–37
  federal government, 121
  insurgent, 37 (*see also* Holston,
    James)
  political, 34, 39–41, 43, 46–47, 60,
    206, 261, 267–68, 271
  republic, 37
  social, 5, 12, 34, 41–45, 53, 56, 57,
    60, 198, 201, 244, 261–62,
    267–68, 271
  See also Constitution, 1988;
    Dagnino, Evelina; Marshall, T. H.;
    Sales, Teresa; Yashar, Deborah
civil society, 15, 33, 47–50, 67–68, 142,
  169–70, 215–22, 236–37, 254–56
civil society organizations (CSOs)
  Alto Vera Cruz, 212–15, 230–33
  authority, 137
  definition, 14
  interlocking institutions, 11
  Morro de Papagaio, 8, 212–15,
    223–30
  participatory budgeting, 99–101,
    119–21, 124, 128, 170–71
  participatory regime, 16, 49–60,
    116, 119, 142, 170–74, 197–201,
    203, 206–8, 246–49, 255–56,
    261, 271
  representation, 56–57, 79
  social justice, 25
  state, 6
  See also health care; housing; Vila
    Viva
clientelism, 3, 10, 14, 42, 76, 115, 270.
    See also participatory clientelism
co-governance (*co-gestão*), 135
collective action
  civil society organizations, 119, 129,
    188, 200, 226
  Morro de Papagaio, 220

  overcome, 251–52
  participatory budgeting, 105
  struggles, 2, 4, 55, 102, 164
community blueprint, 102–4, 117, 211
conference
  definition, 12, 139–41
  government, 13, 86
  health care, 132
  housing, 132–33, 171–72
  mobilization, 57
  participatory regime, 64, 81, 85, 93,
    131, 134, 201, 203, 206–7, 259
  policy, 139–40, 146–47, 266–67
constitution, 1988, 2, 3, 5, 22, 24, 27,
  33–36, 50–54, 60, 245, 252
contentious politics, 4, 195, 121, 181,
  195, 205, 243
coreneis, 34, 38–40, 42, 51
councils
  Belo Horizonte, 141
  budget, 74, 106
  deliberation, 145–48
  health care, 148–56, 201–4
  housing, 132–33, 156–57, 163
  local, 79, 134, 142, 143–44, 239
  municipal, 20, 70, 72, 79, 86, 105,
    134, 141–43, 260
  participation, 12, 19, 22, 64, 85, 142,
    144, 159–62, 168, 175, 263–70
  public policy, 78–79, 92, 133,
    135–40
  regional, 79, 134, 142, 143–44
  social services, 163–67, 187–88

Dagnino, Evelina, 23, 47, 48, 50
deliberation, 22, 49, 55–61, 92, 103,
  134–36, 145–48, 167, 206, 246,
  259–61
democracy
  activating, 168, 176, 261–67
  deepening, 14, 54–61, 167, 271
  deliberation, 58–61

history of, 4, 11, 22, 37
participatory, 5, 23, 55–56, 250
  (*see also* participatory citizenship
  regime)
quality of, 6, 14
representative, 13, 23, 56–58
demonstrations. *See* contentious
  politics

Eakin, Marshall, 65
elections
  campaigns, 192–95, 240–44
  democracy, 13, 182, 270
  history of, 40–46, 67, 267
  legislative, 192
  local, 143–44, 260
  mayoral, 26
  municipal, 68–71, 140, 192, 238, 260
  realignment, 26, 250
  See also mayors of Belo Horizonte:
    Ananias, Patrus
Estado Novo, 44, 46
Evans, Peter, 65

favela
  Alto Vera Cruz, 7–8, 57, 211–44
  Belo Horizonte, 65–66, 98, 159, 212
  community blueprint, 102–5, 117
  definition, 27, 212
  Morro de Papagaio, 9, 18, 209–44
  property titles, 107, 123, 157
  state, 17, 37, 114, 116
First Republic, 34, 36–43

health care, 148–57
Heller, Patrick, 6, 23, 117
Holston, James, 47–50, 158. *See also*
  citizenship regime: insurgent
housing, 156–68
housing *núcleo*, 107, 122–24, 159, 177,
  221, 236
Human Development Index (HDI), 26

interlocking institutions
  Ananias, Patrus, 86
  Castro, Célio de, 87–88
  definition, 16–22
  participatory citizenship regime,
    11, 84–85, 128–29, 143, 152,
    162, 171, 148, 198, 251, 271
IQVU (Quality of Life Index), 80,
  82–83, 101, 126

Keck, Margaret, 6
Kohli, Atul, 21
Kubitsheck, Juscelino, 66

legislature, 70–76, 120, 189–90,
  219–20

Madison, James, 19, 22, 41, 55, 251
Marshall, T. H., 36
Martins, Ana Flavia, 79, 142, 144
Matta, Roberto da, 37
mayors of Belo Horizonte
  Ananias, Patrus, 64, 76–84, 97, 149,
    159, 214, 222, 244, 274n3
    (chapter 3)
  Castro, Célio de, 77, 87–89, 90, 149
  Lacerda, Mario, 90–91, 113
  Pimental, Fernando, 89–90, 108–9,
    113
mayor's office
  Belo Horizonte, 63, 68, 69, 76, 85
  community relationships, 189–90,
    220, 239
methodology
  elite interviews, 29, 174
  mixed methods, 28, 174
  participant observation, 29,
    175–80
  subnational, 27
  survey, 174–81, 233–44
  See also campaigns; elections
mētis, 18–22, 103, 127, 158, 250–51

military regime, 34, 39, 44–47, 66–67, 214, 220
Minas Gerais, 37, 4–43, 64
municipalization, 51–52, 54
municipal legislature. *See* legislature
Murray Li, Tanya, 137

O'Donnell, Guillermo, 35
Ostrom, Elinor, 52
oversight (*controle social*), 135, 137, 139

participation, popular, 78–81
participatory budgeting
  council, 85, 105–6
  definition, 96, 99–101, 106
  digital, 80, 108–9, 125–29
  history of, 64, 78, 95–97
  housing, 80, 106–8, 121
  impact, 109, 112, 116, 118, 121–23, 200, 262–63
  limitations/constraints, 119–21, 123–24, 126–29, 200
  micro-regions, 105, 118–19
  number of participants, 92, 110, 122, 125, 239
  PB delegates, demographic profile, 111
  regional, 98–101, 109–21, 171, 189–200
  social services, 173–74
  See also IQVU (Quality of Life Index); mayors of Belo Horizonte: Pimental, Fernando
participatory citizenship regime, 2, 4–7, 11–12, 16–17, 21, 33–39, 47–61, 76, 92, 105, 129, 134, 154–56, 162–63, 166–68, 176, 197–98, 200–201, 203–4, 206–8, 246, 248–71
participatory clientelism, 170, 258, 268
participatory publics, 48, 49–50, 128, 179, 182
party system, 63, 68, 71, 76

Plotke, David, 56
president
  Cardoso, Fernando Henrique, 87, 267
  "Lula," Luis Inácio da Silva, 18, 75, 89, 122, 166, 267
  Rousseff, Dilma, 18, 89
  Vargas, Getúlio, 44–45, 163, 196
protest. *See* contentious politics
public goods
  Belo Horizonte, 65, 67
  civil society organization, 2, 155, 208
  distribution, 1, 5, 11, 17, 44, 80
  history of, 41
  public budgeting, 97, 108, 118, 121, 243–49, 263
  state, 21, 78, 81

Quality of Life Index. *See* IQVU (Quality of Life Index)

representation, 55–58, 60, 76, 79
  councils, 141–45, 167, 188
  definition, 55–58
  democracy, 60
  legislature, 76
  participatory citizenship regime, 85, 107, 128, 200–201, 246, 259–61
rights. *See* citizenship rights
"right to have rights," 23, 48, 50, 179, 243. *See also* Dagnino, Evelina
Rio de Janeiro, 24, 27, 51, 157, 167, 217

Sales, Teresa, 38. *See also* citizenship rights
São Paulo, 24, 27, 37, 41–43, 51, 66–68, 77, 114, 149, 158, 205
Scott, James, 17–18, 103, 127
social justice, 5, 11, 22–25, 27, 59, 67, 81–92, 105, 112–13
social services, 16, 143–45, 163–70, 173–74, 183–84, 239, 255. *See* IQVU (Quality of Life Index)

state
  Alto Vera Cruz, 7–8
  Belo Horizonte, 64–76, 116
  broadening, 6, 14, 20, 22, 55, 92,
    114, 141–48, 270
  demonopolization, 206
  formation, 11, 21, 37, 41–47, 51,
    63–64, 148–50, 157–59, 163–64,
    167, 198, 242, 253–54
  Minas Gerais, 27, 65
  Morro de Papagaio, 8–10, 213–16,
    230
  participatory citizenship regime, 2,
    6, 17, 47, 121, 249

techniques of access, 64, 82. *See* IQVU
  (Quality of Life Index)

unions, 15, 45, 66–67, 79, 142, 144,
  202, 254

Vila Viva, 117, 143, 227

Workers' Party, 26, 63, 71, 77, 82–92,
  97, 162, 206, 213, 217, 222, 244,
  249, 256, 262, 266

Yashar, Deborah, 36, 42

BRIAN WAMPLER

is professor of political science at Boise State University.

He is the author of *Participatory Budgeting in Brazil: Contestation,*

Cooperation, and Accountability.

www.ingramcontent.com/pod-product-compliance
Lightning Source LLC
Chambersburg PA
CBHW071838270326
41929CB00013B/2040